# SPECIAL ISSUE
# LAW AND LITERATURE
# RECONSIDERED

# STUDIES IN LAW, POLITICS, AND SOCIETY

Series Editor: Austin Sarat

| | |
|---|---|
| Volumes 1–2: | Edited by Rita J. Simon |
| Volume 3: | Edited by Steven Spitzer |
| Volumes 4–9: | Edited by Steven Spitzer and Andrew S. Scull |
| Volumes 10–16: | Edited by Susan S. Sibey and Austin Sarat |
| Volumes 17–33: | Edited by Austin Sarat and Patricia Ewick |
| Volumes 34–42: | Edited by Austin Sarat |

STUDIES IN LAW, POLITICS, AND SOCIETY   VOLUME 43

# SPECIAL ISSUE
# LAW AND LITERATURE
# RECONSIDERED

### EDITED BY

## AUSTIN SARAT

*Department of Law, Jurisprudence & Social Thought and
Political Science, Amherst College, USA*

Emerald

JAI

United Kingdom – North America – Japan
India – Malaysia – China

JAI Press is an imprint of Emerald Group Publishing Limited
Howard House, Wagon Lane, Bingley BD16 1WA, UK

First edition 2008

Copyright © 2008 Emerald Group Publishing Limited

**Reprints and permission service**
Contact: booksandseries@emeraldinsight.com

**British Library Cataloguing in Publication Data**
A catalogue record for this book is available from the British Library

ISBN: 978-0-7623-1482-9
ISSN: 1059-4337 (Series)

Awarded in recognition of
Emerald's production
department's adherence to
quality systems and processes
when preparing scholarly
journals for print

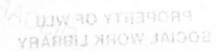

# CONTENTS

# LIST OF CONTRIBUTORS

| | |
|---|---|
| *Rob Atkinson* | Florida State University, Florida, USA |
| *Guyora Binder* | University at Buffalo Law School, Buffalo, NY, USA |
| *Susan Chaplin* | Leeds Metropolitan University, School of Cultural Studies, Leeds, UK |
| *Harriet Murav* | Department of Slavic Languages and Literatures, and Comparative Literature, University of Illinois, IL, USA |
| *Sara Murphy* | Gallatin School, New York University, New York, NY, USA |
| *Teresa Godwin Phelps* | American University, Washington College of Law, Washington DC, USA |
| *Jon-Christian Suggs* | The City University of New York, New York, NY, USA |

# EDITORIAL BOARD

# "E PROBOSCIS UNUM: LAW, LITERATURE, LOVE, AND THE LIMITS OF SOVEREIGNTY"

Harriet Murav

## ABSTRACT

*The phrase "e proboscis unum," a parody on the more familiar Latin phrase that means "out of many one" is taken from the courtroom scene of the 1964 Broadway musical Hello, Dolly! In this scene, the entire cast is under arrest for disturbing the peace, but the young impoverished clerk Cornelius Hackl takes the opportunity to proclaim his love for the milliner Irene Molloy in the song "It only takes a moment." The matchmaker Dolly pokes fun at the judge, the figure of authority, by commenting on the appearance of his nose, which she characterizes as "a flaming beacon of justice" and "living symbol of the motto of this great land," "e proboscis unum." The bickering, fighting crowd, however, in spite of the parody, are transformed into a community as they witness the young man's declaration. As this episode shows, popular culture reads the law and the courts as making possible a space for personal transformation and transformative sociality. The recent debate about same-sex marriage in Massachusetts shows that both individual persons and the law itself are open to a process of mutual transformation. The chapter uses* Hello, Dolly!, *the 2003 Massachusetts Supreme Court decision on same-sex marriage, and Shoshana Felman's* The Juridical Unconscious *to argue*

Special Issue: Law and Literature Reconsidered
Studies in Law, Politics, and Society, Volume 43, 1–20
Copyright © 2008 by Emerald Group Publishing Limited
All rights of reproduction in any form reserved
ISSN: 1059-4337/doi:10.1016/S1059-4337(07)00601-1

*that the study of law and literature is crucial in the current academic environment in which many critics, influenced by Giorgio Agamben, argue that law and the courts are merely the space for the exercise of the state's sovereign power to carry out punishment.*

In *Homo Sacer: Sovereign Power and Bare Life* Girogio Agamben provocatively argues that the basis for the state's protection of human "life is the possibility of destroying it." The constitution of sovereign power is the ability to decide life and death. Agamben provides three fundamental theses at the conclusion of his work:

1. The original political relation is the ban (the state of exception as zone of indistinction between outside and inside, exclusion and inclusion).
2. The fundamental activity of sovereign power is the production of bare life as originary political element and as threshold of articulation between nature and culture, *zoe* and *bios*.
3. Today it is not the city but rather the camp that is the fundamental biological paradigm of the West (Agamben, 1998, p. 181).

The way that political life, or sovereign power, also called state power – creates itself is by expelling a part of itself, which it defines as "bare life." Bare life marks the constantly shifting boundary between what and who is included in political life, and its protections and opportunities, and who is not. Andrew Norris, explicating Agamben, writes "Politics thus entails the constant negotiation of the threshold between itself and the bare life that is both included within and excluded from its body" (Norris, 2000, p. 47). The state of exception, or, the boundary space, is the all-important defining moment of political life for Agamben.

Bare life means human life as nothing more than a mere instrument that performs labor and, as Agamben says, can be killed, but not sacrificed. Bare life is the life of "homo sacer," the "sacred" human. The concentration camp inmate, stripped of all rights, outside of all law, and reduced to a status of a "living corpse" – is the exemplar of bare life for Agamben. The model of the "living corpse" comes from the discussion of the concentration camp in Hannah Arendt, on whom Agamben significantly depends. In *The Origins of Totalitarianism* Arendt relatess the camp inmate to the citizen of the totalitarian state: "the human specimen reduced to the most elementary reactions, the bundle of reactions that can always be liquidated and replaced by other bundles of reactions that behave in exactly the same way, is the model 'citizen' of the totalitarian state; and such a citizen can be produced only imperfectly outside the camps" (Arendt, 1973, p. 456). For Agamben the "bundle of reactions" is the model citizen of and the condition of possibility for the citizen of any state, any form of political life. While recognizing some differences between totalitarian and democratic states, Agamben defines the effects of sovereign power – residing in the people in democratic states – as similar to the effects of totalitarian power. The possibility of safeguards, limits, checks, and balances is excluded.[1] Agamben writes that "the categories whose opposition founded modern politics (right/left, private/public, absolutism/democracy, etc.) ... have been steadily dissolving to the point of entering today into a real zone of indistinction" (Agamben, 1998, p. 4).

The surge of interest in Agamben's *Homo Sacer: Sovereign Power and Bare Life* in American universities coincided with the Bush administration's move to concentrate more power in the executive branch and to limit the rights of those considered to be terrorist suspects. This coincidence helped to spur a remarkable shift in perception in certain academic circles, which increasingly see law as nothing more than the exercise of state power concentrated in the executive branch.[2] This view did not arise all at once. The history of critical theory in the past few decades, while not the only factor, had a significant influence, because the major trends in critical theory, taken together, eroded prior assumptions about individuality, agency, language, narrative, and power. The trends that contributed the most to the deep suspicion about law include a justifiable skepticism about the categories of the self and of the individual and doubt about the capacity of language to articulate the claims of the individual. What aided the process was also a shift toward a postmodern embrace of desubjectification, seen as the result of both the operation of the power/knowledge nexus and by the operation of language itself. This environment is not one in which the law and literature movement, traditionally oriented towards story, language, and interpretation in the name of a humanist ethos, could be expected to thrive. Framing law in the context of narrative, identifying the need for more storytelling in the legal context, diagnosing the problematic nature of first-person, confessional narrative, and calling for more emotion in law – are some of the ways that the law and literature movement has left its mark on the study and practice of law.[3] As has been argued elsewhere, the goal of the law and literature movement has been to humanize the law (Pantazakos, 1995). An increasing mistrust in categories that form the foundation of the law and literature movement, including such notions as the self and agency, and a suspicion about language's humanistic potential makes it difficult to approach literature and law from the perspective of what may seem to be outmoded concepts. Even though Agamben is deeply interested in language and narrative, as his analysis of Holocaust testimony reveals, some aspects of his work in the first volume of *Homo Sacer* fuel the very real challenge to the law and literature movement.

This paper does not attempt a critique of Agamben, and it does not offer a solution to the problem he raises, namely, the zone of indistinction between political life and bare life, but rather uses Agamben and other authors to rethink the challenge to the law and literature movement. I focus on the problem of marriage.[4] An examination of marriage in American legal and popular culture reveals that the expressive, emotional, and ethical potential of law should retain their importance both as a dimension of legal practice and as objects of critical study. It is not only that attention to language, literature, and narrative humanize law, which would remain otherwise merely formalistic or scientific. I am arguing instead that law itself includes the possibility of open-ended meaning. Law, in other words, has-or, can have – the qualities that are more typically associated with literature, and recent developments in marriage law reveal that potential.

It is a commonplace to say that marriage is the foundation of society, and to invoke this cliché suggests a backward looking and traditional society, in which marriage is heterosexual marriage, women are confined to the home, and an unruly population disciplined by the heavy hand of state authority. There are, however, other ways of defining the common thread between marriage and society. In exploring marriage as a form of association freely chosen between two people, it is possible to ask a broader question about law and the state that goes beyond this image of a hierarchically ordered world. Is the basis for both marriage and the state nothing more than violence, whether overt or subterranean, or does its verbal and performative basis include other possibilities? How does access to marriage, and the processes of inclusion and exclusion define what marriage is? Agamben defines the boundary between private and public as a zone of indistinction in which sovereign power dominates. The more traditional definition of the relation between the public and the private insists on a distinction between the two. In this more traditional view, the public institution of civil marriage makes possible a range of particular meanings in private life. It affords a form of human expression and human relatedness not easily achieved outside the sanction of the law. Agamben's point is to show that the benefits given by inclusion in political life depend on what is left on its borders. My argument, while not overcoming the slippery relation of zoe and bios, offers only the suggestion that in the recent history of civil marriage in the U.S. mere life had a significant impact on political life, leading to a redefinition of marriage away from the regulation of bodies and populations. My argument is based on three readings: the 2003 Massachusetts Supreme Court decision regarding same-sex marriage, Shoshana Felman's discussion of Tolstoy's "Kreutzer Sonata" and the O. J. Simpson trial, and the Broadway musical *Hello, Dolly!* (1964), which tells the story of a matchmaker, Dolly Levi, and her clients.

Both the Massachusetts decision and the Broadway musical take cogniz-ance of the role of power and constraint in the lives of individuals. The Massachusetts decision in particular defines marriage as a creature of state, or, to use its language, "police power." The musical also reveals, albeit humorously, an appreciation of the central role of police power in making the pursuit of happiness possible. The young clerk, Cornelius Hackl, virtually a slave to his employer, decides to "live" for an evening. He defines "living" as eating a good meal, having an adventure, almost getting arrested, and kissing a girl. The law plays a central role in Cornelius's definition of "living," or, the good life, because transgressing the law makes for the good life. The fact of state power, and the fact of bare life offer an ever-present contrast to the emotive, expressive, and transformative potential of political life and legal institutions, which, according to Agamben, are made possible by the exclusion of bare life. What is important in this regard is that the Massachusetts decision suggests that individuals on the border between bare life and political life can transform institutions in significant ways. In the Massachusetts decision the exception produces not only more "bare life" in Agamben's sense, but instead, more political life in a positive sense, more opportunities for fulfillment.

Bare life, according to Agamben is the object shared by both totalitarian and democratic states. It is not only in totalitarian regimes that private life, family matters, leisure, and health are regulated. What seems like a safeguard against the incursion of governmental power into everyday life is in fact the opposite. Agamben writes: "It is almost as if, starting from a certain point, every decisive political event were double-sided: the spaces, the liberties, and the rights won by individuals in their conflicts with central powers always simultaneously prepared a tacit but increasing inscription of individuals' lives within the state order, thus offering a new and more dreadful foundation for the very sovereign power from which they wanted to liberate themselves" (Agamben, 1998, p. 121). The argument about the duality of the fight against the intrusion of government power comes from Foucault. Agamben relies on Foucault's insight that individuals are caught in a double bind: the techniques that produce the individual as individual also produce the state's political power. To use Foucualt's language, the "technologies of the self" and the "political techniques" of state power intersect (Agamben, 1998, p. 5). Lang-uage, of course, may be used in service to the technologies of the self.

Marriage is an ideal platform upon which Agamben's argument may be explored, because as an institution it combines three realms: (1) the body, biology, sexuality, and procreation; (2) law, license, and regulation; and (3) expression, cultural meaning, speech, and literature. It is a form of contract and it can be an arena for violence. The phrase "I now pronounce you husband and wife" is the prime example of what John Austin calls performative speech, words that not only posit some quality about something, but actually change the state of affairs, and thereby offering an instance not of biopower, but of language power. Language power depends on sovereign power, but not entirely, and admits of more slippage and less rigidity than otherwise might appear. I will address below the role of same-sex unions in shifting the conventions of such performatives. The new importance of bodies, gender, and sexuality as matters of legal regulation means that marriage can play a central role in debates about state power and law.

The Massachusetts decision is fundamentally a debate about what marriage is, and provides a useful overview of the changing history of marriage. It is significant that the disagreement between the majority opinion and the dissent fall along the lines suggested by Agamben's claims. The opinion in favor of granting marriage licenses to same sex couples separates marriage from procreation, and thus shifts the definition of marriage away from the state's regulation of procreation. A reading of the majority opinion reveals an emphasis on aspects of human existence that transcend "bare life." First and foremost among these human qualities is dignity. The extension of marriage to same-sex couples is consistent with the Massachusetts Constitution, "which affirms the dignity and quality of all individuals" (2003). The opinion asserts that the U.S. Supreme Court that the Fourteenth Amendment protection of human dignity "precluded government intrusion into the deeply personal realms of consensual adult expressions of intimacy and one's choice of an intimate partner" (2003).

The state, however, intrudes nonetheless, because it decides who gets to participate in its sanctioned "consensual adult expression of intimacy." Notwithstanding the emphasis on the personal, private, and individual nature of the choice of a marriage partner, the majority opinion acknowledges the central role of state power in the institution of civil marriage. The state enters the bedroom. "In a real sense, there are three partners to every civil marriage: two willing spouses and an approving State" (2003). Without using the terms "biopower" or "biopolitics" the opinion draws a direct line from the state's regulatory capacity through the institution of marriage to the health of the citizenry. Again, the opinion affirms, "Civil marriage is created and regulated through exercise of the police power" (2003). The object of regulation is the collective body of the population and the individuals who constitute it: civil marriage "is central to the way the Commonwealth identifies individuals, provides for the orderly distribution of property, ensures that children and adults are cared for and supported whenever possible from private rather than public funds, and tracks important epidemiological and demographic data" (2003). The role of civil marriage in the regulation of the bodies of the population coexists with the personal, emotive, and ethical dimensions of marriage:

> Civil marriage is at once a deeply personal commitment to another human being and a highly public celebration of the ideals of mutuality, companionship, intimacy, fidelity, and family. "It is an association that promotes a way of life, not causes; a harmony in living, not political faiths; a bilateral loyalty, not commercial or social projects." (2003)

The last line is from the Griswold case, which prevented the State from barring the use of contraceptives among married couples. The 2003 Massachusetts majority opinion stresses that marriage offers the opportunity for recognition, interconnectedness, reciprocity, and individuality not available by any other means and not flattened out or even significantly reduced by the role of State power in civil marriage, which the opinion fully acknowledges to be central. Again, the opinion clearly and emphatically identifies civil marriage as a creature of State power and names the State as one of the three partners in any civil marriage.

The disjuncture between the celebratory, personal, private, and expressive value of marriage, on the one side, and the role of the State in using civil marriage to regulate conduct, identify individuals, and track data, on the other side – does not disturb the overwhelmingly positive view of civil marriage in the opinion as a whole. It would seem that civil marriage is precisely an instance of the double bind I discussed earlier, that is, "the technologies of the self by which processes of subjectivization bring the individual to bind himself to his own identity and consciousness and, at the same time, to an external power" (Agamben, 1998, p. 5). According to the majority opinion, greater inclusivity changes the nature of the institution of civil marriage, but the harm done to individuals who would otherwise be excluded outweighs the potential harm caused by the change.

The dissent, in contrast, minimizes the personal dimension of marriage and enhances its public and State importance. Marriage, in this view, amounts to little more than the exercise of state power over the bodies of individuals. According to J. Cordy, the author of the dissent, marriage laws in Massachusetts, based on English common law, "were enacted to secure public interests and not for religious purposes or to promote personal interests or aspirations. The primary goal of marriage is procreation and not the expression of emotional support and public commitment" (2003). The dissenting opinion goes on to say that "the institution of marriage has systematically provide for the regulation of heterosexual behavior, brought order to the resulting procreation, and ensured a stable family structure in which children will be reared, educated, and socialized." The language of a case from 1810, which the defense quotes, emphasizes the controlling, regulatory effect of marriage: "intended to regulate, hasten, and refine, the intercourse between sexes; and to multiply, preserve, and improve the species" (2003). The object of marriage law, this language strongly implies, is not individuals and their happiness, but the human population generally. The State's regulation of marriage is a clear instance of the exercise of what Foucault and Agamben would call biopower.

The dissent conjures up a promiscuous world of rampant heterosexual intercourse leading inevitably to the birth of children. Without marriage, fathers would be incapable of being identified, and children would be left without care. The opinion states "a society without the institution of marriage, in which heterosexual intercourse, procreation, and child care are largely disconnected processes, would be chaotic." The process of connecting fathers to children and husbands to wives has another benefit: marriage is the basis for a stable social order; marriage is the "foundation of the family and of society, without which there would be neither civilization nor progress." Binding women to men binds the society together. Just beneath the surface of the text is a claim about the justification for patriarchal power. The real threat to a stable society seems not to be same-sex marriage, but women's reproductive power, which, left on its own, creates chaos. Indeed, feminist attacks on the institution of marriage emphasize its role in the subordination of women, and the correlation between marriage and violence against women.[5]

I want to consider this argument in relation to the broader claims I am trying to make about marriage as a model for a form of association. The arguments about law and expressiveness, emotion, dignity, and human connectedness hardly mean much if we close our eyes to the fact of violence in marriage. The potential for new forms of power and domination to surface even as marriage grows more inclusive is also an issue. This last argument has been made by Anna Marie Smith, who writes that same-sex marriage "might enlarge the privileged married class and contribute to the further marginalization of the unmarried class" and "might contribute to new forms of domination" (Smith, 2001, p. 118). It seems that relations of power and domination are inescapable, however, it also seems that institutions have the capacity to change to respond to the articulation of individuals' desires for their particular forms of happiness. In the Massachusetts ruling on same-sex marriage, making new law does not mean merely reproducing the body politic. The group of people who previously constituted the exception, those who wished to enter marriages but could not, because they chose same-sex partners, now can enter marriage, which itself changes. The change is not merely that same-sex couples may be married, but that marriage is no longer defined primarily in terms of procreation. In Agamben's logic, political life defines itself by what it places along its threshold, namely, bare life. In the Massachusetts decision, in contrast, the exception does not prove the rule, as the saying goes, but changes the rule.

The same-sex couples who unofficially married each other changed the definition of marriage, even before the state granted their petition about civil marriage. It may seem that my emphasis on the performative, celebratory dimensions of marriage ignores Austin's distinction between valid and what he calls "infelicitous" performatives. I rely on Judith Butler's discussion in *Excitable Speech: A Politics of the Performative*. In a valid speech act saying equals doing. If a speaker has no authority to produce a valid speech act, no effect is gained in its utterance. In the absence of the necessary conventions performatives fail. Performatives are forms of speech that are ritual and conventional; they are embedded in a system that allows them to work. Same-sex couples who affirm bonds of commitment to each other outside of the necessary legal context are not legally married, because they violate the necessary conventions. To argue that marriage is less a domain of power and more a performative speech act in which two individuals create a relation between themselves by affirming it in public is to fail to admit to conventions that govern speech acts. The bond of marriage is something that is made in the saying of it, but the saying depends on state power, which either legitimates or denies legitimacy to marriage vows.

To respond to this objection, I am going to make what can be considered a naively empiricist argument. Other kinds of arguments are possible, including for example, the position that the conventions themselves are vulnerable, that they contain what Judith Butler in *Excitable Speech* calls "faultlines." To put in another way, law is not entirely a closed, rigid system in which the prevailing structures of power are endlessly re-inscribed. Butler argues that such structures are vulnerable to "destructuration through being reiterated, repeated, and rearticulated" (Butler, 1997). The very conditions under which the felicity of the performative is given, namely, conventionality, are also the conditions under which slippages can take place.[6]

The empiricist argument, however, is more to the point in this case. The mere fact of the plaintiffs' lives together helped to convince the Massachusetts

Supreme Court to shift its position on marriage. In its discussion of the lives of these same-sex couples, who lived for many years as if they were legally married, the 2003 decision actually departs from its emphasis on marriage as a kind of celebratory statement, and instead makes a particular point of bodies and their needs. The decision describes the length of time the couples spent together (thirty years, thirteen years, seven years) and the kinds of care they provided for their children and for their elderly parents during this time, when, to use Agamben's language, they were in some limited way, living more in the manner of *zoe* cut-off from *bios*. Again, the mere fact of their daily life together made a difference in their legal status. Living outside the space sanctioned by state power changed the kind of space that state power sanctioned. This is not to say that the shift brought an end to the limit separating unsanctioned from sanctioned married life. Various limits still obtain, including limits on the number of partners, the age of the partners, and the species of the partners. It is doubtful whether anyone would want to eliminate such constraints altogether, and the zone of indistinction persists. It does matter, however, and especially to the lives of the Massachusetts plaintiffs, that the limits can shift.

To recap the argument thus far, civil marriage is a form of association that affords the possibility of happiness, by allowing for the emotive, expressive, ethical dimension of human existence to be articulated (the public celebration that the Massachusetts decision points to as one of the central features of marriage). Even though state power makes this form of association possible, the mere life of the same-sex couples who lived together significantly altered the legally sanctioned space of civil marriage. Since I am emphasizing the dimension of expression and language, it is useful to turn to literature as a source for debates about the meaning of marriage. Marriage, and its failures, has been the central theme of the classic nineteenth century novel, including such works as *Madame Bovary* and *Anna Karenina*, both of which offer a strikingly negative picture of marriage.[7] These novels have not traditionally appeared in the law and literature canon, which has favored instead such works as "Billy Budd" and *The Brothers Karmazov*, because they more directly address the problems of law and justice. In comparison to such canonical works of literature as Tolstoy's *Anna Karenina* and especially his subsequent work "The Kreutzer Sonata," the Massachusetts opinion looks extremely naïve. Dolly and Anna are trapped in marriages which give them little happiness, and even the happily married Levin has to hide rope and guns because the temptation to commit suicide is so strong. After her disappointment in love, Kitty comes to the conclusion that marriage is nothing more than the exchange of bodies, as in a market. In *Anna Karenina* the first sexual encounter between Anna and Vronsky is described as something akin to murder: "And as the murderer falls upon this body with animosity, as if with passion, drags it off and cuts it up, so he covered her face and shoulders with kisses" (Tolstoy, 2000, p. 189). I have argued elsewhere that what kills Anna is not her unhappy marriage to Karenin per se, but the loss of her role and identity in society: as "no one's wife" (to use Dolly's language) she has no way to connect her private life, which includes more than just her passion for Vronsky, with her role in public. She is deprived of self and language. She has a voice, but it is only the voice of a jealous woman, not someone entitled to make claims, and devolves into a mere body even before she finally dies. It is of significance that a literary work such as *Anna Karenina*, which defines marriage as the joining of bodies, should demonstrate that gap between "*zoe* and *bios*, between voice and language" that for Agamben constitutes the central problem of politics today. The virtue of literature, from the point of view of those who would study law and literature from Agamben's perspective, is its capacity to represent the gap.

Tolstoy returned to the problem of marriage in his later work, "The Kreutzer Sonata." Here the dismal reading of marriage as the exchange of women's bodies and as an opportunity for nothing more than violence takes center stage. On this reading, marriage provides a very poor model for other forms of voluntary association, because it is fundamentally an institution built on quicksand. The discussion of this work that most closely suits my broader purposes in terms of law and society is that provided by Shoshana Felman in *The Juridical Unconscious: Trials and Traumas in the Twentieth Century*. Felman reads Tolstoy's Kreutzer Sonata together with the O.J. Simpson trial, seeing in both the fiction and the trial law's failure.

"The Kreutzer Sonata" was first published in 1891, although it circulated in other forms beginning in 1889 (Møller, 1988). Its appearance, as Felman argues, caused tremendous controversy. Tolstoy, like Agamben with respect to political life, was interested in stripping away the false veneer of family life and marriage to reveal its underlying horrific core. The truth of marriage is economic exchange and violence. This position is articulated by Pozdnyshev, who murdered his wife out of jealousy. According to the murderer, his act was only the logical extension of what marriage is to begin with: a form of murder. Tolstoy's hero, in a passage Felman quotes, says:

They asked me in court how I killed her [...] Imbeciles! They thought I killed her that day, the fifth of October, with a knife. It wasn't that day I killed her, it was much earlier. Exactly in the same way as they're killing their wives now, all of them.[8]

This thorough indictment of all of culture, typical of late Tolstoy, is similar to Agamben's unmasking of the secret relation between the sacredness of life and bare life, the secret relation between totalitarian and democratic society. In Tolstoy's story, the law protects marriage and sanctions murder, yet marriage is nothing more than a form of murder. For both Tolstoy and Agamben, there is no difference between what the law enshrines and protects and what it excludes.

For Tolstoy's murderer, there is no basis for marriage aside from violence. Felman stresses Tolstoy's use of the term "abyss," citing several passages in which Pozdnyshev states that an abyss lay at the heart of the relation between himself and his wife, as in the line "It all happened because of that terrible abyss there was between us." The gap that he is referring to is never spelled out concretely, but it has to do with the difference in power between men and women. The fundamental violence and alienation separating women and men (and blacks from whites in Felman's discussion of the O. J. Simpson trial) is more than a mere set of superficial disagreements or differences of view. It makes individuals in society monsters to each other.

Law, according to Felman, does not recognize, much less address this underlying and permanent upheaval in human relations. Felman writes:

> In its pragmatic role as guardian of society against irregularity, derangement, disorganiza-
> tion, unpredictability, or any form of irrational or uncontrollable disorder, the law, indeed,
> has no choice but to guard against equivocations, ambiguities, obscurities, confusions, and
> loose ends.[...]Under the practical constraints of having to ensure accountability and to
> bring justice, the law tries to make sense of the abyss or to reduce its threat (its
> senselessness, its unintelligible chaos) by giving it a name, by codifying it or by subsuming
> its reality (which is inherently nameless and unclassifiable) into the classifying logic and into
> the technical, procedural coherence of the trial. (Felman, 2002, p. 95)

Felman's image of the law is surprisingly similar to its definition in the dissenting opinion of the Massachusetts Supreme Court decision on same-sex marriage. Both represent the law as bringing order to chaos. I quote from the dissent: "The alternative, a society without the institution of marriage, in which heterosexual intercourse, procreation, and child care are largely disconnected processes, would be chaotic" (2003). Felman is far less sanguine about law's efficacy, because she sees the chaos erupting within the legal institution of marriage and within the legal process of the trial, yet she and the Massachusetts dissent share the view that law, particularly when it comes to marriage, is or seeks to be a form of control over what would otherwise be the unruly, chaotic, and incoherent sexual life of individuals. In both the Massachusetts dissent and in Felman human beings are fundamentally incapable of forming bonds between themselves. They cannot form associations and cannot function in any kind of public. In this regard – in the absence of the potential for community – Felman and the Massachusetts dissent, to a certain extent, share Agamben's dismal view of political life without foundations. For Agamben, as we recall, rejects the image of the human being in political life as a rational, deliberative creature who freely enters relations with others. In contrast, the model citizen of Agamben's political world is bare life, the replaceable bundle of reactions.

It is only a short set of steps from Felman's foundationless and fundamentally chaotic law to Agamben's argument about sovereign power. To help explicate this point, I turn to Andrew Norris's discussion of Agamben. As Norris points out, the figure behind Agamben, in addition to Arendt, whom Agamben does not mention, but relies on heavily, nonetheless is Carl Schmitt. The sovereign, or, sovereignty, in Agamben as in Schmitt, defines the boundary between the realm of law and what is outside it (bare life). Law does not work when there is chaos. Law only works when there is such a thing as everyday, normal life. Norris cites Schmitt, who writes, "There is no norm applicable to chaos. For a legal order to make sense, a normal situation must exist, and he is sovereign who definitively decides whether this normal situation exists."[9] If all we have is chaos, groundlessness, and a lack of foundations, Felman, Agamben, and Schmitt agree, mere law alone is helpless to do anything.

According to Felman literary texts unmask the chaos and trauma that the law attempts to hide. Literature, in contrast to law, enables us to encounter what the law covers over, as Felman puts it, "the purpose of the literary text is to show or to expose again the severance and the schism [...] to wrench apart what was precisely closed or covered up by the legal trial" (Felman, 2002, p. 95). The literary work "transmits the force of the story that could not be told (or that failed to be transmitted or articulated) in the legal trial" (Felman, 2002, p. 96). For Felman, the literary text uses language to reveal what the legal trial's use of language conceals: the violence that is present in marriage. Pozdnyshev's story – the literary work and the confession of its hero – is a form of "discourse and a speech act [...]a speech performance" that continues to have significance beyond Tolstoy's time because it conveys the underlying trauma of gender, incapable of being addressed or reconciled by law and thereby doomed to repetition. I understand Felman to be saying that Tolstoy's literary work stages a speech performance in another sense, having to do with the narrative structure of "The Kreutzer Sonata." Pozdnyshev's confession is embedded in the first person narrative of a traveler on a train who hears his story. The confession is a performance because it is a reiteration. The hero confesses over and over again, without ever being absolved. The literary work exposes in its repetition what the law is condemned to repeat, the fundamental trauma that underlies political life.

A more Agambenian reading of the text would see Pozdnyshev as the exception that defines the rule, marking the boundary between mere life and the good life. Although a court acquitted him, Pozdnyshev lost custody of his children, and lost his standing in society. Formal and informal networks of regulation are more important than the outcome of the legal trial in his case. Tolstoy's hero rides the train without ever arriving at any destination, traversing a liminal space that can be understood to be located metaphorically on the border of the city and what lies beyond it. He possesses language, because he confesses, but at times, he slips into mere voice, the strange sigh that marks the opening of his discourse. Tolstoy's work reveals the fracture between zoe and bios, because he represents in language the zone of indistinction between what is and what is not language. "The Kreutzer Sonata" reveals what is beyond law and beyond language but makes them possible.

Felman highlights the capacity of literature to represent what escapes law. In her view, law imposes order both by means of language and by means of force on that which fundamentally escapes its control. Literary language splits open, exposes, and performs what law closes, orders, and hides. Tolstoy's "Kreutzer Sonata" and the O. J. Simpson trial reveal that literary language is true, but law is false – not because it is duplicitous, but because it is unequipped to handle the violence that grounds the traumatic relation between men and women and blacks and whites. Where I disagree with Felman has to do with law. Civil marriage, as the 2003 Massachusetts Supreme Court defines it, is an open-ended speech act whose language shares the qualities that Felman ascribes uniquely to literature. Law's language, in this reading of marriage, is neither true nor false, because it is a performative speech act. We do not just have groundlessness, chaos, the abyss, and trauma. The zone of indistinction in which the same sex couples lived led to a shift in the language of marriage.

The shift produced new language, which reads something like this: marriage is the commitment of two people to pursue happiness together. I am inspired to use this formulation by Stanley Cavell's 1981 *Pursuits of Happiness: The Hollywood Comedy of Remarriage*, a study of philosophy and American films of the 1930s and 1940s.[10] There are striking similarities between the 2003 Massachusetts decision on same-sex marriage and Cavell's definition. Marriage, in both, is a way of life and a form of association between people that joins the private and the public in a particular way. Its fundamental purpose is not procreation, but association, and it is in this regard, as a form of association – not as a power hierarchy – that it is in itself a "little community." The "form of association" has an erotic dimension, but the meaning of marriage, according to Cavell, is not to be reduced to this aspect alone. Cavell cites Milton's discussion of the meaning of marriage to buttress his claim. According to Milton, God solved the problem of Adam's loneliness by giving him a spouse to talk to, in Milton's words, which Cavell cites, "in God's intention a meet and happy conversation is the chiefest and noblest end of marriage" (Cavell, 1981, p. 87). Cavell does not refer the 1965 Griswold decision, which, again, declares that marriage is "an association that promotes a way of life, not causes; a harmony in living, not political faiths; a bilateral loyalty, not commercial or social projects." He echoes the thrust of this decision nonetheless when he describes marriage as achieving "purposefulness without purpose" (Cavell, 1981, p. 89). There is no pre-ordained content to the association called marriage, what is more important is that the two spouses want the association. Human beings make and re-make themselves by the pledges and agreements they make with each other. For Cavell, there is no ground or foundation for this mutual constitution of marriage, or of democratic society, for that matter, and in this regard he differs significantly from Robert Cover. Cover argues for the foundational significance of the narratives that give law and legal institutions meaning (Cover, 1983). The groundlessness, however, does not signal for Cavell, as it does for Felman, law's permanent state of trauma. The association without content, purpose, or foundation only requires the pledge and consent between the individuals who make the marriage and the society.

In *The Coming Community*, originally published in 1990, Agamben argues for a form of foundationless association in terms that resonate with Cavell's argument and with the claims I am making about the 2003 Massachusetts Supreme Court decision. In the essay entitled "Tianamen" Agamben raises the possibility of a politics based on the absence of all content, what he calls "whatever singularity." The demonstrators at Tianamen threatened state power because they formed a community that did "not possess any identity to vindicate nor any bond of belonging for which to seek recognition" (Agamben, 1993). It is true that the same-sex couples in Massachusetts sought recognition as married couples, however, marriage, no longer conceived as the legal framework for procreation, has no fixed content or meaning, but is instead an open-ended and undefined form of living together.

I conclude by rehearsing the issues I have raised through a reading of the musical *Hello, Dolly!* First performed on Broadway in 1964, the work is

based on Thornton Wilder's play, "The Matchmaker."[11] Wilder wrote, "My
play is about the aspirations of the young (and not only of the young) for a
fuller, freer participation in life" (Wilder, 1957). In the play and the musical
that was based on it, marriage is the vehicle for this "fuller, freer
participation in life." Life without this possibility is reduced to the endless
and uneventful cycle of production, consumption, and death that is
characteristic of Agamben's bare life. Cornelius Hackl (whose name reveals
his instrumentality; "Hackl" suggests one who chops, or, hacks) is a thirty-
three-year-old clerk. His entire existence is defined by his employer's grain
and feed store. Cornelius goes to bed at nine in the barn room of the store,
rises at six to mind the supplies, never has an evening off, and never sees his
wages, because Horace Vandergelder, his boss, keeps them. The first
appearance that Cornelius makes emphasizes his lowly, downtrodden
existence. Horace bangs his foot on the floor, and a trapdoor opens to reveal
the clerk, who says, "You stomped, Mr. Vandergelder?" If Cornelius's life
does not conform to the camp inmate's, it does correspond to Agamben's
model of bare life in his replacability, lack of individuality and freedom, and
his confinement to his job. Time has no shape in Mr. Vandergelder's feed
store; Cornelius is repeatedly promoted to chief clerk. The repetition of his
daily life is only underscored by the repetition of his meaningless
advancement. He merely exists, but does not "live" – this is the play's
term for "the good life," which it defines in a passage from which I have
already quoted, "really living" means, according to Cornelius, having a
good meal, being in danger, risking arrest, spending all your money, and
kissing a girl. Cornelius accomplishes everything on his list. To merely get all
these things and experiences, however would not be to change anything.
Nothing new would enter his world. Cornelius's concept of really living
undergoes a significant shift. The musical includes a notion of a public,
communal life in its vision of what the truly living means. In order to
achieve his private happiness, the clerk has to enter the public realm. His
attempts to arrive at the sanctioned space of the good life reveal the zone of
indistinction on which the good life is based.

The highlight of the musical, from the perspective of this paper, is not
Dolly's triumphant return (the song, "Hello, Dolly!") to the Harmonia
Garden's restaurant, but Cornelius's moment of transformation. Having
fallen in love with the milliner Irene Malloy, he declares his love to her from
the prisoners' dock in a courtroom. He and all the other patrons of the
Harmonia Gardens are under arrest for disturbing the peace. His song, "It
Only Takes a Moment" describes the transformation that love brings by
emphasizing time. Cornelius searches for the right word to describe the

instant of time that it took to fall in love, rejecting "minute" and "second" as too long before settling on "a moment:"

It only takes a moment

For your eyes to meet and then

Your heart knows in a moment

You will never be alone again

It only takes a moment

To be loved a whole life long

And that is all

That love's about

And we'll recall when time runs out

That it only took a moment

To be loved a whole life long

(Stewart & Herman, 1964, pp. 102–103)

In the musical, the articulation of what "only takes a moment" requires a public space. The courtroom setting for this song reveals an understanding of law as affording the opportunity for the expression of the emotive and ethical dimensions of human existence and for their articulation *to someone*. Those living outside political life have little opportunity for any kind of community. The law gives a public space for a private *moment* – as the song says – and this moment changes everything. The 1969 film version of *Hello, Dolly!* lacks the courtroom scene, setting the song instead in Washington Square park in New York, in which a small group of witnesses gather, including a policeman. The park and the presence of a policeman lend a similar legal and public setting for the song.

Instead of the endless cycle of production, consumption, and death that marks life in Vandergeler's feed store, the song marks the transformative event as taking no time. The new thing that changes everything takes no time, lifting those who experience it outside of time. In Agamben's writing, death provides the framework for the political; one of the synonyms for "biopolitics" is "thanatopolitics," the politics of death. Agamben's point is the zone of indistinction between life and death that the state regulates. The song, like the musical and the play, do not ignore the fact of death: Dolly,

Vandergelder, and Irene Malloy have each lost a spouse. The significance of death here, however, has to do with remembering and returning to what life made meaningful.

Cornelius's speech to the judge emphasizes what I described earlier as the contentless pledge of marriage. The young man hardly knows Irene Malloy, indeed he has no real idea of who she is; she, like all women, is "mysterious." Cornelius says

> I bet you could know a woman a hundred years without ever being really sure whether she liked you or not. Today I've lost so many things. My job, my future, everything that people think is important, but I don't care! Even if I have to dig ditches for the rest of my life, I'll be a ditch digger who once had a wonderful day. (Stewart & Herman, 1964, p. 102)

The loss of his future means the loss of knowledge of the future based solely on the past. What he has gained is the possibility of something new that he previously did not know. Included most importantly in this new, unknown and unknowable life is Irene herself, who like all women, will never let him know for certain that she likes him, but who will require that he promises to try to make her like him over and over. There is no foundation for Cornelius's happiness, only the possibility of pursuing it.

This chapter has argued for a reconsideration of the law-literature relation not for the purpose of reinscribing the opposition between the two, but instead, for the purpose of bringing them closer together. The force and efficacy of statements as means of bringing about connections among individuals without any other ground for their association is one of the features of language that law and literature share. These statements may be deliberative and rational, or they may be emotional, but what is important is the conventions governing the efficacy of utterance can shift, and that their utterance creates a relation between the speakers, a public, in a sense.[12]

A musical, unlike a literary work that is read in private, is, of course, performed in public. In *Hello, Dolly!* the private moment that Cornelius articulates in public has two publics: one formed by the other characters in the play who listen to him in the courtroom, and the second formed by the audience viewing the performance. The doubling of the public audiences in this scene can be read as reiterating the all-important threshold between mere life and political life. There's no love, even in Broadway musical, without the police. There is another possible reading, however. Cornelius says that even if he were to be a ditch digger for the rest of his life, he would be a ditch digger who once had a wonderful day. No recognition from state power is required in order for Cornelius to be a ditch digger who once had a wonderful day. We can imagine the audience watching the play in a similar light, as ditch diggers, so to speak, caught up in the perpetual cycle of production and consumption for whom the interlude of watching *Hello, Dolly!* was something like Cornelius' wonderful day.

## NOTES

1. I am grateful to the anonymous reader of an earlier version of this essay, who offered an invaluable critique of its shortcomings. I am also grateful to Bruce Rosenstock for discussing its problems with me, and to Penelope Rosenstock-Murav for her performance in Champaign's Central High School's 2006 production of *Hello, Dolly!* For a discussion as to why Agamben ignores the possibility of safeguards, see Hussain & Ptacek (2000).
2. I am basing my observation on a semester-long seminar on governmentality in 2006 sponsored by the Unit for Criticism at the University of Illinois at Urbana-Champaign. I am grateful to my colleagues, for their discussions during this seminar, and in particular, to its convener, Michael Rothberg.
3. I am referring to such works as Cover (1983), Brooks (2000), Brooks and Gewirtz (1996), Scheppele (1998), White (1994), Sarat and Kearns (1994) and Weisberg (1984).
4. For a discussion of Agamben that defends the role of poetry in political life, see MacNamee (2002).
5. For a discussion of this critique, see West (1993). Felman provides bibliography of the key work in Felman (2002).
6. This is similar to Derrida's argument about Austin. For a discussion, see Murav (1998).
7. For a discussion of the classic novels of marriage and adultery in the broader context of human social order, see Tanner (1979).
8. Leo Tolstoy, "The Kreutzer Sonata," cited by Felman (2002).
9. Carl Schmitt, "Definition of Sovereignty," in *Political Theology*, trans. George Schwab, cited by Norris (2002).
10. I am indebted to my husband Bruce Rosenstock for my discussion of Cavell, which is based on his article (see Rosenstock, 2005).
11. Wilder wrote an earlier version of the play, which was called *A Merchant of Yonkers* (1938). Wilder's work was based on the Austrian playwright Joann Nestroy's *Einen Jux will es sich Machen* (1842). The hero of the Austrian play wants to have a "fling" and not a marriage, and as Wilder points out, there is no Dolly Levi in the Austrian play.
12. For an argument about the act of speech and the act of reading as creating multiple publics, see Warner (2002).

## REFERENCES

Agamben, G. (1993). *The coming community*. Minneapolis: University of Minnesota Press.
Agamben, G. (1998). *Homo sacer: Sovereign power and bare life*. Stanford: Stanford University Press.

Arendt, H. (1973). *The origins of totalitarianism.* New York: Harcourt Brace Jovanovich.

Brooks, P. (2000). *Troubling confessions: Speaking guilt in law and literature.* Chicago: University of Chicago Press.

Brooks, P., & Gewirtz, P. (1996). *Law's stories: Narrative and rhetoric in the law.* New Haven: Yale University Press.

Butler, J. (1997). *Excitable speech: A politics of the performative.* New York: Routledge.

Cavell, S. (1981). *Pursuits of happiness: The Hollywood comedy of remarriage.* Cambridge: Harvard University Press.

Cover, R. (1983). The supreme court 1982 term, forward: Nomos and narrative. *Harvard Law Review, 97,* 4–68.

Felman, S. (2002). *The juridical unconscious: Trials and traumas in the twentieth century.* Cambridge: Harvard University Press.

Goodridge v. Department of Public Health (2003). In 440 *Mass.* 309.

Hussain, N., & Ptacek, M. (2000). Thresholds: Sovereignty and the sacred. *Law & Society Review, 34,* 495–515.

Møller, P. U. (1988). *Postlude to the Kreutzer sonata: Tolstoj and the debate on sexual morality in Russian literature in the 1890s.* Leiden: E. J. Brill.

Murav, H. (1998). *Russia's legal fictions.* Ann Arbor: University of Michigan Press.

Norris, A. (2000). Giorgio Agamben and the politics of the living dead. *Diacritics, 30,* 38–58.

Pantazakos, M. (1995). "Ad humanitatem pertinent": A personal reflection on the history and purpose of the law and literature movement. *Cardozo Studies in Law and Literature, 7,* 31–71.

Sarat, A., & Kearns, T. R. (Eds). (1994). *The Rhetoric of Law.* Ann Arbor: University of Michigan Press.

Scheppele, K. L. (1988). Forward: Telling stories. *Michigan Law Review, 87,* 2073–2098.

Smith, A. M. (2001). Missing poststructuralism, missing Foucault: Butler and Fraser on capitalism and the regulation of society. *Social Text, 19,* 103–125.

Stewart, M., & Herman, J. (1964). *Hello, dolly!.* New York: DBS Publications.

Tolstoy, L. (2000). *Anna Karenina.* New York: Penguin.

Weisberg, R. (1984). *The failure of the word: The protagonist as lawyer in modern fiction.* New Haven: Yale University Press.

Wilder, T. (1957). *Three plays.* New York: Harper and Row.

# WHAT IS IT LIKE TO BE LIKE THAT? THE PROGRESS OF LAW AND LITERATURE'S "OTHER" PROJECT

Rob Atkinson

## ABSTRACT

*A central interest of the modern law and literature movement has been how literature can show lawyers what it is like to be different from what they are – in a word, "other." This essay examines the course of that "other" project through three critical phases: the taxonomic, which purported to give lawyers an external account of others, the better to serve their own clients; the empathetic, which has tried to give lawyers an internal account of others, the better to enable lawyers to improve the lot of those others; and the exemplary, which holds up models of how lawyers themselves might be more firmly and effectively committed to the commonweal, particularly the good of others less well-off. It argues that the law and literature movement should embrace this third phase of the "other" project. Although analytically last, this phase is chronologically first, anticipated in Plato's* Republic. *This essay concludes by placing the*

Special Issue: Law and Literature Reconsidered
Studies in Law, Politics, and Society, Volume 43, 21–52
Copyright © 2008 by Emerald Group Publishing Limited
All rights of reproduction in any form reserved
ISSN: 1059-4337/doi:10.1016/S1059-4337(07)00602-3

*exemplary phase of the "other" project at the center of the law and literature movement's mission, with the* Republic *at the core of the movement's canon.*

And so the lawyer, whose highest problems call for a perfect understanding of human character and a skillful use of this knowledge, must ever expect to seek in fiction as in an encyclopedia, that learning which he cannot hope to compass in his own limited experience of the humans whom chance enables him to observe at close range.

John Wigmore, *A List of One Hundred Legal Novels.*

My central subject is the ability to imagine what it is like to live the life of another person who might, given changes in circumstance, be oneself or one of one's loved ones.

Martha Nussbaum, *Poetic Justice.*

It is this particular that makes the study of history salutary and profitable: patterns of every sort of action are set out on a luminous monument for your inspection, and you may choose models for yourself and your state to imitate, and faults, base in their issue as in their inception, to avoid.

Livy (1962), *A History of Rome.*

# INTRODUCTION

This essay explores what is, in two senses, the law and literature movement's "other" project. In the first and most significant sense, a central interest of the modern law and literature movement, from the beginning, has been how literature can show lawyers what it is like to be different from what they are: in a word, "other." As Thomas Nagel asked fellow philosophers to redefine consciousness by asking themselves "What is it like to be a bat?" (Nagel, 1974), so the emerging law and literature movement asked the legal profession to re-orient itself by experiencing the inner life of others in listening to their stories.

This interest in the "other," however, has never been the law and literature movement's only project[1] and, over time, that project has become, at best, peripheral. This is the second sense in which it is the movement's "other" project. The "other" project has become something of a neglected stepchild, if not quite an embarrassing illegitimate, in the movement's extending family of tropes and themes.

My thesis is that the law and literature movement's "other" project, if properly appreciated, should move from the margin to the center, not only of the law and literature movement, but of a much wider front, inside academia and out. To sustain that admittedly ambitious claim, this article examines three phases, roughly chronological, of the "other" project: the taxonomic, the empathetic, and the exemplary. The first offers a scientific, or at least quasi-scientific, taxonomy of character types; the second, a medium and method for empathizing with others, particularly "outsiders"; the third, a pantheon of moral exemplars and a pandemonium of villains. These three perspectives are reflected, respectively, in my epigraphs; we will consider each of them in turn in the paper's three parts.

The relationship among the three phases of the "other" project, we shall see, is one of increasing complexity and ambitiousness. Examining that relationship will illuminate the limits, even dangers, of the "other" project, even as it reveals that project's very great, but still largely unrealized, promise. Behind the promise and the peril is a paradox. To overcome its problems, the "other" project must become both more and less than it has been: less, by acknowledging a legitimate division of labor between literature and other disciplines; more, by transcending the confines of imaginative literature as conventionally understood.

Unpacking this paradox will take us back to an earlier, even more ambitious integration of reason and imagination that was the goal of Plato's *Republic* (Plato, 1968). On the one hand, it will require a re-reading of the *Republic* informed by a post-modern skepticism about the eternal values supposedly announced there. On the other hand, it will both require and expand the possibility of renewed commitment to radically improving the lot of humanity. It thus will be a re-reading that tries to do for our post-modern time nothing less than what Kant attempted in the first post-Enlightenment generation: restore a right balance between faith and reason.

# 1. THE TAXONOMIC PHASE: CATALOGING LIFE'S CHARACTERS TO HELP OUR CLIENTS

The first phase of the "other" project came well before what most consider the beginning of the contemporary law and literature movement in the 1970s (Binder & Weisberg, 2000, p. 3). Its paradigm, now nearly a century old, is John H. Wigmore's "A List of One Hundred Legal Novels." This will serve as a useful starting place because it is not only chronologically first, but also theoretically simplest.

## 1.1. Description

Wigmore, himself a distinguished law school dean and legal scholar, wanted not only to list the novels most useful to lawyers, but also to set out the criteria for their inclusion. Among those criteria he mentions becoming familiar with classical descriptions of law and lawyering and developing a historical sense, both of the background of particular legal developments and of historical eras more generally (Wigmore, 1922, pp. 27–29). These are all themes to which we will return. "But," in Wigmore's words

> there is a higher standpoint yet. For the novel – the true work of fiction – is a *catalogue of life's characters*. And the lawyer must know human nature. He must deal understandingly with its types, its motives. These he cannot find – all of them – close around him; life is not long enough, the range is not broad enough for him to learn them by personal experience before he needs to use them. For this learning, then, he must go to fiction, which is a gallery of life's portraits. (Wigmore, 1922, p. 31)

From his prototype of this gallery, Balzac's *Human Comedy*, Wigmore borrows a second, and more telling, metaphor: the taxonomic treatise. He notes, with approval, that Balzac saw his project as doing for human society what Buffon had done for the animal kingdom: systematically ordering and presenting the various species. In their principal usefulness to lawyers, according to Wigmore, the great novelists, very like the great zoologists, are taxonomists.[2]

## 1.2. Assessment

If we are to appreciate the place of Wigmore's taxonomic approach in the broader scheme of the "other" project, we must note three salient features: its external perspective, its static focus, and its narrowly instrumentalist purpose. The first two of these features are methodological; the third is functional.

### 1.2.1. Methodology

Most significantly, the perspective Wigmore takes toward others in strictly external. We are to see other people, his operative metaphor suggests, as scientists see animals. We are, to be sure, to come to understand their motives, but in a distinctly behavioralist sense. Nowhere are we asked to feel as they feel, or even see as they see. As we shall see, the latter two phases of the "other" project take a very different turn here, asking us quite explicitly to share others' experiences, to come to appreciate their humanity as essentially like our own.

Wigmore's particular choice of biological metaphors is significant in another way. In choosing Buffon, the late-eighteenth-century culmination of the Enlightenment's encyclopedist taxonomy, over Darwin, the mid-nineteenth-century pioneer of evolutionary ecology, Wigmore emphasizes the static over the dynamic. This is even clearer in his other metaphor, the portrait gallery. Both tropes suggest that what we lawyers need is a frozen-frame point of reference. Perhaps we can do with no more than the two dimensions of a print or painting, at most we need the three dimensions of a stuffed specimen in a drawer or diorama. But in no case must we have a narrative account of how the individual develops, how it comes to be as it is. Here again, the later phases of the "other" project take a very different line.

### 1.2.2. Function

These two methodological aspects of the taxonomic approach, its external perspective and its static frame of reference, cast its principal functional feature into high relief. Just as we are to see others from the outside as static specimens, so are we to manipulate them without reference to their own wishes or purposes. If the method of the taxonomic mode is the aloofness of scientific observation of the external world, so its function is purely instrumental manipulation of others in that world. In an inversion of the second formulation of Kant's categorical imperative, the taxonomic approach invites lawyers to treat other people solely as means to their clients' ends, rather than as ends in themselves. Thus, each of Wigmore's illustrations of his method involves a lawyer's using the insights literature provides into particular character types to prevail against someone of that type on behalf of his client. Here, yet again, we will see that the empathetic and exemplary phases of the otherness project are in sharpest possible contrast.

### 1.3. Summary

As a matter of method, then, the taxonomic phase of the "other" project invites lawyers to see others from the outside, as we might see animals in a zoo or, more precisely, as we might see stuffed animals in a diorama or pictures of animals in a taxonomic text. As a matter of function, the taxonomic phase invites lawyers to use other people as means to their clients' ends. In the next section, we shall see that the empathetic phase of the "other" project differs, quite self-consciously, in both method and purpose. It invites lawyers to see the world from the perspective of others, and it urges them to improve the lot of those others who, from that internal perspective, appear to be particularly in need.

## 2. THE EMPATHETIC PHASE: EXPERIENCING OTHERS' LIVES, THE BETTER TO HELP THEM

If the Wigmore's taxonomic project was a fairly distant precursor of the modern law and literature movement, the second phase of the "other" project, the empathetic, was very much a part of that movement's birth (Binder & Weisberg, 2000, p. 3). Indeed, for many prominent figures in the law and literature movement, it is still near the core. Typical of them is the classicist and moral philosopher Martha Nussbaum, whose position I quoted in my second epigraph: "My central subject is the ability to imagine what it is like to live the life of another person who might, given changes in circumstance, be oneself or one of one's loved ones" (Nussbaum, 1995, p. 5). This part first outlines the empathy project, then critiques it.

### 2.1. Description

In this section, we will examine the basic features of the empathy project against the background of its precursor, the taxonomy project. Here, as in our consideration of that prior project, we will examine two aspects, the methodological and the functional. As a matter of methodology, the empathetic project can be seen as a broadening and deepening of the taxonomic; we are to experience the other's life from the inside, not just see it from the outside. As a matter of basic function, by contrast, it is a radical re-orientation, we are to help others themselves, not use them for our clients' advantage.

#### 2.1.1. Methodology
As Nussbaum's statement makes clear, the empathetic approach, in stark contrast to the taxonomic, emphasizes an internal, rather than external, perspective on others. This second approach invites us to see the world as others see it and, beyond that, to see others as they see themselves. And, even as the empathetic approach explicitly shifts from the external to the internal perspective, it also shifts, equally significantly, from a static to a dynamic mode of viewing. We are encouraged, that is, to experience with the

other what it is like to have become themselves, to share with them the experiences that have shaped their characters and their personalities, their motives and their desires.

It is important to notice that, although the empathetic approach differs from the taxonomic in these two related ways, these particular differences are methodological, not functional. They go, that is, to the way the otherness project works, not to what it works for, the use to which its methods and insights are to be put. Seen in that light, these differences are not so much refutations of the taxonomic method as corrections or adjustments of that method. Here Wigmore's own zoological metaphor is instructive. The discipline of taxonomy is refined, not rendered obsolete, by the insights of evolutionary biology; informed by genetic studies, taxonomists now have a much better sense of how the various species are related – indeed, of what it actually means to speak of a species, and of the relatedness of species. Similarly, the empathy project's internal perspective augments, rather than displaces, the taxonomic project's stock of external knowledge about others.

This latter point is nicely captured in a sportsmen's cliché: If you want to catch fish (or bag game), you must learn to think like your quarry. If, as we have seen, the function of the taxonomic method is to effectively manipulate other people on behalf of one's client, then the internal and evolutionary perspective of the empathetic movement is a great improvement upon that method, not a grave threat to it. The more you know how your clients' opponents have come to be as they are, and the more you can see as they see, think as they think, the better you can beat them in court and otherwise bend them to your clients' ends.

### 2.1.2. *Function*

It is in this turn from the methodological to the functional, from the descriptive mode to the normative, that we come to a much more basic difference between Wigmore's taxonomic phase of the "other" project and the contemporary empathetic phase. The empathetic phase is, in two important respects, a conscious reaction to the instrumentalism of the taxonomic method. It rejects, first, the predominantly client-oriented outlook of Wigmore in favor of a more immediately public-oriented model of lawyering. Second, and more explicitly, it rejects the mode of assessing and advancing public benefit recommended by an academic movement that emerged long after Wigmore's time, the economic analysis of law.

*2.1.2.1. Rejection of the Morally Neutral Model of Lawyering.* From the perspective of the early twenty-first century, the taxonomic method's implicit adoption of client ends as normatively appropriate seems particularly crass. But here we must be historically sensitive, if we are to be fully fair. In Wigmore's time, it was every bit as tempting as it is today for lawyers to equate the service of client desires with the advancement of public ends; back then, however, that equation was a very great deal more plausible. Wigmore wrote at a time doubly different from our own. In his day the early nineteenth century's more directly public-spirited model of lawyering had just collapsed (Pearce, 1992; Gordon, 1984), and the invisible-hand, client-oriented model that emerged in its wake had not yet been fully tried and found wanting. Wigmore and his contemporaries had at least some reason to believe that single-minded service of client's ends would, through the instrumentality of the adversarial system, redound more or less automatically to the public good. We today have very little reason to believe that account and very many reasons to believe the opposite.

As the modern law and literature movement gained momentum, scholars of legal ethics devastatingly criticized the model of lawyering that had come to dominate theory and practice since Wigmore's time (Simon, 1978; Schwartz, 1983; Luban, 1986; Shaffer, 1987a, 1987b). In its place, they have erected a model that calls for lawyers actively to weigh the public good against private client ends, rather than passively to leave that balance to the external outworkings of the adversarial system (Luban, 1988; Simon, 1998; Shaffer, 1987a, 1987b). This morally activist model is, by and large, the implicit paradigm of the law and literature movement. Under that model, conscientious lawyers consider not only the will of their clients, but also the effect that doing the will of their clients will have on others, including the public at large.

*2.1.2.2. Reaction to Neo-Classical Economic Analysis of Law.* Since Wigmore's time, the normative outlook of lawyers has shifted in another way as well. If most of the conscientious among us no longer trust the morally neutral model of lawyering implicit in Wigmore's client-first orientation, neither do we believe we can go back to the Neo-Classical, or classically republican, model of lawyering it displaced. That earlier model rested on a more or less monolithic conception of the public good, which lawyers were directly to serve in their representation of their private clients. In our post-Realist, post-modern era, that conception of the public good is, of course, very much in doubt. In our current situation, most of us find any objectively valid definition of the public good to be immensely problematic in practice, if not completely impossible in principle.

In the face of that impasse, in the time between Wigmore's day and ours, one branch of legal scholarship, the law and economics movement, has offered an amazingly tempting escape (Posner, 1973, 2003). That escape involved three radically simplifying steps (Leff, 1974). First, all desires are radically democratized. In the mode of the pre-Millian Utilitarian movement, no desires are qualitatively better than any others; it is no better to be Socrates satisfied (much less dissatisfied!) than a pig satisfied. Second, the origins of desires, on both the individual and social levels of analysis, are ignored; where desires come from, their phylogeny and their ontogeny, is simply deemed irrelevant.[3] Third, all desires are quantified according to a single metric. As an answer to two intractable problems of older Utilitarians – how to measure and how to limit desires – the law and economics movement came up with a metric that is also a cap: money. For your desire to count in the re-calibrated felicific calculus, you have to be not only willing, but also be able, to pay for its satisfaction. Pigs, being impecunious, are out – along with a lot of people. The desires of those without money literally do not count for anything; the starving thus have no demand for bread, technically speaking (and speaking technically was to be the order of the new day). That radical subtraction leaves only simple addition. The public good is the sum of all money-backed bids, for everything – including, in some of the more thorough-going analyses, ourselves and each other.

The modern law and literature movement began, in very large part,[4] as a response to what many saw as the law and economics movement's de-humanizing, pseudo-scientific rationality (Binder & Weisberg, 2000, p. 3). Literature was to offer law a corrective to economics' new, crasser mode of policy analysis, in which everyone is merely a means toward the satisfaction of the aggregate, undifferentiated desires of no one in particular (provided, critically, that those desires are backed with the money required to register in the market's amoral calculus).

As an antidote to this narrowness of vision (not to say meanness of spirit), the law and literature movement proposed narratives, especially long, fictitious narratives. These were to show lawyers two closely related aspects of human reality relevant to public policy making: first, the fate of the people left behind, the have-nots whose real needs and desires are defined out of the new economic calculus; and, second, the face of the desires left veiled, particularly their frequent psychopathology and their place in historic patterns of oppression. This dual demonstration is the central mission of the empathy phase of law and literatures "other" project.

## 2.2. Assessment

This mission, for all its merit, poses a host of problems, some inherent in the empathy project itself, some an accident of its historical origins. This section sketches out these problems and the answers that the empathy project has given (or might give). Binder and Weisberg put the point nicely: The empathy project needs "to urge not more, but better, narratives" (Binder & Weisberg, 2000, p. 261). To date the empathy project has not done particularly well at identifying "better." To do that, it will almost by definition have to transcend itself.

### 2.2.1. Methodology
Proponents of the empathy project face two basic methodological problems, what materials to include in their readings and what effects those readings can be expected to have on their audience. The first is an embarrassment of riches; the second, an issue of recruitment.

*2.2.1.1. The Embarrassment of Riches.*   Let us assume, with the empathy project, that literature delivers what it promises to law, a useful corrective to economists' current tendency to over-quantify social reality and to ignore the traditionally oppressed and excluded. Accepting this basic claim immediately presents an embarrassment of riches, in two directions. Intramurally, within the field of literature, we must choose among a wide range of arguably relevant material. Extramurally, we must consider the parallel claims of other disciplines that deal in concrete narratives: in particular, the social sciences of anthropology, sociology, and psychology and history, that long-contested ground between social science and the humanities. The empathy project has done well with the first problem; it is doing relatively well – though not nearly as well as it could – with the second.

*(a) Intramural problems.*   The empathy project's intramural embarrassment of riches has had two related aspects, the question of which genre to superordinate and the subsidiary question of which works within that genre to select. The first question has been resolved, more or less satisfactorily, in favor of the novel. The question of which novels has proved much more contentious, but one of the movement's earliest proponents, Richard Weisberg, has offered a plausible, if not widely accepted, accommodation, and a further accommodation is at least implicit in the movement's central focus.

*(i) The genre question: novels over everything else.* Imaginative literature comes, of course, in many forms: lyric and epic poetry; comedic, tragic, and historical drama; short stories, novellas, and novels, to list only the larger headings of the more generally recognized genres. For plausible reasons, the empathy project has focused largely on longer non-dramatic narrative works, particularly the novel. Martha Nussbaum nicely makes the case: "The novel is a living form and in fact still the central morally serious yet popularly engaging fictional form of our culture" (Nussbaum, 1995, p. 6).[5] Beyond that, the novel's very structure is especially suited to showing us the rich and textured interior life of others (Nussbaum, 1995).

Implicit in Nussbaum's argument for focusing on the novel is a critical exception. If we are best to appreciate fiction's insights into others in our own time, we must see them through our culture's major form. In that respect, Tolstoy may have been right: "The ancients have left us model heroic poems in which heroes furnish the whole interest of the story, and we still are unable to accustom ourselves to the fact that for our epoch histories of that kind are meaningless" (Tolstoy, 1992). But what if the others we want to see are not only from our time, but also from the past, and not just from our own culture, but from others as well? And what if we want to understand people of our time as the products of an evolving, historically conditioned culture, a culture vitally in contact with other cultures? Then, presumably, we would need to look at the principal fictional forms of other times and places as well. These would include, for example, the epic, the saga, and various forms of drama.

*(ii) The canonicity crisis: radicalizing the classics.* But to answer the genre question in favor of the novel (and, by extension, the principal fictional forms of other times and places) is only to raise the next question, which is structurally subsidiary but substantively more problematic: What novels (or comparably revealing works of other eras and cultures) to include? As Wigmore realized at the very outset, there are too many great novels for any of us, least of all busy practitioners, to read them all. What, then, should be the standard of selection?

The first point here was one that Wigmore had already noted in 1922: The list of best novels for lawyers would not necessarily coincide with the best novels, tout court. The law and literature canon, that is, need not be a subset of the literary canon (whatever the latter might be). For Wigmore, the most appropriate novels for lawyers should have as their subject either lawyers or the law; we find an echo of that sentiment even now when "law *in* literature" is contrasted with "law *as* literature" (Binder &

Weisberg, 2000, p. 3). This hardly seems an appropriate criterion, however, if we are looking for what Wigmore said we need: studies of humankind in all its variety and complexity. Indeed, to take one of his own examples, what he found to be the most insightful literary study of a miser came from Balzac's *Eugenie Grandet* (Wigmore, 1922, p. 32), which involves lawyers and the law only peripherally. Thus, one of the principal apologists for the empathy project, Richard Weisberg, argues that any law and literature syllabus should include Toni Morrison's first novel, *The Bluest Eye* (Morrison, 1994), for its insights into the life of a horrifically disadvantaged African-American girl, even though no lawyers appear in the book and law itself is present only as deep and little-illuminated background (Weisberg, 1992, p. 117).

On the other hand, and more to the present point, novels may be included in the literary canon for reasons largely extraneous to the core of law and literatures "other" project. At the highest level of generality, a work might have gained justified renown not for its "sense," but for its "sound" (Phillips & Cornett, 2003). The empathy project, by contrast, needs novels that primarily reveal their subject matter, rather than display their style, novels that take, in John Barth's revealing metaphor, the "windex," as opposed to the "stained glass," approach (Barth, 1988). Thus, Martha Nussbaum chooses Anglo-American realist novels that focus on social and political themes, particularly the distorting effects of pure economic instrumentalism and the emotional damage wrought by inequality, discrimination, and hatred (Nussbaum, 1995, pp. 10–11).

To that extent, then, the empathy project need not have become directly implicated in the late-twentieth-century's crisis of the canon. And yet the empathy project could not remain entirely outside that fray, either. Even though the texts best suited for the empathy project, for reasons we have seen, would not be coterminous with the literary canon writ large, yet, among those novels that do deal with the relevant subject matter, the inner lives of others, particularly the oppressed, an obvious question arises: Wouldn't otherwise canonical books be best?

Richard Weisberg has offered an answer that is both conciliatory toward critics of the canon and consistent with the needs of the "other" project. Canonical books would likely be best for the "other" project precisely because a major criterion of canonicity is the capacity to show others as they really are (Weisberg, 1992, p. 121). On this point, even Richard Posner, one of the law and literature movement's great skeptics and one of Weisberg's most trenchant critics, whole-heartedly agrees (Posner, 1988, p. 304).

And there is another answer, equally consistent with the aims of the empathy project and even more appealing to critics of the canon. Let us take the most radical anti-canonists at their word and grant that the canon has been, to a very large extent, tendentiously selected for its capacity to produce and reproduce elite values and to ensure subordination and exclusion of others. For the purposes of the empathy project, we would, for that very reason, want to read canonical works. They have made us – the oppressors and the oppressed – who we are; fully to understand ourselves, we must continue to read them, albeit with a far more critical eye.

Consider a single example, from the letters of the Apostle Paul. On the one hand, if we are to understand the universalizing and democratizing tendencies of Christianity, we must know Paul's resounding egalitarian declaration: "There is neither Jew nor Greek, there is neither bond nor free; there is neither male nor female: for ye are all one in Christ Jesus" (Galatians 3:28, King James Version). On the other hand, if we are to understand the persistent inequity of much of our culture, including our law, we would do well to ponder also two other Pauline dicta: "Wives, submit yourselves unto your husbands, as unto the Lord, for the husband is the head of the wife, even as Christ is the head of the Church," (Ephesians 5: 22–23, King James Version); "Servants, be obedient to them that are your masters according to the flesh, with fear and trembling, in singleness of your heart, as unto Christ" (Ephesians 6:5, King James Version).

If we are to know who we are, and why we are as we are, we must, as these passages suggest, read the whole of the canon, not just the parts that are loveliest according to our present lights. And, as this example also suggests, the canon we must read cannot simply be the literary canon. This latter prospect raises the empathy project's next set of problems.

*(b) Extramural problems.*   We saw in the last section that, even if we accept the basic premises of the empathy project, we must choose among the wide range of available literary works. This choice, however, can be made on the basis of a largely internal criterion: Which works best suit the purpose of the movement, which most effectively reveal what it is like to be other than we are? But, even as that "internal" criterion promises to narrow the range of choices within the field of literature, it also threatens to expand the range of choices beyond that field. Aren't those precisely the insights promised not only by literature, but also by social science and history, if not philosophy and theology? In principle, what, if anything, makes literary narratives better suited to the purpose of the empathy project than other forms of narrative?

The answer to this question reveals both the empathy project's common ground and very significant, if largely ignored, divisions within the project between what we might call its more ambitious and its more modest claims. We examined the common ground in the prior section, and need only summarize here: Literature offers a uniquely accessible and compelling "inside" perspective on the lives of others.

The more modest claims for the empathy project do not go far, if at all, beyond this common ground. For these modest claimants, of whom Nussbaum is the prototype, literature is a supplement and corrective.[6] Its empirical claims must be tested against history and social science, including economics; even as its normative claims must be tested against moral and political philosophy (Nussbaum, 1995). The more ambitious position – that of Robin West and Richard Weisberg – stakes out much wider territory for literature at the expense of other disciplines. As they see it, social science has failed descriptively, even as philosophy has failed normatively, to give us what imaginative literature alone can provide: an accurate picture of authentic human nature (West, 1993; Weisberg, 1992).

We will take up the normative side of both the modest and the ambitious claims of the empathy project in the next section; that analysis takes us beyond the project's methodology to its function. Here we need to examine the descriptive side of the ambitious claim, West and Weisberg's assertion that literature can reveal to us realities of the human condition unavailable to other disciplines, to "reclaim a kind of post-critical real as a viable basis for legal ethics" (Peters, 2005, p. 447). The basic question is this: Does literature reveal others and ourselves to us as we really are? In classical terms, how are we to distinguish the apparent from the real?[7]

In answering that crucial question, the empathy project's more ambitious claimants have been seriously deficient. I want to point out first that deficiency and its dangers, then a way around it, a way that has taken the project's more modest claimants back into a comfortable alliance with social science and history. Other disciplines have developed criteria for verification of their narratives, tentative, and disputed though those criteria may be. Literature, as a source of substantive data about ourselves and others, has no such pedigree, and the more ambitious claimants of the empathy project have provided none.

To see why this is a problem, think back to Nagel's question, "What is it like to be a bat?" One plausible answer would be, "Wow! It's a real trip, flying through the forest in extremely low-light conditions, nabbing insects on the wing, all without snagging on branches, much less bumping into trees!" Now consider a parallel response to an analogous question: "What is it like to be a unicorn?" "Well, it's a bit of a bother, really, keeping your horn out of the brambles and bushes, even in broad daylight, barely at a canter, never mind a gallop ... ." This latter account is at least as accessible as the former, if not more; it is fairly easy to imagine the difficulties of an added appendage, but pretty hard to imagine the advantages of another mode of perception. But, of course, for better or worse, bats are real mammals; unicorns, but mythical beasts.

From those comic examples, let us move – appropriately warned! – to the tragic. Compare "What is it like to survive the fire-bombing of a city" with "What is it like to be abducted by aliens?" Kurt Vonnegut describes both, movingly enough, in *Slaughterhouse Five* (Vonnegut, 1953). No one discounts the trauma of those who report having experienced alien abductions, but virtually all serious scientists deeply doubt that any such abduction has actually occurred.

This, of course, is an extreme case, but it runs closely parallel to other cases that pose serious epistemological problems for literature as a guide to public policy making. Consider, in that respect, three other situations to which we might address "what is it like" questions: recovering the memory of a remote experience, lying for years in a 'permanent vegetative state,' and floating in one's mother's womb. Imaginative literature could give – perhaps has given – compelling "inside" accounts of all three situations. But those accounts would still leave us in the dark about three other, and quite different, questions: "Are memories of remote events recoverable?" "Do people in permanent vegetative states have the capacity for any conscious life at all?" "When does a fetus become self-aware?" Before we can safely use literary insights to shape the law in these and other areas, we need to know the answers to the latter questions as well as the former. We need to know whether particular imaginable experiences are really possible, not just what such imaginable experiences might be like.

In the face of that challenge, autobiography and its close fictional analogues offer an appealing way out, a way that has been tried by several legal scholars sympathetic to the empathy project (Delgado, 1989; Williams, 1991; Bell, 1992; Delgado, 1995). It is tempting to think that we can avoid the problem of verifying internal accounts if we listen to the stories others tell about themselves. This appears to give a Cartesian answer to doubts about internal accounts: We cannot doubt that we feel the way we feel. But autobiography is at once too fine a filter, and too coarse.

It is too coarse a filter, for two related reasons. On the one hand, we cannot be sure how accurately an autobiography reports external reality. A perfectly honest and accurate internal account of an event is not reliable evidence, by itself, that the event actually happened – remember the case of alien abductions. On the other hand, even where an autobiographical account corresponds quite closely to external events independently verified, it may not be typical of the reaction of others similarly situated (Farber & Sherry, 1997). The autobiographies of African-American slaves, to take a much-discussed example, are almost by definition the accounts of literate, and to that very extent Westernized, slaves (Binder & Weisberg, 2000). Autobiographical internal accounts, then, are no guarantee of either their own relation to external reality or the typicality of the reporter's internal experience.

If the filter of autobiography is sometimes too coarse, it may, at other times, be too fine, too limiting of who gets to tell whose stories. This is often seen as trenching, for better or worse, against the artistic freedom of men of European ancestry to tell the stories of others: classically and perhaps most poignantly, the entitlement of William Styron, twentieth-century descendant of European-American slave-owning Virginians, to recount the autobiography of Nat Turner, African-American leader of a nineteenth-century Virginia slave revolt (Styron, 1994; Clarke, 1987). But autobiography as the test for authenticity can strain out others as well, including others who are members of traditionally disfavored groups.

Consider Toni Morrison's *The Bluest Eye* which, as we have seen, Richard Weisberg takes as a paradigmatically canonical work of the empathy project. Its principal narrator is Claudia, a young African-American girl growing up in the Great Depression in Lorraine, Ohio; her background is very like Morrison's own. But Morrison also tells, in the same novel, not only the story of Pecola, a much more disadvantaged African-American girl, but also the stories of twentieth-century men of African-American, Caribbean, and Eastern European descent, all, to a large extent, from an internal perspective. And in other, more widely acclaimed novels, she tells the stories of nineteenth-century African-American slaves, male as well as female.

If we limit ourselves to hearing only the stories others tell about themselves or those in all relevant respects like them, we lose not only Styron's Nat Turner, but also many of Toni Morrison's characters. Indeed, if tightened to its logic limit, the filter of autobiography becomes a hermetic seal, and the "other" project itself cuts each of us off from every other, locking us into solipsism. As Socrates said (albeit in gendered language that should put us on our guard): "if the feelings of every human being were peculiar to himself and different from those of every other human being, instead of our all possessing, for all the diversity of our experience, something in common, it would not be easy for one man to make his own situation clear to another" (Plato, 1985, p. 75).

Thus, the more ambitious claims of the empathy project not only fail to justify their effort to displace other disciplines; they also pose the risk of very real abuse of both fictional and autobiographical narratives themselves. Having made that concession, however, it is important to note that it leaves the more modest claim of the empathy project entirely intact. Even within the confines of that narrower position, literature can play an immensely useful role for law. Even if it cannot legitimately claim a superior role here, neither need it be consigned to an inferior, much less merely ornamental, position. Rather, its role would be essential to a full understanding of law and would be co-ordinate, in that respect, with social science and history. The "other" project, as part of the more general literary criticism of law, would become an essential part of a still broader "cultural criticism" of law (Binder & Weisberg, 2000, pp. 462–539).

It is important to see, at least in outline, how that co-ordination might work. Here again, it is useful to think of Nagel's question, "What is it like to be a bat?" History and the human sciences give us the verifiable contours of possible experience, the parameters of what has happened, and can happen. But the perspective of these disciplines is, by its very nature, external, that which can be verified from the position of neutral observers. Literature, by contrast, gives us an internal perspective, lets us see what it would be like to be a particular person, to live a concrete life other than our own. The two perspectives, the internal and the external, can thus complement each other, as claimed.

We must be careful, however, to notice that both perspectives are tentative or hypothetical in different but related ways. The external, objective perspective of the human sciences and history is subject to revision under the canons of the relevant disciplines. Memories may not be recoverable in the ways we once thought; it may turn out that aliens have regularly visited our planet; Washington now seems never to have chopped down his father's cherry tree, and further research may show that accounts of his crossing the Delaware were greatly exaggerated, too. The internal perspective, at least insofar as it is useful for law reform, is subject to precisely these corrections, but in a different, derivative way. What literature tells us it may be like to be a certain way, or to have experienced a certain state or event, may be fully imaginable yet historically untrue or humanly impossible, as tested against our ever-tentative scientific and historical knowledge.

*2.2.1.2. The Recruitment Problem.* The modest version of the empathy project offers a plausible way to resolve the relationship between literature and other narrative disciplines, a way that preserves the claim for a unique contribution from the literary perspective. Here, however, we face two further questions, both of them about the reception of the tentative, hypothetical accounts that literature offers: First, will reading those accounts morally transform, not just intellectually inform, their readers? Second, and more basically, will those accounts attract those readers in the first place? Proponents of the empathy project tend to focus on the first question, to the virtual exclusion of the second. And, in their answer to the first, they tend to be unduly optimistic. In both respects, their approach reveals a disappointing inclination to adopt the very sort of liberal moral psychology from which they promise, at least implicitly, to deliver us.

*(a) Will proper narratives morally transform their readers?* To this first question, the empathy project's standard answer has been winningly simple: Reading the right accounts of others will not only provide empathy with their plight; it will also, in and of itself, bring readers to their side. Thus, for example, Richard Weisberg maintains that "Stories about the 'other' induce us to *see* the other, and once we do so, we endeavor consistently to understand the world from within the other's optic" (Weisberg, 1992, p. 46). Similarly, Richard Delgado concludes that "Hearing stories invites hearers to participate, challenging their assumptions, jarring their complacency, lifting their spirits, lowering their defenses" (Delgado, 1989, p. 2440). In very much the same vein, Robin West makes an even bolder claim: "The narrative voice can convey the subjective feel of experiences in a way that triggers understanding of others and an empathetic response to their plight, thereby changing our moral beliefs and our moral assessment of the law" (West, 1993, p. 11). Reading the right stories will, in short, move readers in the right direction.

But proponents of this view seldom get much beyond asserting that this desired effect – enlisting powerful readers on the side of the oppressed – will inevitably follow. They never quite get around to showing how this will work, and, what is perhaps worse, they never face the grim prospect that it may not only fail, but work in the wrong direction. As alien abduction narratives suggest, morally appealing "inside" accounts may move sympathetic listeners to credit the empirically implausible, if not the demonstrably false. Here we have to consider the converse problem: Factually accurate narratives may fail to move conscientious readers to re-orient themselves in the morally desirable direction. Worse than that, descriptively accurate narratives may be put to bad use, rather than to good. Might not the study of past modes of oppression be the education, not just of future liberators, but also of future oppressors? This is, at bottom, the problem of Plato's *Gorgias*: Shall we put powerful tools for shaping public policy into the hands of those who are ignorant of, or indifferent to, whether the policies they pursue help or harm the public (Plato, 1985, p. 39)? Hitler, as Posner pointedly reminds us, had unequalled powers of persuasion, doubtlessly drawing on an immense capacity for empathy (Posner, 1998). Perhaps worst of all, might not searing accounts of sufferings be, for the truly sick among us, not deeply repellant, but darkly attractive? The very name for that attraction, after all, comes from an author well ensconced in the canon of a paradigmatically literate nation.

Literature, we have reason to hope, may make those inclined to helping others to do just that; it may, in other words, be the means of making the good better, more beneficial to the badly off. But we have at least some reason, too, to fear that literature will make the bad worse, more capable of causing – even enjoying – harm to those already most hurt. To assume that literature will always have the desired moral effect is to assume an oddly optimistic version of the position, often attributed to Plato, that those who really know the good will invariably choose the good (Plato, 1976).

Even if this is Plato's position, and even if Plato is right, this is certainly not all he had to say on the point. Plato also raises a logically anterior question, sometimes implicitly, sometimes explicitly: How are those who see the good, and choose it, able to do that? Sometimes, as Jesus's parable of the sower tells us, the seeds fall on dry and stony ground, where, even if they sprout, they wither and die (Matthew 13:3–9, King James Version). This should make us wonder: How does the right ground, where the seed flourishes and bears fruit, come to be ready?

*(b) What makes people heed, not just hear, the right stories?*   The empathy project tends to ignore this second question, so much at issue in both classical Greek and Latin philosophy and the canonical Jewish and Christian scriptures. The project's assumption – a glaringly liberal assumption – is that, when presented with stories about others' plight, we either choose to heed their call, or we do not. Those who choose to follow are virtuous; those who turn away, vicious. By implication, we who choose well have every reason, not just to congratulate ourselves, but also to condemn our straying fellows.

A more subtle psychology – again, that of the Scriptures and the Classics – suggests a more complex process. Although the choice is quite real, it is not wholly unconditioned; although the virtuous choose the right path, they cannot choose the capacity for that choice. That capacity comes from outside, at least initially independent of their will. For Plato and Aristotle, it is the result of proper education; in the tradition of Jews and Christians, it is a gift of grace[8]; in our post-modern idiom, it is socially constructed. Whatever their differences, these three perspectives share this much common ground: The virtuous are made, not born (and they cannot make themselves).

If that more complex moral psychology, at once both pre- and post-modern, is correct, then we must not just tell the right stories; we must also prepare those whom we would have listen to those stories. This raises a final question for the empathy project: Why do we feel entitled to make others the way we want them to be, responsive, through the call of our stories, to the needs of others?

This question, of course, is the challenge of the egoists and anti-altruists, ancient and modern (or, if you prefer, post-modern). Theirs is the response of Thrasymachus and Callicles to Socrates, of Nietzsche not only to Socrates, but also to Jesus and the other Jewish prophets. In a word – Nietzsche's word – it is *ressentiment* (Nietzsche, 1969). Callicles's indictment of the classical Athenian education system might easily have been addressed to today's empathy project: "Our way is to take the best and strongest among us from an early age and endeavor to mold their character as men tame lions; we subject them to a course of charms and spells and try to enslave them by repetition of the dogma that man ought to be equal and that equality is fine and right" (Plato, 1985, p. 79).

### 2.2.2. Function

We saw, earlier on, that the more ambitious view of the empathy project and the more modest view divide on normative as well as descriptive matters. In the prior section, we saw that, on descriptive matters, the more modest view is the more compelling. The insights of literature are most helpfully seen, not as a replacement for the failures of other descriptive disciplines, but as a supplement, with each offering its respective strengths, the "external" and the "internal" perspectives on ourselves and others.

In normative matters, by contrast, the better view lies not with the more modest claims of the empathy project over against the more ambitious, nor even somewhere between the two. It lies, rather, beyond, and in a sense behind, both, at the very beginning of classical literature and philosophy, in works in which the law and literature movement itself is rooted. Those deepest roots are the dialogues of Plato.

*2.2.2.1. The Metaethical Impasse.* As the modest view of the empathy projects invites us, in the descriptive realm, to test the external aspects of our stories with social science and history, so it invites us to test our stories' normative insights with the findings of moral and political philosophy. But here, the more ambitious view points up a very real problem: Traditional philosophy has failed to give us externally grounded norms, and its current practitioners offer us no prospect of improvement.

In the face of that impasse, we find one of the empathy project's most ambitious claims, and one of its most conspicuous failures. Its adherents purport not only to displace social science with an accurate description of human nature as it is, descriptively, but also to displace moral and political philosophy with a vision of humanity, as it ought to be, normatively. Here, the more ambitious have sought to deliver the dream of philosophers at least since Aristotle: normative human nature. If they could deliver on that claim, they could answer the question we raised in the last section: By what right do we make people as we want them to be, that is, capable of being moved by stories to empathetic, loving response to the needs of the worst off of our fellow-folk? If we can prove that that is how people ought to be, then it may be our right, even our duty, to make them that way. But the promise to deliver that proof has emphatically not been fulfilled.

*2.2.2.2. The Skeptical Escape.* There is, however, a way out, a way deeply implicit in the empathy project itself. Their ungrounded but appealing categorical imperative, "Do unto others as you would have them do unto you," has an alternative, existentialist reading: "Eschew trying to prove the rightness of a certain end; choose, instead, to be a certain way, to become the kind of person who helps others, particularly the neediest of others." This shifts analytic focus from the objects of our care, the others we help, to the subject, our own becoming what we take to be our better selves.

To a considerable extent, the empathy project has already done this. Along with its images of those who are suffering, it has also given us examples of those who have taken it upon themselves to alleviate suffering. This aspect of the empathy project, its presentation of the liberator as well as the liberated, brings us to the third phase of law and literatures "other" project, the exemplary project. As we shall see in the final part of this chapter, the exemplary project can both accept the principal mission of the empathy project, helping others, and advance that mission by placing it on a sounder metaethical foundation and by giving it a more sophisticated moral psychology.

# 3. THE EXEMPLARY PHASE: RE-READING
# PLATO'S *REPUBLIC*

This part sketches, in barest outline, one form that the exemplary phase of the "other" project might take. Imaginative literature, of course, holds up many possible exemplars; here, we focus on the ones that best complement the empathy project's goal of helping the neediest others. To parallel the prior parts, this part first describes that exemplary project in terms of its method and function, then subjects both to critical analysis.

## *3.1. Description*

Methodologically, the exemplary phase, as we have seen, holds up role models, in long narrative presentations, for the powerful, particularly those who will be lawyers, to emulate. Functionally, its goal is to win the powerful – again, particularly those who will make and apply the law – over to the side of the disadvantaged.

## *3.2. Analysis*

I have presented the exemplary phase of law and literatures "other" project as both an extension and a correction of that project's empathy phase, which itself is, similarly, a strengthening and focusing of the taxonomic project. In analyzing this last phase, accordingly, we will focus on how it meets the problems of the other two, particularly the second.

### *3.2.1. Methodology*
### *3.2.1.1. The Embarrassment of Riches*
*(a) Intramural*

*(i) The appropriate genre.* The exemplary project has, in principle, no problem adopting the empathy project's choice of the novel as the appropriate genre, with the caveat we noted above: We must, if we are to understand other cultures, also include with the novel the equivalent genres from those cultures, genres that have done for them what novels do for us. For my particular version of the exemplary project, it will be especially important to include Plato's dialogues, foundational works of the classical culture that is both different from and predecessor to our own.

*(ii) The exemplary canon.* Like the empathy project, the exemplary project must choose from within its preferred genres the works that best show us what others are like from the inside, the particular works that best reveal the relevant individuals. The empathy project, as we have seen, shows us principally those whom it would have us help; the exemplary project, by contrast, shows us those who it would have us become. This latter could, in principle, include role models incompatible with, even antithetical to, those of the empathy project. It could, that is, choose role models who are indifferent, even opposed, to the needs of the powerless: Nietzsche's Plutarchan heroes, for example (Nietzsche, 1957, pp. 41–42), or Ayn Rand's egoist icons (Rand, 1999; Rand, 1946). Homer's epics were the education of Hellas, even as the sagas were the study of the pagan north. But their heroes are hardly those of the empathy project.

That project's heroes, by contrast, are close, at least in their alignment, to those of the chivalric literature of the Christian middle ages, with its nine noble knights as embodiments of strength serving the weak, a trilogy of trinities from the Hebrew scriptures, the Greco-Roman classics, and the medieval courtly romances (Keen, 1984). Closer still, in both time and temperament, are modern lawyer heroes. These could include fictional characters like Thomas Shaffer's Atticus Finch (Shaffer, 1987a, 1987b) or my Gavin Stevens (Atkinson, 1999) and historical figures like those presented by legal ethicicist David Luban: Louis Brandeis as "the people's lawyer," Clarence Darrow as "lawyer for the damned" (Luban, 1988). And any pantheon of lawyer heroes should include examples of the modern lawyer-statesman (Kronmann, 1993), chief among whom might well be Abraham Lincoln (Jaffa, 1982).

For the ideal of rational control of power for the public good, however, we must go farther back than these modern examples, and to a different source of western culture from the Jewish and Christian scriptures. We must look back to the dialogues of Plato as our canonical texts, and the Platonic Socrates as our paradigmatic person. In the *Gorgias*, Plato has Socrates raise the core question of modern law and legal education: Must our leaders be trained merely in methods of persuasion, or must they also learn, more fundamentally, to distinguish good policies from bad? In the *Republic*, Plato has Socrates give – more precisely, live – the answer.

The *Republic* is the paradigm of this particular exemplary project for several related reasons. It gives us the ideal moral person, the ideal political community, and the proper relationship between the two, all through a persuasive narrative form. With respect to "others," the relationship between the ideal person and community is essentially this: Any kind of other who is (or, significantly, can be made) capable of engaging in dialogic resolution of normative questions is to be engaged (or enabled to engage) at the very highest level, the governance of the polity. In a very real sense, the only criterion for fullest citizenship is this minimum: the ability meaningfully to address normative questions with others who share that ability. Correspondingly, the minimal mandate of that society is this: Enable every potential member to become a full member. In the conversations within the Dialogues, in their realistic portrayal of existing Athenian society, this moral community included not only the educated male citizens and future citizens of Athens, but also educated foreigners in Athens (Plato, 1985). In the society imagined in the Dialogues, particularly in the republic set out in the *Republic*, this also included all the children of the underclasses, female and male alike.

The final book of the *Republic*, of course, is notoriously hard on its competitors, the then-prevalent genres of drama and lyric. But we must bear in mind that Plato's infamous ban on the poets is explicitly subject to their showing, through dialogue, the public benefits of their craft. Beyond that, his ban is implicitly subject to a showing – again, through dialogue – that the ban itself is counter-productive. This is the showing that has persuaded us of Plato's error; it is the showing that Aristotle began in his *Poetics*, in the very next generation, and that Milton offered, metaphorically before the Areopagus, the appropriate Athenian tribunal (Milton, 1868). Most significantly, Plato, in presenting the *Republic* to us, not as a treatise, but as a story, violates his own ban, even as Socrates does within that story, by following his exclusion of the poets with his own recitation of a myth. The *Republic* thus doubly announces, not the death of imaginative literature, but its rebirth.

*(b) Extramural.* But how can we know whether such transformations, individual and social, are, in fact, really possible? Here the method of the dialogues is open, in principle, to the insights of discourses outside its own, even those of disciplines that existed only in embryonic form in Plato's time. Socrates routinely refers matters of physical health to doctors; he might have been surprised to learn how much mental health is also in their ambit, but that knowledge need not have discomfited him. At every step he explicitly makes his model open to the charge of practical impossibility; if means or even ends can be shown unworkable, he is committed to considering others, on the same conditions. In that way, the implicit openness of his republic, and Plato's *Republic*, to rational correction is perfectly compatible with the explicitly interdisciplinary version of the

empathy project that Nussbaum has developed. Plato, thus viewed, is not the archetypical enemy of an open society (Popper, 1945), but rather its principal architect.

*3.2.1.2. The Problem of Recruitment.* The Platonic dialogues, particularly the *Republic*, give us a doubly instructive solution to the recruitment problem. Socrates in the reported dialogues, and Plato in reporting the dialogues, begin with the very limited human material they have at hand; from there, they try to show how that material might be improved, made better to serve better ends. On the one hand, both Socrates and Plato address those, in the present regime, who have not only the power to change society in the desired direction, but also the capacity to commit themselves to making that change. In that respect, the dialogues are essentially conservative or realistic; they begin with their audience where they are, imbedded in their society as it is.

On the other hand, the *Republic* recommends an ideal society that is radically different from the existing society whose elite members it addresses, even as it invites members of that elite to become, through dialogue with Socrates, different from what they themselves now are. The ideal society would, at its foundation, involve the full enfranchisement of everyone capable of full enfranchisement; its rulers would, as their most basic commitment, exercise power only for the public good. The present elite are transformed precisely to the extent that they enlist in that imaginative recreation of society in league with Socrates. Plato shows us how, within the dialogue, Socrates successfully recruits the aristocratic brothers Glaucon and Adeimantus; in that showing, Plato brings the *Republic*'s readers themselves into dialogue with Socrates, and thus recruits us, too (White, 1983).

But to prove that individual or social transformations are possible, as Part 2 reminds us, is not to prove that they are good. If, as the *Republic* insists, both good citizens and good regimes are made, not born, what entitles us to make either in our image? For that, too, the *Republic* has the answer; indeed, one could fairly say, it *is* the answer. It may not be, however, the answer we have come to think we will find there, nor, for that matter, the answer that we have come to think we are looking for.

*3.2.2. Function*
The shared goal of the exemplary and empathy projects is rational control of power for the public good. The Platonic dialogues – again, particularly the *Republic* – purport to demonstrate the goodness of this goal in objective, rational, and universal terms. In the conventional reading of Plato, the

good, the beautiful, and the true are one, and that one is both eternal and external, beyond time and independent of the human will. That normative unity and universality, of course, is precisely what, in the wake of various waves of post-modern criticism, most of us now deeply doubt.

At a deeper level, though, what the dialogues seem to present as an objectively grounded normative system is always open to question, its proof always subject to dispute. The dialogues' recommendation of the life of reasoned discourse as the model for individual virtue and political justice is, at bottom, presented, not as some externally imposed prototype or logical proof, but rather as what we its readers want and, in that very desiring, already have. If we could show that the rational proofs of the *Republic* were weak, that would produce a critical paradox. Our demonstration of their weakness, by the process of dialogic discourse, would necessarily involve our commitment to the mode of discourse that lies at the republic's foundation. Socrates says explicitly to his interlocutors in the dialogues, and Plato says implicitly to us through the dialogues, that what ultimately matters is not the rational proof of any argument, but our willingness to resolve our disagreements, and thus build our polity, through dialogue.

At every critical turn in the dialogues, Socrates asks his interlocutors if they agree with him. If they do not, he moves back to a more basic agreement; if they do, he moves forward to a further, more refined point of agreement. He suggests – perhaps he and Plato both believed – that the source of this kind of agreement was shared insight into some external, rational order. But the method by which they proceeded did not depend on this; all it requires is shared normative commitment, not external normative reality. In practice, then, Plato shows us how to bridge the post-modern gap between the fact of desire and the supposed norm of the truly desirable: if we reach back to, and proceed forward to, points of normative agreement, the divide, as a practical matter, disappears. The difference between impersonal, objective normative reality and shared, though merely subjective, normative preferences becomes, to use an ironically apt expression, merely academic.

Sometimes, of course, we will not reach such agreement, within our own culture or with other cultures with which we come in contact.[9] We then face an intractable dilemma: They will force us, or we will force them. It was precisely through the horns of this dilemma that the *Republic*, in its very opening pages, proposed to offer its *via media* of dialogic agreement. When that agreement fails, we come to the ultimate stumbling-block of all process-oriented systems, modern civic republicanism as much as any other: What do those who are fundamentally committed to rational discourse do in the face of intractable disagreement on substantive questions, either among themselves or with outsiders?

At this point, in our critical re-reading of Plato, commitment to the process of dialogue itself becomes a matter of substance; what citizens of the republic are committed to is sustaining and expanding their normative dialogue. And that commitment becomes its own foundation, both descriptively and normatively. This, in turn, gives us the basis for determining when to submit, and when to fight, within and outside the commonwealth. Socrates risked his life in battle to defend Athens; he forfeited his life to submit to Athens's legal process. Defending its empire, we are inclined to believe, was hardly the high point of Athenian democracy; the execution of Socrates certainly seems among its lowest. In both these cases, as in all others, we have his example of how he himself made the normative assessment: In dialogue with those who shared his commitment to dialogue, whatever the personal cost. It is a culture committed, in large measure, to that dialogue that has made us who we are; it is our commitment to that dialogue, at the deepest existential level, upon which that dialogue ultimately rests. The foundation of a republic that is a government of laws and not of men is dialogue about that very republic – even as we are taught in the *Republic*.

As the *Republic* itself acknowledges, the ideal city may exist no where on earth; in that sense, the *Republic* is, literally, the first Utopia. It is enough, Socrates and his interlocutors agree, if its model exists in Heaven, as a basis for our actions here below. In our post-modern reading of the *Republic*, however, Plato may, intentionally or not, have proved something more: Commitment to the republic Socrates describes can rest on that description itself, without any metaphysical underpinnings or quasi-mathematical normative proofs.

As Nietzsche reminded us, at the very beginning of our post-modern era, it was Socrates's own persistent questioning that ultimately led us to call his faith in reason into doubt (Nietzsche, 1967). At the bottom of that doubt, to which Nietzsche quite rightly directed us, is the prospect that our concern for the badly off may really be rooted, not in our better, Socratic selves, but in our worst, our *ressentiment* toward the very kind of epic heroes that Socrates sought to displace (Nietzsche, 1969). If we can still believe in his republic, despite all our post-modern doubts about both the ultimate proof of any norm and the absolute purity of any motive, then we will have not only become its foundation, but also proved that it has always been ours.

## CONCLUSION: *THE REPUBLIC* CONSTITUTING
## THE REPUBLIC

The *Republic*, critically re-read, would be a fitting foundation for the canon of the law and literature movement's "other" project. It shows us how to be different from what we are in the way that we take to be the best, the most passionately committed to making power serve the public good as determined in rational discourse among all those who can be enabled to participate. The *Republic* at once draws us, its readers, into dialogue ourselves, and brings us to commit ourselves fundamentally to including others. It promises to make us better than we are, by engaging us in the service of the common good. It is, then, not only the core of our law and literature canon, but also the heart of our legal constitution. In the *Republic*, more than anywhere else, we can learn the lessons literature has for law.

## NOTES

1. In saying this, I whole-heartedly concur in my anonymous commentator's cautionary note: "The 'other' project is indeed one of the movement's strongest strands, but it isn't the only one."
2. Norman Stein rightly observes that Wigmore tends to overlook two additional, if subordinate, sorts of taxonomers: those like Wigmore himself, who compile and organize the novelists' taxonomic canon, and those like us, who read both his article and his novelists.
3. As Norman Stein reminds me, one branch of the law and economics movement has itself begun to address these issues; in his words, "law and economics has moved into a new phase concerned with actual human behavior rather than the idealized view of human behavior enshrined in neo-classical theory." That development conceded (and welcomed!), the fact remains that the originators of the empathy project faced an economic analysis of law that was much less-empirically attuned than today's.
4. It is fair to agree, with my anonymous commentator, that this is more typical of scholars who came from legal backgrounds and less true of those who came from literary, historical, or cultural studies.
5. Here Norman Stein raises an objection that Martha Nussbaum herself concedes, if a bit begrudgingly: Dramas retain considerable power in our era, and movies may well be the distinctive narrative genre of our time. As Stein suggests, lawyers, philosophers, and literary critics may well undervalue these other genres because our primary orientation is verbal rather than visual; in his words, "all crafts people are partial to the tools of their particular craft."
6. In taking Nussbaum as prototypical, I do not mean to deny that she is in a large company; indeed, as my anonymous commentator points out, "there is a sense in which law and literature, to the extent that it has now been subsumed under the rubric of 'culture,' has explicitly joined forces with anthropologists, political

scientists, sociologists, and historians." This perspective of the cultural studies movement is nicely captured in Sarat and Simon (2003, p. 4): "We see cultural analysis more as valued supplements ... than as competitors to the multitude of intellectual programs that already operate in the what might be called the post-realist legal landscape, including varieties of realism, its moderate legal-process critics, as well as more the more radical recent discourses ... ."

7. As my anonymous commentator points out here and elsewhere, my concern with the "reality" and "verifiability" of fictional accounts is not shared by many who identify themselves as "post-modern" and "postrealist." At least some of them, as my commentator notes, hold that "the 'real' is the product of social agreement: simply put, it is made-up," and, in a similar vein, that "the self, like the proscenium of the real upon which it is enacted, is a fiction ... ." Let me be clear: I do not agree, as to either the world or the self; indeed, I cannot see how discourse, even life itself, is possible without something out there for me, here, to talk about. I am unable to operate outside what Sarat and Simon identify as "the continuing constraints" of "the realism of legal realism" Sarat and Simon (2003, p. 7). We may be very wrong about what is out there and in here, about the world and ourselves – culturally conditioned, demonically deluded, otherwise falsely conscious – but we cannot have our doubts, much less share them, without some substratum that is "me" and "you" and "it." With Paul Kahn, "in the capacity for critical distance, I find a free self that is always beyond the reach of any symbolic form to exhaust," which takes me, too, "back through Kant and Plato and the origins of Western philosophy," Kahn (2003, p. 182); with Julie Stone Peters, in "the exhaustion of questions about the real," I "have come to realize that to expose the made-upness of a thing is not necessarily to dim its prestige, let alone to do away with it" Peters (2005, p. 451). (My particular thanks to my anonymous commentator for both these references.) On metaethical matters, on the other hand, I am a much deeper skeptic, as I imply at various points in the text. To put the matter as tightly as possible, I believe in the fact/value distinction, and I believe in objective facts, but not in objective values. (As this implies, I also believe, at least minimally, in me.)

8. Both Norman Stein and my anonymous commentator question whether grace is a Jewish as well as Christian concept. As a student of both the Jewish and Christian scriptures, I am convinced that grace is central to both, but I come at them from the Augustinian tradition, which is quite orthodoxly Christian but at best only very heretically Jewish.

9. I quite agree with my anonymous commentator: "there clearly are some differences in worldview that cannot be reconciled through reason and that have proved tragically resistant to dialogue." As I try to show in the text that follows, however, I believe that Plato's dialogues, especially the *Republic*, and the example of Socrates, both in the dialogues and in historical Athens, give us a viable and principled, though not rationally provable, way of dealing with these apparent normative impasses.

# ACKNOWLEDGMENTS

In the legal literature, it is customary to thank those who have helped with one's work. My thanks to Austin Sarat for letting me honor that custom here and, much more importantly, for inviting me to participate in this symposium and for guiding me all through the process. Bernard O'Donnell, Brian Sites, Paul Washington, and Arthur Zimmet, my research assistants at Florida State, were invaluable. I owe special thanks to Norman Stein, my colleague during a semester's visit at the University of Alabama, and to my anonymous commentator at Studies in Law, Politics, and Society, for their extensive, insightful, and kindly comments. Unfortunately but understandably, the parameters of the symposium could not accommodate their thoughts as separately published comments; accordingly, I have tried to acknowledge their contributions and continue our dialogue in my endnotes. Had I had more time and space (not to say that Studies has not been generous with both), I would have answered them more fully, and my chapter would have been much the better for it.

# REFERENCES

Atkinson, R. (1999). *Liberating lawyers: Divergent parallels in* intruder in the dust *and* to kill a mockingbird. *Duke Law Journal, 49*(3), 601–748.

Barth, J. (1988). *The floating opera and the end of the road.* New York: Anchor Books.

Bell, D. (1992). *Faces at the bottom of the well: The permanence of racism.* New York: Basic Books.

Binder, G., & Weisberg, R. (2000). *Literary criticisms of law.* Princeton, NJ: Princeton University Press.

Clarke, H. (1987). Introduction. In: H. Clarke (Ed.), *William Styron's Nat turner: Ten black writers respond.* Westport, CT: Greenwood Press Publishers.

Delgado, R. (1989). Storytelling for oppositionists and others: A plea for narrative. *Michigan Law Review, 87,* 2411–2441.

Delgado, R. (1995). *The Rodrigo chronicles: Conversations about America and race.* New York: New York University Press.

Farber, D. A., & Sherry, S. (1997). *Beyond all reason: The radical assault on truth in American law.* New York: Oxford University Press.

Gordon, R. (1984). The ideal and the actual in the law: Fantasies and practices of New York city lawyers, 1870–1910. In: G. Gawalt (Ed.), *The new high priests: Lawyers in post-civil war America.* Westport, CT: Greenwood Publishing Group.

Jaffa, H. (1982). *Crisis of the house divided: An interpretation of the issues in the Lincoln–Douglas debates.* Chicago: The University of Chicago Press.

Kahn, P. (2003). Freedom, autonomy, and the cultural study of law. *Sarat and Simon,* 155–187.

Keen, M. (1984). *Chivalry.* London: Yale University Press.

Kronmann, A. (1993). *The lost lawyer.* New Haven: Yale University Press.

Leff, A. A. (1974). Economic analysis of law: Some realism about nominalism. *Virginia Law Review, 60,* 451–482.

Livy (1962). *A history of Rome: Selections.* (M. Hadas & J. P. Poe, Trans.). New York: The Modern Library.

Luban, D. (1986). The lysistration prerogative: A response to Stephen Pepper. *The American Bar Foundation Research Journal*, 637–649.

Luban, D. (1988). *Lawyers and justice: An ethical study*. Princeton, NJ: Princeton University Press.

Milton, J. (1868). *Areopagitica*. London: Alex. Murray & Son.

Morrison, T. (1994). *The bluest eye*. New York: Penguin Books.

Nagel, T. (1974). What is it like to be a bat? *The Philosophical Review*, *83*(4), 435–450.

Nietzsche, F. (1957). *The use and abuse of history*. New York: Library of Liberal Arts Press.

Nietzsche, F. (1967). *The birth of tragedy and the case of Wagner*. (W. Kaufmann, Trans.). New York: Vintage Books.

Nietzsche, F. (1969). *The genealogy of morals and ecce homo*. (W. Kaufmann & R. J. Hollingdale, Trans.). New York: Vintage Books.

Nussbaum, M. (1995). *Poetic justice: The literary imagination and public life*. Boston, MA: Beacon Press.

Pearce, R. (1992). Rediscovering the republican origins of the legal ethics code. *Georgetown Journal of Legal Ethics*, *6*, 241–282.

Peters, J. S. (2005). Law, literature, and the vanishing real: On the future of an interdisciplinary illusion. *PMLA*, *120*, 442–453.

Phillips, J. J., & Cornett, J. M. (2003). *Sound and sense: A text on law and literature*. St. Paul, MN: Thomson/West.

Plato (1968). The republic. In: A. Bloom (Ed.), *The republic of Plato*. New York: Basic Books, Inc. Publishers.

Plato (1976). *Protagoras*. (C. C. W. Taylor, Trans.). Oxford: Clarendon Press.

Plato (1985). *Gorgias*. (W. Hamilton, Trans.). Middlesex, England: Penguin Books.

Popper, K. (1945). *The open society and its enemies volume 1: The spell of Plato.* , New York: Routledge.

Posner, R. (1973). *Economic analysis of law*. Boston, MA: Little, Brown & Company.

Posner, R. (1988). *Law and literature: A misunderstood relation*. Cambridge, MA: Harvard University Press.

Posner, R. (1998). *Law and literature: The revised and enlarged edition*. Cambridge, MA: Harvard University Press.

Posner, R. (2003). *Economic analysis of law* (6th ed.). New York: Aspen Publishers.

Rand, A. (1946). *The fountainhead*. New York: Penguin Books.

Rand, A. (1999). *Atlas shrugged*. New York: Penguin Group.

Sarat, A., & Simon, J. (2003). *Cultural analysis, cultural studies, and the law*. Durham, NC: Duke University Press.

Schwartz, M. L. (1983). The zeal of the civil advocate. *The American Bar Foundation Research Journal*, *3*, 543–563.

Shaffer, T. (1987a). The legal ethics of radical individualism. *Texas Law Review*, *65*, 963–991.

Shaffer, T. (1987b). *Faith and the professions*. Provo, UT: Brigham Young University.

Simon, W. H. (1978). Ideology of advocacy: Procedural justice and professional ethics. *Wisconsin Law Review*, *1978*, 29–150.

Simon, W. H. (1998). *The practice of justice: A theory of lawyers' ethics*. Cambridge, MA: Harvard University Press.

Styron, W. (1994). *The confessions of Nat Turner*. New York: The Modern Library.

Tolstoy, L. (1992). *War and peace*. New York: Everyman's Library.

Vonnegut, K. (1953). *Slaughterhouse five*. New York: Dell Publishing.

Weisberg, R. (1992). *Poethics and other strategies of law and literature*. New York: Columbia
    University Press.
West, R. (1993). *Narrative, authority, and law*. Ann Arbor, MI: University of Michigan Press.
White, J. B. (1983). The ethics of argument: Plato's Gorgias and the modern lawyer. *Chicago
    Law Review, 50*, 849–895.
Wigmore, J. H. (1922). A List of one hundred legal novels. *Illinois Law Review, 17*,
    26–41(Reprinting and correcting the original essay that was published in *Illinois Law
    Review, 2*, 574 (1908)).
Williams, P. (1991). *The alchemy of race and rights: Diary of a law professor*. Cambridge:
    Harvard University Press.

# THE LAW, THE NORM, AND THE NOVEL

Sara Murphy

## 1. THE USES OF THE VICTORIANS

In *Poetic Justice*, Martha Nussbaum (1996) offers one version of an argument frequently repeated in the history of law-and-literature scholarship; to wit, that the literary imagination performs a salutary function with regard to many domains of modern public life. While law and economics are governed by logics of bureaucratic rationality and utilitarian calculus, literature, in particular the novel, presents a counterdiscourse, inviting us to empathize with others, expanding our moral sense, emphasizing the importance of affect and imagination in the making of a just, humane, and democratic society. Nussbaum's broad goal is a commendable one; concerned that "cruder forms of economic utilitarianism and cost-benefit analysis that are ... used in many areas of public policy-making and are frequently recommended as normative for others" are, in effect, dehumanizing, she argues for the importance to public life of "the sort of feeling and imagining called into being" by the experience of reading literary texts (1996, p. 3). This sort of feeling and imagining, Nussbaum explains, fosters sympathetic understanding of others who may be quite different from us and a deepened awareness of human suffering.

Nussbaum's book exemplifies a practice among law-and-literature scholars of making arguments about the importance of literature to legal

Special Issue: Law and Literature Reconsidered
Studies in Law, Politics, and Society, Volume 43, 53–77
ISSN: 1059-4337/doi:10.1016/S1059-4337(07)00603-5

thought. A number of scholars have criticized the polarization of law and literature that this approach entails, arguing that this type of argument assumes an image of the literary as an unproblematic locus of sympathy and virtue over against a conception of law as a soulless body of rules and proscriptions (Baron, 1999, 2004; Binder, 1999; Sharpe, 1999; Peters, 2005). In a recent article, Julie Stone Peters has pointed out that the effects of these assumptions are anything but interdisciplinary: studies in law and literature, she argues, "sought to break down disciplinary boundaries, but through the imaginary projection by each discipline of the other's difference, [they] exaggerated the very boundaries [they] sought to dissolve" (2005, p. 499). To the extent that this is an accurate description of things, we might be better served by displacing efforts to break down boundaries in favor of investigating the constitution and development of the boundaries themselves. This chapter represents a modest effort at indicating some ways such an investigation might be framed.

*Poetic Justice* presents a particularly compelling instantiation of boundary delineation. Nussbaum's analysis is structured around what appears an inexorable chasm between modern modes of social control and the field of the imagination, a faculty understood here to have particularly moral potentialities. Because she relies so intensively on examples drawn from the mid-Victorian period, Nussbaum's discussion, perhaps unwittingly, focuses our attention on a particular scene of mid-Victorian disciplinary formation in which literature and governmental institutions are often represented as not simply different, but in some central ways opposed to one another. Part of what I want to argue here is that in so far as this particular nineteenth-century opposition forms her interpretive horizon, Nussbaum simply reiterates a set of relations between law, literature, and the economic that we might instead interrogate. Viewed from another angle, however, we can see that what is at stake among the Victorians is not really a clear-cut opposition but a complicated struggle over the production of social norms.

Nussbaum relies heavily on a formalist reading of Charles Dickens' novel *Hard Times* (1853), a fiction that itself develops an argument for the importance of imagination over against a satirical image of mid-nineteenth-century utilitarianism. For Nussbaum, *Hard Times* exemplifies the kind of dichotomous relation between the world of imagination – personified in the novel by young Sissy Jupe and her circus background – and the world of facts and figures, personified by the philanthropic industrialist and future M.P. Gradgrind. Dickens represents the dominance of utilitarian political economy as effecting a complete perversion of morality: Bitzer, the star of

Gradgrind's charity school, grows into a self-interested dolt; the industrialist Bounderby turns out to be a callous liar; and Gradgrind's son Tom is so successfully educated by his father that he makes the rational choice to become a thief. The saving grace of Coketown, Dickens' industrial city where fact and calculation rule and workers starve, is little Sissy Jupe, whose rich imagination and vibrant powers of sympathy unite characters of diverse background, offering the novel's only glimpse of potentially more humane and just future.

Like Dickens, Nussbaum takes a liberal-humanist view; Nussbaum, argues that "sympathetic emotion ... is essential to public judgment" (1996, p. 77) and that furthermore, "it is this sort of emotion that literary works construct in their readers, who learn what it is to have emotions, not for a 'faceless undifferentiated mass' but for the 'uniquely individual human being'"(1996, p. 78). Dickens can indeed be read as advocating for the "uniquely individual human being"; but his fiction can also be read as constituting that paradoxical entity, the unique human being who is also the instantiation of a normative subject. Sissy Jupe herself provides us with an example: by the end of *Hard Times*, the little circus girl has forsaken the circus and the horses, the improper speech, the inappropriate alliances that characterized her life there and has settled into life as a paradigmatic mid-Victorian "angel in the house."

Michel Foucault's exploration of norms as a means of social regulation in modern societies complicates our vision of the boundaries between imagination and institutions considerably. In the closing section of the *History of Sexuality v. 1*, Foucault contrasts pre-modern forms of juridical power, located in the sovereign will, with what he terms "bio-power." Unlike the form of power "to take life or to let live" that characterized monarchical systems, modern power concerns itself, he writes, "with living beings, and the mastery it would be able to exercise over them would have to be applied at the level of life itself; it was the taking charge of life, more than the threat of death, that gave power its access even to the body" (1980, p. 143). In Foucault's theory of modern power as diffuse and de-centralized, the exercise of this power over life entails the "growing importance assumed by the action of the norm, at the expense of the juridical system of law" (1980, p. 144). This is by no means to suggest that law is of no further importance in modern societies. In fact, it is a description of the emergence of the functions and limits of modern legal systems, whose force, Foucault argues, is primarily a regulatory one.

As the sociologist Francois Ewald points out, "normalization tends to be accompanied by an astonishing proliferation of legislation ... The norm is not opposed to law itself but to what Foucault would call 'the juridical'," that is to say, the kind of sovereign power that characterizes monarchical regimes (Ewald, 1990, p. 138). Foucault points out that "the law operates more and more as norm, and the judicial institution is increasingly incorporated into a continuum of apparatuses ... whose functions are for the most part regulatory" (1980, p. 144). According to this analysis, law in modern societies functions principally through formulating, upholding, and advancing normative visions of behavior, social relations, and subjectivity itself – but it is not the sole or even necessarily the prime norm-making agent. In his "continuum of apparatuses," Foucault mentions the medical and the bureaucratic, but we could add to this culture and perhaps particularly the novel. Ewald poses the question of the relation between law and norms; but since Foucault insists that law is not the sole, nor perhaps even always the central, normative practice in modern societies, he invites us to broaden the question to interrogate the function of culture in constituting and reproducing norms in relation to legal institutions.

To make her argument, Nussbaum might also have chosen any one of several mid-nineteenth-century texts in which large social and political structures are represented as opposed to "uniquely individual human beings" and in which can be read calls for sympathy, a prepolitical fellow-feeling that crosses the boundaries that determine social and economic identities.[1] Dickens' own later fiction, especially, is run through with the theme: one thinks of the deadly Court of Chancery in *Bleak House* and the near-psychotic Office of Circumlocution in *Little Dorrit*. Poetic justice is frequently represented as derived through individual bonds of affect and concern, bonds negatively defined in relation to the institutions of law, government, and economy. And poetic *justice* is the appropriate appellation; in many nineteenth-century fiction the relations of the institutions of law to the abstract entity of justice are extensively explored. Tony Sharpe points to two distinct novelistic strategies in this regard: the "competitive emulation of law by literature," on the one hand, and on the other, "the implicit (or explicit) comparison within the literary text between legal methodology and its own ways of working" (Sharpe, 1999, p. 91). In either instance, nineteenth-century fiction can be seen as developing a metanarrative on the relations between law and normative modes of behavior, affect, and disposition.

For instance, were we to turn our attention to *Bleak House*, Dickens's fulsome critique of the Court of Chancery, we might read into its development of an apparent schism between sympathetic bonds and law an oddly akimbo relation instead; years before the Judicature Acts, which officially reordered the legal system such that the functions of equity merged administratively with those of law, Dickens seems to be proposing the absorption of those functions historically associated with equity into the domestic sphere. In the figure of Esther Summerson, law's ancient supplement is distributed far better than the fog-hobbled Chancery can manage; she repairs the broken hearts of children, sits with the dying, heals the sick and injured, and calls attention, through her actions, to the fact that justice cannot be done by law alone. Equity is returned to its ancient meanings only by being detached from government and rewritten in the terms offered by middle-class domesticity. While at one register, one can read this as another instance of the opposition upheld and explored in Nussbaum, this form of poetic justice can also be read as reinforcing the law as a modern, scientific discipline. The functioning of law is aided and abetted by the production of subjects whose sympathies are carefully taught and well-ordered, for whom the normative relations imagined by law between action and will are not simply comprehensible, but naturalized.[2]

On this reading, the novel becomes a modality for instantiating and encouraging the reproduction of a norm. Equity, associated with archaic forms of sovereign power, can only function within a modern bureaucratized society if it is repositioned as the kind of care, love, and sympathetic emotion exercised by Esther Summerson: a form, we might say, of Foucaultian "bio-power" that is specifically bound to gendered and classed norms.

*Bleak House* poses the question not only of the relation of law to norms, but the more specific issue of the relation of law, literature, and the norm in nineteenth-century culture – and arguably, in our own. This is evidently not an issue that can be resolved adequately here; however, what I propose to do is to sketch out some ways we might reread the reified opposition between law and literature that has explicitly or implicitly characterized so much law-and-literature scholarship as part of a larger struggle over social norms and what kind of subjects will be constituted through them.

By turning to some Victorian-era texts, we find that what initially might appear as an opposition dissolves into a dense debate over models of subjectivity and modalities of mediating between groups and individuals in an increasingly complex industrial society.

## 2. THE NORM, THE LAW, AND JAMES FITZJAMES STEPHEN

Noting that Foucault's thought "encourages us to distinguish law and its formal expression from the juridical," Ewald points out that "law can ... function by formulating norms, thus becoming part of a different sort of power that 'has to quantify, measure, appraise, and hierarchize rather than display itself in its murderous splendor' " (1990, p. 138). While Robert Cover, in other words, was certainly correct to say that "legal interpretation plays on a field of pain and death" (Cover, 1986, p. 1601). Foucault insists that this field is reconfigured in important ways for modern societies. "In the age of bio-power," Ewald writes, "the juridical, which characterized monarchical law, can readily be opposed to the normative, which comes to the fore most typically in constitutions, legal codes, and the clamorous activity of the legislature" (1990, p. 138).

But what exactly is a norm? If the etymological roots of the word are found in terms of tools of measurement, the meaning of the term ceases to be synonymous with "rule" in the early nineteenth century; when "it comes to designate both a ... variety of rules and a way of producing them and perhaps most significantly ... a principle of valorization" (Ewald, 1990, p. 139). The norm, Ewald argues, is related to power, but "it is characterized less by the use of force or violence than by an implicit logic that allows power to reflect upon its own strategies and clearly define its objects" (p. 139). The production of the norm is related to the rise of statistics as a discipline, which enabled the constitution of the figure of the "average man," by definition identifiable with no particular individual but functioning as a point of comparison for everyone. Normative practices are therefore compatible with, and perhaps inextricable from a certain kind of law: as a condition of possibility for communication in a moment when universal values are at an end or at least in crisis, "the norm is a means of producing social law, a law constituted with reference to the particular society it claims to regulate and not with respect to a set of universal principles" (p. 155). This could serve as one way of framing a description of a problematic facing jurists and legal scholars in the mid- to late nineteenth century: if law can no longer pretend to uphold universal values, what is its role? If it has long ceased to function in the way that Foucault describes as "juridical," exercising primarily the right of death, how and on what grounds does it legitimate itself?

Julie Stone Peters has recently delineated a broad and complex history of social and epistemological formation at stake in the relation between law and literature: "Literature [became] ... a separate aesthetic field ... precisely because of its claim on the humanist tradition in the face of utilitarianism and academic scientism ... The separation of literature from law might be seen not only as attempts to free the aesthetic sphere from the utilitarian world, but also as attempts to rationalize the legal sphere by ridding it of the critical natural-law and customary-law traditions" (Peters, 2005, p. 449). This rationalization of the legal sphere is underwritten by occult or explicit arguments about law's role in modern society; for many jurists and legal philosophers an apprehension of law's role was inseparable from questions about its relationship to moral norms.

It helps us to recall that early nineteenth-century utilitarianism positioned itself as inextricable from moral philosophy – or at least as the modality through which questions traditionally posed by moral philosophy could be best asked and answered.[3] Martin Wiener, pointing to the interlacing of Evangelical and Utilitarian thought in early Victorian legal reform, remarks that "despite the frequent anticlerical insistence on the distinction between law and morality" heard in the work of jurists and philosophers, "law was nonetheless used to advance a program of broad moral reform" (1990, p. 53). We might replace the "despite" here with a "because"; in a society where it had come to seem, at least by the mid-century, that traditional religious authority was increasingly compromised or diffused, law could, if not fill a vacuum, at least produce parameters for conduct and at best instigations and incentives to normative moral behaviors.

To discuss this in more detail, I want now to turn to the work of James Fitzjames Stephen. As a specialist in the criminal law, public intellectual, political philosopher, and eventual judge on the Queen's Bench, Stephen's varied and copious writings not only reflect mid- to later-Victorian thinking on the relation of law to society and culture, but also bear witness to a particular utilitarian-influenced moderate liberalism that sought to respond, often with fair trepidation, to the upheavals facing a modernizing and imperial nation-state. For Stephen, law was "essentially an 'organ of the moral sense of the community,' giving expression to and advancing public morality" (Wiener, 1990, p. 53). Much of his work can be read as a project entailing the careful delineation, not so much of law from morality *tout court* but of the moral reach of law, the delineation of law as the realm of a specifically modern moral rationality. In Stephen's writing, I want to suggest, we can read a mapping of the process by which, as Judith Butler has put it, "power becomes productive; it transforms the negative constraints of the juridical into the more positive controls of normalization" (Butler, 2004, p. 49).

Although Stephen was, like his contemporary Oliver Wendell Holmes and other nineteenth-century Anglo-American jurists, wary of the risks entailed in conflating law with morality, he insisted that "indefinite and unscientific as the terms may be in which morality is expressed, the administration of criminal justice is based upon morality" (Stephen, 1863, p. 82). In the preface to the second edition of his work on political philosophy, *Liberty, Equality, Fraternity* (1873), Stephen asserts that "law ... affects all human conduct directly or indirectly, and is in itself connected with and affected by all the principles which lie deepest in human nature, and which would usually be called spiritual. Though in this sense law applies to things spiritual just as much as theology, its application must of necessity be limited considerations which arise out of its nature as law. It can only forbid or command acts capable of accurate definition and specific proof, and so on" (Stephen, 1993, p. 248). While theology deals with the things unseen and realms unknowable by ordinary means, law, by providing a normative picture of human mental states and the conduct that proceeds from them, can produce temporal knowledge in support of social order.[4] In this modern rationality enabled by law, morality and social order are articulated together.

In Stephen's writing, we see the articulation of the domain of modern law as a distinct realm that, in part because its language is a transparent medium of communication, can claim primacy as the regulator of social meanings. Stephen combined his claims for the place of law as an arbiter of morality with the legacies of Austinian analytic jurisprudence. Again and again, across his writings, we find him railing against the detrimental effects of fuzzy or imprecise language, particularly in so far as concerns sentiment and morality. For Stephen, following Bentham, "the principle of sympathy and antipathy never can, from the nature of the case, be so applied as to lead to any definite result" (1993, p. 224). Utilitarian thought comes to the aid of law in disambiguating those moral sentiments that are frequently expressed in language that is never "free from metaphor:" "A moral intuition, or any other intuition, that does not go so far as to enunciate definite propositions in express words, is only a fine name for those inarticulate feelings which utilitarians recognize like everyone else and which their system attempts to name, to classify and to arrange" (1993, p. 225). We might see the desire expressed here as going beyond simply "naming, classifying, and arranging." By stipulating relations between conduct and mental or emotional states, linguistic convention produces normative subjectivities, against which deviations can be measured, potentially codified, and accordingly punished.

Naming, classifying, and arranging "inarticulate feelings," of course, is also a central project of literature; for Victorian writers, the novel is often represented as a privileged vehicle through which the feelings of diverse social groups and individuals can be conveyed, with the goal of cultivating sympathetic bonds outside what Matthew Arnold might call one's "ordinary" self. Literature's province is "language never free from metaphor" and therefore, even in its most conservative instances, it runs the risk of exceeding norms, throwing them into crisis, or indicating the limits of the knowable.

In his literary criticism of the 1850s and 60s, Stephen joined the long-ongoing debate about reading, literature, and affect, but from a point of view that we can link to some aspects of his writings on law. In several essays, Stephen took up the question of the role and efficacy of the modern novel, and while he discusses a range of popular mid-century fictions, he takes Dickens in particular to task. For Stephen, it is not simply Dickens' pervasive critique of social and political institutions that is offensive; it is the appeal to sentiment in which that critique is couched that is deeply troubling. Dickens is insisting on a particular form of literary subjectivity as the only viable means of mediating between and among individuals and groups; it is a form of subjectivity characterized by sympathetic connection that links persons, despite differences of age, sex, and class, to one another. For Stephen, Dickens's substantial popularity stemmed from "his power of working upon the feelings by the coarsest stimulants, and his power of settling common occurrences in a grotesque and unexpected light" (quoted in Colaiacco, 1983). Dickens' evocation of sentiment was the product of a "feminine, irritable, and noisy mind;" an excess of sentiment risked inciting dissatisfaction and social disorder. Dickens' fiction is execrable, according to Stephen, because it not only represents but inculcates mental states that are potentially disruptive and dangerous. Coupled with the harsh depictions of political and legal institutions, especially in Dickens's later work, there was hazardous potential impact on public opinion. For Stephen, these exceptionally popular fictions constitute an example of the irresponsible critique of English institutions which, while no doubt requiring reform, were by no means the ominous shelters of incompetence and executors of injury portrayed in the novels. It is, in effect, Dickens' representation of an opposition between institution and individual mental state that Stephen often finds so troubling; by making us laugh at government institutions, cry with Amy Dorrit, and even perhaps pity, rather than despise, her lazy improvident father, Dickens is fostering more than disrespect; he is cultivating social disorder.

Stephen is not a particularly literary-minded reader, to be sure; yet he was sensitive to the role played in the shaping of public opinion by the novel. In his responses to Dickens's fiction, Stephen acknowledges the novel's normalizing capacity and suggests that it lies in the particular use of literary language to stimulate emotional response and identification in its readers. Ewald would have it that "the norm relates the disciplinary institutions of production – knowledge, wealth, finance – to one another in such a way that they become truly interdisciplinary"; norms render transparent practices, entities, and individuals that might otherwise remain opaque, "[making] it possible to translate from disciplinary idiom to another" (1990, p. 141). Stephen's struggles with Dickens' fiction suggest, however, that beyond the sphere of statistical norms calculated with the mathematical tools, the production of norms themselves takes on agonistic character. If the norm has a mediating function, the discipline which has primacy in defining becomes a sort of master discourse.

In his writing on literature, Stephen implies the general tenet that grounds his jurisprudence: law is potentially the most effective mediator of social relations. Yet, he recognizes that this goal can only be fulfilled effectively if law can claim a conception of subjectivity, of mental states and affect; part of the Stephen's problem with Dickens' representation of mental life, one might suggest, is not so much that the novelist is so interested in the internal states and conditions of his characters, but that he represents complex mental states as pure emotion and in doing so, that he underplays the individual as an entity capable of will and self-direction, a "sovereign self," as Simon Petch has put it, anchored by a conscience (Petch, 1999). If this resonates with the Arnoldian hope for "our best self,"[5] Stephen saw that self fostered better by law than by literary works. Law, equipped with a Benthamite distrust of the vagaries of metaphorical expression of emotion and an analytical approach to the meaning of words, is far more effective an instrument than literature for the project of inculcating moral standards that Stephen saw as of paramount importance to Victorian society.

Foucault remarked in his lecture, "Truth and Juridical Forms" that he believed juridical practices to be among the most important forms "by which our society defined types of subjectivity, forms of knowledge, and consequently relations between man and truth" (1997a, p. 4). In the study of penal practices, Foucault argued in this lecture from the era of *Discipline and Punish*, one could locate the "emergence of new forms of subjectivity." At least, we can say the emergence of particular sets of norms for subjectivity is visible in nineteenth-century legal and penal debate. Perhaps there is no site upon which the battle over the delineation of normatively responsible subjects more visible than in discussion of the mental states productive of criminal acts.

Martin Wiener notes that "a crucial supposition underlying early Victorian legal changes was that the most urgent need was to make people self-governing and that the best way of doing this was to hold them sternly and unblinkingly responsible for the consequences of their actions" (1999, p. 477). This required the production of a normatively responsible subject, an entity articulated in terms of a stable relation to him or herself and a stable relation to well-defined institutions. The development of such a subject is central to the smooth working of a hegemonic state; yet there was in the Victorian period by no effective consensus on what constituted that subject, as the discourse of criminal responsibility and the common law principle of *mens rea* suggest. As Lisa Rodensky points out, and as Stephen's own struggling with questions of responsibility over the course of his career demonstrates, "there was [disagreement], particularly around questions pertaining to criminal states of mind and to the relation between states of mind and acts" (Rodensky, 2003, p. 3).

It would be hasty to declare, as does Peter Hutchings, that the nineteenth century saw "the eclipse" the common law principle of *mens rea*; more accurately, perhaps, attention was increasingly called to its vagueness and need for precision and refinement.[6] By disambiguating Coke's classic formulation – *actus non facit reum, nisi mens sit rea*, "the uncouth maxim," as one judge described it[7] – a normatively responsible subject of law could emerge. While an increase in the number of strict-liability offenses had the effect of excluding legal consideration of mental states, and indexed as well an increasing intolerance for various forms of violent and antisocial behaviors, the limit case was insanity. In 1843, the McNaughtan rules articulated legal insanity as a disturbance in cognition, a "defect of reason" on account of which the accused had either not known what he was doing or not known that what he was doing was wrong. In negative, the subject of law is delineated as a rational knower – and a normatively moral individual. In his *General View of the Criminal Law in England*, Stephen seeks to define meticulously the nexus of relations between volition, action, and intent; his investigation leads him to isolate the term "malice" for further specification: "The etymological meaning of the words malice and malicious is simply wickedness and wicked ... The consequence of making malice in general terms a necessary element of crime is ... that certain acts are declared to be *prima facie* wicked actions, though circumstances may exist by which their wickedness is either removed or diminished ... Thus in the case of murder, when one man kills another, the presumption is that he did so maliciously; and so committed murder; but this presumption may be rebutted by showing that the act was done in self-defense, or under certain specified provocations, or by certain forms of negligence" (Stephen, 1863, pp. 83–84). Acts rise up first quasi-independently of doers; while an act can be safely declared wicked in itself by public morality, the specific mental state of the doer can be adjudged according to conventionally specified criteria. It is not so much that *mens rea* is out of the picture; but that there is a formalization of the legal understanding of the role mental states are to play in adjudicating crime. Rather than undefined, abyssal entities comprised of emotion, varying degrees of reason and desire, mental states are, as Stephen's formulation suggests, to be defined so to speak from the exterior, largely through inference, by measuring their congruence with specifically-defined legal forms.

In his 1863 discussion of madness and law, Stephen cautions his readers that sanity "is a state neither of the mind nor the body, but of the conduct" (1863, p. 87). Questions bearing on the relations of mind to body are for medical professionals to decide, but "they are foreign to law." From this, Stephen insists, one must infer that "lawyers and physicians mean two different things by the word 'madness' " (1863, p. 87). The domain of law is disambiguated from that of medicine; while physicians can worry about disease entities, it is for lawyers and judges to concern themselves with whether the conduct such entities produce is liable to punishment. What emerges from Stephen's analysis of law and forensic psychiatry is the normatively responsible subject as a sort of legal fiction; this fiction produces as its negative a residue of subjectivity that is specifically excluded by law.

Historians of madness and the criminal law point out, in fact, that after the McNaughtan rules were instituted, successful insanity pleas did become less frequent. New categories and concepts of madness, however, present challenges to law as these concepts reinscribe the relations between mind, body, and conduct. For instance, the idea of "irresistible impulses," discussed by the English psychiatrist Pritchard early in the century, seemed to present a lurking challenge to the McNaughtan test. One could hypothetically know what one was doing, know it was wrong, and still be powerless to stop from doing it; in other words, one could meet the strict cognitive criteria for a rational, responsible legal subject and nonetheless be volitionally impaired to the point of criminal acts. In 1863, Stephen takes up "irresistible impulses," his tone almost dismissive: "The only question ... in the administration of criminal justice is whether the impulse in question was irresistible as well as unresisted" (p. 95). The tenor of the discussion, unsurprisingly, implies a greater concern with the implications for law of asserting that some individuals may lack volitional control than with entertaining new research on madness.[8] But questions about the relation between states of mind and acts were pressing on those outside the legal profession as well; in the 1860s, sensation fiction seemed to be taking up precisely the kind of questions law had not simply foreclosed from consideration but in a sense defined through the constitutive exclusions in its image of normative subjects.

## 3. "MAD TODAY AND SANE TOMORROW": SENSATION FICTION AND THE LAW

Towards the end of Mary Elizabeth Braddon's *Lady Audley's Secret*, barrister Robert Audley gets a lesson in the law from the mad doctor Dr. Mosgrave. Audley has come to consult with Mosgrave on the fate of Lady Audley who, it has been revealed, has not only abandoned her only child, faked her own death, assumed a false identity, committed bigamy, but possibly murdered her first husband as well. Audley wants to avoid what Mosgrave delicately terms "an *esclandre*," a smear to his family name, by having the doctor certify her as legally insane. Evaluating what he knows of the case, the doctor refuses, as he explains to Audley,

> because there is no evidence of madness in anything she has done. She ran away from home because her home was not a pleasant one and she left it in hope of finding a better. There is no madness in that. She committed the crime of bigamy because by that crime she obtained fortune and position. There is no madness there. When she found herself in a desperate position, she did not grow desperate. She employed intelligent means, and she carried out a conspiracy which required coolness and deliberation in its execution. There is no madness in that. (Braddon, 1998, p. 379)

That the mad doctor has to provide the barrister with the definition of legal insanity is only one of the several ironies at work here; the broader one, of course, has to do with the fact that Lady Audley's ceaseless violations of normative feminine behavior cannot be codified as madness according to the legal criteria. Defined out of the norm for a "lady" and that for the legally mad, Lady Audley's fate is nonetheless grim; the doctor sees in her a latent insanity, possibly hereditary, and arranges for her to be locked up in a Belgian asylum, doubly exiled from her homeland as well as polite society, dead to the world.

Braddon's fiction of female will and desire is only one of the most well-known of the sensation novels of the 1860s. But as this scene intimates, it exemplifies these novels' concerns with law, social norms, and questions of legal and moral responsibility. Most closely associated with the novels of Wilkie Collins, whose *Woman in White* (1860) is said to have initiated the genre, sensation novels offered readers a racy plot-driven revitalization of the gothic, combining "crime, mystery, passion, social commentary, and questions of identity, in a contemporary setting" (Helsinger, Sheets, & Veeder, 1983, p. 122). In the fictions of Collins and Mary Elizabeth Braddon, what we find is a subversion of many of the conventions of domestic realist fiction: rather than being the secure bourgeois space outside of market values and violence that it often is in English realism, the domestic space of sensation fiction is precisely the most dangerous one of all. Theft, imprisonment, bigamy, false identities: all lurk under the surface of pastoral, calm, and often aristocratic domestic arrangements.

In their frequent representations of law sensation novels explore the underside of the normatively responsible legal subject, in the process taxing and interrogating the dominant standards of responsibility and subjectivity as articulated in law. Characters in sensation fiction commit crimes that might appear as effects of madness, only to be found, as is Lady Audley, for legal purposes completely rational. Law-abiding citizens find themselves to have committed crimes, either by negligence or oversight; characters find themselves to have done terrible deeds while sleeping or under the influence of drugs. In the sensation novel, the true criminal is often a character that cuts against the grain of emergent mid-nineteenth-century stereotypes. We have a vivid representation of what Peter Hutchings calls "the criminal specter" that haunted nineteenth-century culture as the dark side of the volitional, responsible subject (Hutchings, 2001). Rather than the Fagins of fiction or the profiles adumbrated by the new discipline of criminology, however, these characters are well-regarded, upper middle-class or aristocratic. This is articulated with another motif common to these novels; in sensation fiction, law makes its way out of the public sphere of Parliament and contemporary debates over legal reform, codification, the status of the common law, out of the ominous and darkened streets of the urban center, out of the Inns of Court, and into the private spaces of the home, where its regulatory effects inform the furthest reaches of subjectivity.

If James Fitzjames Stephen, in his legal writing of the 1860s, insists that mental states be stipulated on the basis of acts, sensation fiction of the same decade sides, in a manner of speaking, with Foucault, when he describes the later nineteenth-century transition in penal law and criminal psychiatry from a focus on acts to one on "dangerous individuals" (Foucault, 1997b). But as Dr. Mosgrave's assessment of Lady Audley suggests, sensation fiction often demonstrates the limits of law's ability to regulate those dangerous individuals. The norms propagated by law, according to the logic of the sensation novel, either culpabilize the innocent or liberate the guilty; if the frequent and ambivalent presence of the mad doctor or psychologist in sensation novels suggests anything generally, it is that law is inadequate to plumb the depths of the modern subject whom it seeks to normalize.

D.A. Miller remarked that something about the sensation novel allows it to "say certain things for which our culture has yet to develop another language" (Miller, 1988, p. 148).While the suspenseful plots and melodramatic oppositions of the genre call up the full semantic span of the word "sensation," I want to suggest that the focus on the somatic has broader – and perhaps stranger – implications. To pursue this, I want to turn to another sensation fiction concerned with problems of legal responsibility and mental states, Collins' *The Moonstone* (1868).

Within the narrative of *The Moonstone*, the question of bodily sensation is mapped onto issues of volition, consciousness, and desire within the framework of a whodunit. The more conventional usage of "sympathy" – that abstract affect with potentially ethical consequences for the reading subject – is displaced onto the mysterious interrelations between mind and body, an instance of which will not be named as "*Trieb*" within the context of psychoanalysis for another half century. While Collins resolves the narrative into a happy ending redolent of domestic realism – justice meted out, order restored, a happy couple secure in a happy home – the novel evokes something else entirely, "a certain thing for which our culture has yet to develop another language," the sublime alterity of the much-vaunted normatively responsible subject of modern law.

The eponymous gem is an extremely valuable Indian diamond, allegedly stolen from its rightful owners by a colonial officer years before the central action begins. Thus, a story of imperial violence and theft operates not only as a framing device for the central narrative, a story of theft in a country house, but evokes the spectral presence of British imperial endeavor in everyday domestic life and underwrites the epistemological force of Collins's narrative strategies: those things excluded from one's direct knowledge may impact one's life as much, or more, than one's empirical knowledge.

The narrative is shaped as legal testimony, with a variety of characters who in some way witnessed the events surrounding the theft of the diamond recounting it "as far as our own personal experience extends and no farther" at the behest of a central character, Franklin Blake, who in consultation with the family solicitor, has decided that the story "ought, in the interests of truth, be placed on record in writing" (Collins, 1999, p. 60). But if the narrative vaunts at once the isomorphous relation between truth and writing and that between truth and the epistemological necessity of surveying a number of different, limited points of view, it finds different ways of challenging both as it goes along. The parade of narrators offering testimony rarely sticks entirely to what they directly witnessed with regard to the theft. Rachel Verinder, the last possessor of the diamond and the one character who could have given decisive information about the theft, is conspicuously left out of the group of witnesses. The key to the diamond's theft will be found in the curious situation of a subject who truly does not know what he willed, performed, or experienced. The crucial information leading to the resolution of the theft emerges neither through the agencies of the law, nor through the readerly perusal of witness accounts, but because of the good graces of a marginalized, Creole psychologist with one foot in the grave.

The miming of the state's dominant strategies for extracting truth functions to exclude them as valid methods. As becomes conventional in detective fiction, when the local police fail, there is repair to a famous detective. But Sergeant Cuff, "the celebrated Cuff" of the London Detective Police, impeccable as his methods of inferential reasoning may be, fails to solve the crime and is sent away into his much-desired retirement. Cuff – "there isn't the equal in England of Sergeant Cuff!" one character apostrophizes (p. 155) – has an eagle-eye for detail: noticing a small smear in fresh paint on a door in Rachel Verinder's bedroom, he concludes someone in the house must have a paint stain on their linen. He's correct, it turns out, but the stained nightdress cannot be found. Importantly for our purposes, Cuff is an astute student of behavior; he studies comportment and infers mental states. This leads him to make Rachel his prime suspect; he believes she stole her own diamond, a birthday present, to pay off putative gambling debts that she had secretly accrued. Certainly Rachel's behavior is curious: she refuses to cooperate with Cuff, she refuses to speak with anyone about the night of the theft, and she flees as quickly as she can to a relative's home. But it turns out she is not guilty of having stolen the diamond. Cuff's inductive methods have been sound enough to have ensured his reputation, but in the case of the Moonstone, his ascription of mental state to perceptible behavior runs aground.

Cuff's failures at ascription are signal for the novel's thematization of law as an instrument for knowing subjects and understanding the relation between volition and action. While other characters, including her mother, vouch for Rachel's innocence, advocating over against the eyes of the law a kind of personhood knowable intuitively and through enduring contact, the novel's larger point has to do with the unknowability of mental states and their apparently contingent relation to comportment. And it goes much deeper than the detection of lies. Rachel is indeed hiding something; but even she, it turns out, is not actually sure about what she is hiding. Franklin Blake, her cousin and would-be lover, is sincerely vigorous in his pursuit of the thief; but it will turn out that he is himself the culprit, having taken the diamond from a cabinet in Rachel's room in the middle of the night while under the influence of a dose of opium covertly mixed into his drink by the village physician.

Miller's reading of this novel argues that the expulsion of outsider Cuff indicates that the small community of the country house can effectively police itself; even the most famous police detective is unnecessary in the modern disciplinary regime. But we might question this reading, noting that while the formal agencies of law are inadequate to their appointed task, Foucaultian surveillance comes up short as well, defeated by a disturbing modality of subjectivity that exceeds even the force of modern discipline. The community around the Verinder estate does transform itself into an amateur detective corps, usurping the observant eye of Cuff and all he represents with a mode of surveillance grounded in familiarity and faith in each other's bona fides. But by itself, this community cannot solve the mystery any better than Cuff can.

It is a complete outsider, not simply to the estate's community but to English society more generally, the physician's assistant and would-be psychologist Ezra Jennings who finally helps Franklin Blake learn who stole the diamond by reproducing the scene of the original theft in a "scientific" experiment that would stand in no court of law, but which satisfies all involved that, asleep and under the influence of laudanum, Blake could enter Rachel's room, steal the diamond, and be so suggestible as to hand it over to the novel's real villain, Ablewhite.

What I want to suggest here is that there is an excess circulating through Collins' novel with regard to questions of responsibility, identity, and consciousness; while at one level, it is the excess produced through and against contemporary discourses on criminal responsibility, on another it exceeds even what the novel itself can say directly, lapsing as it does into a rational scientifically sanctioned explanation of Blake's conduct the night of the theft. A discourse on desire, the body, and consciousness is recuperated here into a narrative of the ill-effects of a dose of laudanum; it is indeed perhaps too obvious to point to the proto-Freudian subtext concerning a young man stealing a virgin's jewel while she is asleep in her bedchamber. But the broader issue posited by *The Moonstone* is one that both fiction and law will have to contend with in the second half of the nineteenth century, ironically perhaps as the disciplinary boundaries between them stiffen. How to conceptualize a mind that is not simply reducible to consciousness? Is the subject who has no consciousness of performing an act still the agent of that act? And if he is not, whose act is it?

Franklin Blake, the hero/culprit of the novel, fits no legal criteria of insanity; nor for that matter, *pace Stephen*, does he appear to conform to any clinical definitions. However, he is a somewhat unstable personality, a fact that the Verinders' house steward, Gabriel Betteredge, one of the dominant narrators of the novel, credits to an upbringing in a foreign boarding schools: "He had his French side, and his German side, and his Italian side – the original English foundation showing through every now and then, as much as to say 'here I am, very much transmogrified, as you see, but there's something of me left at the bottom of him still' " (pp. 98–99). Betteredge's grammar here, in which his hypothetical self-description of Blake involves a splitting between the first and third persons, indicates not only the elderly steward's nationalistic prejudice by claiming Blake's "I" for England and representing his other "sides" as superficial, contingent; it also hints at the lack of continuity and cohesion in Blake's identity. Before the theft, Blake is already divided into "I" and "him." After the theft, that "I" slowly becomes more dominant; his various European sides seem to lapse into abeyance as, with great focus and determination, he seeks the thief. Yet the whole time, the reader will discover, he is really looking for some version of that "him" that shows up early on in Betteredge's peculiar prosopoeia.

Collins, the would-be barrister, produces a fictional version of a problem that would show up in the law courts increasingly after 1843: defendants who for one reason or another claimed to be entirely unaware of their actions. Sleepwalking murderers, thieves in the grip of epileptic vertigo, "split" personalities whose "alters" committed the crime in question: these not only "refused to stay confined in their post-McNaughtan categories," as Joel Peter Eigen puts it (2003, p. 8), but they challenged the very fundamentals of normative subjectivity. It was one thing to say that a defendant who had been under the grip of a delusion was not guilty by reason of insanity; this kind of delusional thinking was specifically addressed by post-McNaughtan medico-legal thinking. The deviation from the normatively responsible subject was clear. But what if the killer of X had no memory at all of the killing, no apparent intention to kill, could make no account of himself whatsoever with regard to the event?

In his recent study of Old Bailey trials, Eigen discusses the increased incidence from 1843 to 1876 – the first date he has found a verdict of "not guilty by reason of unconsciousness" – of defendants arguing that were in fugue states, absent, sleepwalking, or otherwise unconscious at the moment of their alleged crime. While many of the cases Eigen surveys are much more violent than Franklin Blake's somnambulist theft, the structure of these cases is the same: in every instance, the legal definition of a criminal action is in some sense put on trial. It is worth recalling Stephen's definition: "... an action consists of voluntary bodily motions combined by the mind toward a common object. Intention is in every case essential to action, and every crime is an action" (1863, p. 81). Are these "unconscious" deeds in some sense voluntary? Is there some intention involved? And if neither voluntary nor intentional – nor even recalled – by the subject who performed them, whose actions were they anyway?

Eigen raises the question of why so many defendants during the period under consideration sought to plead various forms of automatism, amnesia, and absence. Bracketing the question of whether there were just more unconscious people wandering around mid-century London than there had been before, he takes up the increased and often agonistic role of forensic psychiatrists: "Eager to assert and maintain their cognitive territory in the courtroom, medical witnesses found in the varying states of consciousness a conceptually attractive language to counter the restrictive criteria imposed by the McNaughtan rules ..." (2003, p. 156). Yet he finds this answer alone unsatisfying and turns to Parliamentary and procedural reforms in the early part of the century, including the entrance onto the courtroom stage of the defense attorney. Other factors he discusses suggest that the emergence of the unconscious defendant is intricately related to the Victorian production of the normatively responsible legal subject – not simply the production of such a subject, but the juridical interest in constricting the scope of that subject. "Judges compelled jurors to raise the bar for reasonableness to create an objective standard for the 'reasonable man'" (Eigen, 2003, p. 160). As the field of possible defenses one could make and still represent oneself as "reasonable" contracted, so did the field of insanity defenses; the effects may well have included fewer specious defenses, more convictions, and more criminals off the streets and into the new penitentiaries. But other effects seem to have also emerged, almost as the constitutive other of these clearly defined legal entities, the reasonable man and his stepbrothers, the delusional, the lunatic, the monomaniac. Here is the "I," the subject of apparent perfect sanity, in whom something or someone other acts.

Here in short is our poor Franklin Blake, whose determined narrative we follow throughout *The Moonstone*, but who does not even know that he is the culprit. He does not know why his would-be fiancée, Rachel, turns away from him. He does not even know that Mr. Candy, the village physician, slipped him a dose of laudanum, which caused him to enter the somnambulistic trance state in which he stole Rachel's diamond. Critical, indeed, that Franklin does not take laudanum voluntarily or habitually; if he is not entirely the paradigm of the juridical "reasonable man," he is at least a well-behaved one, according to legal norms. Blake raises the question that the law is simultaneously trying to negotiate and cannot hear: Can even a well-educated, sane, morally responsible young man be overtaken by a trance state in which he commits a crime?

One might argue that *The Moonstone* makes claims against law's ability to address mental and psychic aberrations. Literature on this reading becomes the site upon which social anxieties and questions excluded by law are represented and worked through. Certainly the removal of the crime, its investigation, and its resolution from the bounds of law seem to argue for this reading. Further, within the context of the agonistic relations between medicine and law, it is surely not insignificant that Candy gives the critical dose as a good-natured riposte to Blake's denigration of medicine nor that Blake's savior is Ezra Jennings, whose extralegal reconstruction of the event a year later convinces all concerned – including, crucially, Rachel – that while Franklin stole the diamond, it was not *his act*. In the battle between medicine and law over which discipline can best determine guilt, medicine here appears victorious.

At the same time, however, we cannot avoid the suspicion that the novel, like the law, has by 1867 discovered things it can neither explain nor successfully recuperate into conventional narrative templates. Once the theft is reconstructed, Rachel feels free to marry Franklin. Betteredge, the house steward, is content to go back to reading his favorite novel *Robinson Crusoe*. Poetic justice is attained when the "real" thief, Geoffrey Ablewhite, is killed by the noble Indians who have forsaken caste to come to England to retrieve their holy diamond. The good are rewarded; the evil are punished. But the vicissitudes of desire and irrational impulses are figuratively mapped into the text: Franklin has desired Rachel and worried that his cousin Geoffrey might ask for her hand. Betteredge had also provoked Franklin's concern – or concern in one of his "sides" at any rate–about giving the "cursed" diamond to Rachel. He had every un-reason, one could say, to want to make sure that Rachel did not keep that diamond, whether the jewel is understood literally or metaphorically.

There is another issue of unconsciousness and forgetting that *The Moonstone* evokes, with its epistolary frame telling the story of "The Storming of Seringapatam" (1799). Extracts from "a family paper" tell the story of how Herncastle, the grandfather of Franklin, Rachel, and Geoffrey, stole the diamond from its sacramental location in India. The diamond is said to be cursed, an object sacred to the Hindus, violently and illegitimately removed from its setting, transported to England under mysterious circumstances, and allegedly resulting in Herncastle's alienation from family and friends, upon leaving India. Assigned to bring the diamond to Rachel as a birthday present, Franklin finds himself debating with Betteredge whether, by leaving the diamond to Rachel in his will, Herncastle meant to transfer the curse to Lady Verinder and her daughter or saw it as a gesture of last reconciliation, implying a critical articulation of the familial with the imperial. There is here a violent history hidden, forgotten, repressed and in so far as Franklin's unconscious theft seems to repeat, in precisely Freud's sense, Herncastle's, there is the sense that in the residue of the civil subject one discovers history as precisely that which is excluded by the normative practices that constitute it. In the structurally analogous relation between Franklin Blake's situation and that of his grandfather with regard to theft of the jewel, perhaps the problem posed has to do with more than individual subjects driven to crime by impulses of which they are not aware, but entire nations whose history has been subject to selective forgetting – or perhaps, we might say, the workings of the unconscious.

## 4. A MISUNDERSTOOD RELATION

"I must say," writes Stephen in 1883, "that the provisions of the existing law have, as it seems to me, been greatly, though perhaps not unnaturally, misunderstood by medical men, who cannot be expected either to appreciate the different degrees of authority to be described to different judicial declarations of the law or to understand the rules for their interpretation or to recognize the limitations under which they are made or to appreciate the fact that when made they cannot be altered at will" (Stephen, 1883, vol. 3, p. 126). Stephen here is railing against some of the writings of "mad-doctors" on criminal responsibility, but it would not be much of a stretch, perhaps, to substitute "literary scholars" and "philosophers" for "medical men" and envision these words uttered by a visitor to Martha Nussbaum's law and literature seminar – Richard Posner, for example.[9]

What I have tried to suggest in the preceding sections is that this position and Nussbaum's as well are not so much wrong as they are part of the "story" itself, a narrative not so much about law and literature but about the ways in which two of the dominant discourses of modernity develop normative models for subjectivity and citizenship in the course of the nineteenth-century. A central way of approaching the relation between law and literature, without reifying them as opposed entities, might be to examine the ways both engage in the production of social norms, sustaining them at times and subverting them at others.

Indeed, it can appear, especially if we take as our principal examples nineteenth-century novels, that law and literature rigorous oppose each other, policing boundaries, militating for disciplinary integrity. But a closer look will often suggest the relationship is far more complex and dialectical than that. Not only does law both formally and thematically shape nineteenth-century fiction, that fiction often explores precisely what jurisprudence has foreclosed from consideration, but which nonetheless circulates around the courts like so many homeless spirits. In this sense, law actually constitutes the literary as a distinct field of linguistic action operating on concerns that are precisely those that law's language cannot speak. It is plausible to suggest that fiction played a role in reshaping notions of criminal responsibility as well as in publicizing the need for legal reform in other areas. But it is also important to see that there are areas of human experience that neither law nor literature find themselves equipped to address fully, though they may both in their respective ways, try – and there, in the breakdown between poetical language and the law's violence, emerge new disciplines of knowledge and new normative practices – for instance, psychoanalysis.

# NOTES

1. In her preface to *Mary Barton* (1848), Elizabeth Gaskell offers an exemplar articulation of how "sympathy" is construed by the middle-class writer at mid-century. Describing how she came upon her topic, she says "I had always felt a deep sympathy with the care-worn men, who looked as if doomed to struggle through their lives in strange alternations between work and want; tossed to and fro by circumstance, apparently in even a greater degree than other men." Later in the preface, she takes a vaguely monitory tone, implying that sympathy, transferred through the novel from author to reader, might have important political effects: "... the idea which I have formed of the state of feeling among too many of the factory-people in Manchester ... has received some confirmation from the events which have so recently occurred among a similar class on the Continent."

2. For two excellent readings of *Bleak House* that develop similar arguments, see Petch (1997) and Dolin (1999).

3. This is something Nussbaum indeed recognizes, discussing the differences between contemporary "rational choice" theory and the "extremely exigent and revisionary moral theory" propounded by Bentham and Sidgwick (14–15 and *passim*). She also avows having been deeply influenced in her work by Adam Smith's *Theory of the Moral Sentiments*.

4. For suggestive, if brief, discussion of the "domain of theology" with relation to the state in nineteenth-century Britain, see Mary Poovey (1995).

5. Stephen had written critically, mostly in the *Saturday Review*, about some of Arnold's work, but as Smith (1988) notes, "the difference of view between Arnold and Stephen on the state of the nation's intellectual well-being was less in substance" than some of their sniping in periodicals might suggest. "They shared a deep anxiety over the outcome of an enlarged franchise, particularly whether the result of a political leveling would truly be a general cultural leveling too" (p. 106).

6. Hutchings (2001, p. 3): "The eclipse of equity goes hand in hand with the eclipse of *mens rea*, but the resulting, apparently purely secular, positivist law, is itself a split formation, irrevocably structured by the leap it has made from religious spirit to legal letter." In the main, perhaps, Hutchings' point here is not inaccurate; but I find it nonetheless a very compact representation of a long, complex historical and social process.

7. See the opinion of Cave, J. *R. v. Tolson* (11 May 1886) All ER Rep. 26 [1886–90].

8. Stephen found himself obliged to address contemporary research in forensic psychiatry by the time of his 1883 *History of the Criminal Law in England*. There he devotes a meticulously researched chapter to criminal responsibility, madness and the law, paying especial attention to the works of Maudsley, whose work on criminal responsibility clearly infuriates him and Griesinger, to whom he gives much more credit. We might see this, as biographers of Stephen have been inclined to do, as evidence of his broadness of mind; there is no contradiction, to my opinion, between taking that point of view and seeing that this chapter also constitutes an effort to contain and regulate the growing influence of psychiatric witnesses on judges and juries.

9. In her acknowledgement and dedication, Nussbaum recalls Posner as "the Mr. Gradgrind" of a lecture she gave on the material of *Poetic Justice*. But it strikes me that Posner's *Law and Literature* is more Stephensian than Gradgrindian at the end of the day.

# REFERENCES

Baron, J. (1999). Law, literature and the problems of interdisciplinarity. *Yale Law Journal, 108*.

Baron, J. (2004). Law's guilt about literature. In: M. Anderson (Ed.), *Studies in law politics, and society: Toward a critique of guilt* (Vol. 36, Special Issue). Oxford: Oxford University Press.

Binder, G. (1999). The law-as-literature trope. In: M. Freeman & A. Lewis (Eds), *Law and literature: Current legal issues*. Oxford: Oxford University Press.

Braddon, M. E. (1998). *Lady Audley's secret*. Oxford and London: Oxford University Press.

Butler, J. (2004). *Undoing gender*. New York: Routledge.

Colaiacco, J. (1983). *James Fitzjames Stephen and the crisis in Victorian thought*. New York: Saint Martin's Press.

Collins, W. (1999). *The moonstone*. Petersborough, ON: Broadview Press.

Cover, R. (1986). Violence and the word. *Yale Law Journal, 95*.

Dolin, K. (1999). *Fiction and the law*. Cambridge: Cambridge University Press.

Eigen, J. P. (2003). *Unconscious crime: Mental absence and criminal responsibility in victorian London*. Baltimore: The Johns Hopkins University Press.

Ewald, F. (1990). Norm, discipline and the law. *Representations, Special issue: Law and the order of culture, 30*(Spring).

Foucault, M. (1980). *The history of sexuality* (Robert Hurley, Trans, Vol. 1). New York: Vintage.

Foucault, M. (1997a). Truth and juridical forms. In: Faubion, J. (Ed.), *Power: The essential works of Michel Foucault, 1954–1984* (Vol. 3), Robert Hurley et al., (Trans.) New York: New Press.

Foucault, M. (1997b). The concept of 'the dangerous individual' in nineteenth-century forensic psychiatry. In: Faubion, J. (Ed.), *Power: The essential works of Michel Foucault, 1954–1984* (Vol. 3), Robert Hurley et al., (Trans.). New York: New Press.

Helsinger, E., Sheets, R. L., & Veeder, W. (1983). *The woman question: Society and literature in Britain and America* (Vol. 3, Literary Issues). Chicago: University of Chicago Press.

Hutchings, P. (2001). *The criminal spectre in law, literature, and aesthetics*. London and New York: Routledge.

Miller, D. A. (1988). *The novel and the police*. Berkeley: University of California Press.

Nussbaum, M. (1996). *Poetic justice: The literary imagination and public life*. Boston: Beacon Press.

Petch, S. (1997). Law, equity and conscience in Victorian England. *Victorian Literature and Culture*, 123–139.

Petch, S. (1999). The sovereign self: Identity and responsibility in Victorian England. In: M. Freeman & A. Lewis (Eds), *Law and literature: Current legal issues*. Oxford: Oxford University Press.

Peters, J. S. (2005). Law, literature, and the vanishing real: On the future of an interdisciplinary illusion. *PMLA, 120*(2), 442–453.

Poovey, M. (1995). *Making a social body: British cultural formation 1830–1864*. Chicago: University of Chicago Press.

*Regina v. Tolson* (1886). All ER Rep. 26 [1886–90].

Rodensky, L. (2003). *The crime in mind: Criminal responsibility and the victorian novel*. Oxford: Oxford University Press.

Sharpe, T. (1999). Perversions of law and literature. In: M. Freeman & A. Lewis (Eds), *Law and literature: Current legal issues*. Oxford: Oxford University Press.

Smith, K. J. M. (1988). *James Fitzjames Stephen: Portrait of a Victorian rationalist*. Cambridge: Cambridge University Press.

Stephen, J. F. (1863). *A general view of the criminal law of England*. London and Cambridge: Macmillan.

Stephen, J. F. (1883). *A history of the criminal law of England* (3 vols). London and Cambridge: Macmillan.

Stephen, J. F. (1993). *Liberty, equality and fraternity*. Indianapolis: The Liberty Fund.
Wiener, M. (1990). *Reconstructing the criminal: Culture, law and policy in England 1830–1914*. Cambridge and London: Cambridge University Press.
Wiener, M. (1999). Judges and jurors: Courtroom tensions in murder trials and the law of criminal responsibility in nineteenth-century England. *Law and History Review*, *17*(3), 467–506.

# AESTHETIC JUDGMENT AND LEGAL JUSTIFICATION

Guyora Binder

## ABSTRACT

*Although criticized as illegitimate, literary elements are necessary features of legal argument. In a modern liberal state, law motivates compliance by justifying controversial prescriptions as products of an appropriate process for representing the will of society. Yet because law constructs the will of individual and collective actors in representing them, its representations are necessarily figurative rather than mimetic. In evaluating law's representation of society, citizens of the liberal state are also shaping their own ends. Such self-expressive choices, subjective but non-instrumental, entail aesthetic judgment. Thus the literary elements of rhetorical figuration and aesthetic appeal are fundamental, rather than merely ornamental, to legal justification.*

In the modern liberal state, law is seen as legitimate in so far as it successfully represents popular and individual will. Liberal legal thought tends to equate law's legitimacy with the objectivity and mimetic accuracy of this representation. Thus, law achieves legitimacy by fulfiling democratic will, satisfying preferences, or protecting rights.

Critics of liberal legal thought often respond that law is illegitimate because (1) it does not achieve its claimed objectivity or because (2) its

Special Issue: Law and Literature Reconsidered
Studies in Law, Politics, and Society, Volume 43, 79–112
Copyright © 2008 by Emerald Group Publishing Limited
All rights of reproduction in any form reserved
ISSN: 1059-4337/doi:10.1016/S1059-4337(07)00604-7

formality precludes it from fully and authentically representing the subjectivity of society's members. In making these arguments, critics of liberal legal thought deploy the analogy of law to literature in antithetical ways. Thus, critiques of the first kind insist that law is too literary – that is, too figurative and imaginative to represent objectively. Critiques of the second kind, however, charge that law is not literary enough – that is, insufficiently sensitive and expressive to represent authentically. Both of these arguments treat the literary as an anomaly within law, although for different reasons. The first critique accepts the modern liberal state's aspiration to represent society objectively, and berates it for falling short of this ideal. The second critique presumes the modern liberal state's success in achieving objectivity, but rejects this standard of mimesis in favor of authenticity. Both accept the liberal premise that law should accurately reflect society in its deliberations and decisions, without changing society. Each criticizes part of modern liberal legal thought's program of objective representation, at the price of endorsing the remainder.

Drawing on pragmatic epistemology, post-structuralist literary theory, and institutionalist critiques of rational choice theory, this chapter rejects liberal legal thought's aspiration to mimetic accuracy. Moreover, it rejects both forms of criticism as expressions of the same flawed aspiration. It treats the charge that law is insufficiently objective as a form of skepticism, and treats the complaint that law effaces authentic subjectivity as a form of sentimentalism. Both critiques are unpragmatic, demanding of law what it cannot possibly – and should not aspire to – deliver. Rather than evaluating law as a mimetic representation of society, this chapter reinterprets law's allocation of decisionmaking authority as a necessarily figurative and constructive representation of society's will. It understands legal argument to make a rhetorical appeal to aesthetic judgment rather than an empirical claim to mimetic accuracy. And it treats the larger question of the legal system's legitimacy as a similarly aesthetic question of expressive validity. Thus, rather than treating the literary as anomalous within law, this chapter treats the literary as inherent in the construction and operation of legal authority.

Like much imaginative literature, law represents subjectivities and their desires. But, also like these types of literature, law's relationship to what it represents is figurative and performative rather than straightforwardly mimetic. Law constructs subjectivities in the process of representing them. In this way it composes and portrays the characters on which it relies for its authority. On this view, legal systems should be judged as much on the basis of the desires and characters they cultivate as on the basis of their efficiency in gratifying those desires or their accuracy in representing those characters. Law's portrayal of society is "true" only in so far as we choose to make it so by identifying ourselves with it. Thus legitimacy involves a performative element, depending on the commitment of those who choose to identify with the law. Law can never simply reflect our authentic selves. Instead, it enables us to express ourselves in certain ways, and thereby precludes us from expressing ourselves in other ways. The question of who we should become is neither simply a question of ethical duty nor an arbitrary matter of consumer choice. Democratic self-fashioning poses value questions, but these value questions call for aesthetic judgment.

One of my aims in laying out this aesthetic account of legal authority is to clarify the conceptual architecture of my book written with Bob Weisberg, *Literary Criticisms of Law* (Binder & Weisberg, 2000). The book reviewed and critiqued the emergent law and literature scholarship of the late twentieth century. It incorporated our earlier article "Cultural Criticism of Law" (Binder & Weisberg, 1997), and drew on other work of ours, including Bob's well-known article "The Law-Literature Enterprise" (Weisberg, 1988). Threaded through *Literary Criticisms of Law* was an argument that, (1) in the modern liberal state, law represents society rhetorically rather than mimetically and (2) the authority of law and the validity of particular legal arguments depend upon aesthetic judgment. In reviewing law and literature scholarship in that volume, we had two aims. One was to collect and explicate works that revealed law's rhetorical and aesthetic dimensions. The other was to expose and critique the skeptical or sentimental premises of much law and literature scholarship. This chapter explicates the critical perspective developed in *Literary Criticisms of Law*, but does not attempt to illustrate or apply that perspective. It does not address the state of law and literature scholarship because what I have to say on that subject, I have said.

My account of the role of the literary in legal authority will proceed as follows. First, I will develop and explain a conception of literature as rhetorical (i.e. figurative) discourse presented for aesthetic judgment. Second, I will offer a conception of law as a relatively coercive, formal, and justificatory institution. In so doing, I will contrast two models of justification within such an institution: a modernist model that seeks foundations in physiological or psychological facts, and a pragmatist model that tests claims by their implications for practice and evaluates these implications aesthetically. Third, I will offer an account of legal argument as a rhetoric offering narratively structured figurative representations of subjectivity for aesthetic judgment and expressive identification. Finally, I will characterize the skeptical and sentimental critiques of law as expressions of legal modernism and urge that legal justification be accepted as a pragmatic discourse which necessarily employs the literary elements of rhetorical representation and aesthetic judgment.

# 1. LITERARY DISCOURSE AND AESTHETIC JUDGMENT

Let us define literature as any kind of discourse that presents figurative representations or "rhetoric" for aesthetic judgment. Using such a conception, we can identify and analyze literary elements in many kinds of cultural practices, including law.

By figurative or rhetorical language, I mean language that is not purely propositional. Rhetoric refers obliquely, substituting one proposition or other verbal sign for another, rather than substituting a proposition for a state of affairs or a set of sense data. An important claim of post-structuralist literary theory is that all language is figurative. This claim rests on ideas drawn from structuralist linguistics and pragmatist philosophy of language. Structuralism treats language as an organization of the experienced world rather than a set of labels for prelinguistic objects or sensations. On the structuralist view signs are given their meanings not by the sense-experience they organize, but instead by their relations to and differences from other signs within a system (de Saussure, 1959; Culler, 1975). In this sense, every proposition is a trope, evoking all the other propositions it differs from.

Pragmatist philosophy of language shares the premise that thought apprehends the world through language (Peirce, 1931–1935). It holds that scientific data, for example, must be identified and recorded in a language laden with theoretical assumptions (Quine, 1963; Rorty, 1979). In contrast to structuralism, however, pragmatism envisions language as an evolving practice rather than a stable structure. On this view, the meaning of any utterance is its use – the actions and utterances to which it responds, and which predictably follow it. Because verbal meaning is merely customary, subject to evolving patterns of use, the concepts that organize thought can have no stable essence. Utterances are moves in a "language game" with no predetermined outcome (Wittgenstein, 1968). Such a game presupposes that interlocutors are bound together by activities and institutions; but as the practical context for speech changes and as players respond to utterances in surprising ways, the use and meaning of particular sentences change. Thus every utterance differs not only from other words that might be said on this occasion, but also from the same words that might have been said on previous occasions, but with a different meaning (Hurley, 1989). This temporal differentiation means that every time we speak we are reusing past utterances to stand for new propositions, with open-ended meanings. For post-structuralists this constant reuse of language in an always-different context is a substitution of one sign for another, so that all utterances are rhetorical figures that invite the hearer to interpret an indeterminate meaning (Binder & Weisberg, 2000; Derrida, 1976; Culler, 1983). The contingency of meaning on the responses of others makes every move in a language game a gamble, requiring what legal theorist Karl Llewllyn called "situation-sense," a kind of interpretive judgment and gestural grace (Llewellyn, 1960, pp. 60–61).

This view of language as inevitably instable and rhetorical has some fairly straightforward implications for law. Thus, it suggests we are unlikely to control official discretion, or to secure a stable, predictable environment for individual choice, merely by issuing detailed rules (Tushnet, 1988; Levinson, 1988; Lieber, 1839). The qualities of regularity and predictability are not relations of correspondence between prescribed and achieved states of affairs, but instead are feelings that officials have used language and exercised choice in tolerably legitimate ways. Such a feeling is likely to depend on a relatively peaceable context without rapid changes in social status or social norms. In other words stable social practices make it possible to "follow rules," rather than the other way around (Fish, 1989). More importantly, the feeling of regularity is not the product simply of observation or measurement, but of a necessarily subjective and evaluative judgment on the part of some socially situated observer. This is an ultimately aesthetic judgment about the way that officials perform their roles.

If all speech is rhetorical, any speech can function as literature – can have literary meaning – in so far as it is subjected to aesthetic judgment. By aesthetic judgment I mean a conception developed by Kant in the *Critique of Judgment*, considered the foundation of the modern field of aesthetics (Kant, 1986). Kant took the appreciation of art as the paradigm for aesthetic judgment, but did not limit the concept to such judgments. According to his conception, aesthetic evaluation requires a subjective, concrete, disinterested, judgment of intrinsic value. For Kant, a *judgment* was an evaluation subject to discursive contestation and justification. Kant certainly did not agree that there is no disputing taste: in principle, one should be able to offer persuasive reasons for an aesthetic judgment, supported by invoking an interlocutor's experience of the sensuous qualities of the object being judged. Yet, neither could logic or empirical evidence ever prove an aesthetic evaluation, or finally settle an aesthetic dispute. Thus aesthetic judgments are *subjective* rather than objective: they are not determined by logic or by characteristics of the object judged. Ultimately, each individual must be the judge of his or her own aesthetic experience.

An aesthetic judgment is *concrete* in the sense that it is a judgment of a particular object, unmediated by any concept, rule, or general criterion. Joseph Heller's *Something Happened* is a fine novel, not because it exemplifies the praiseworthy quality of suspense, but because of the particular way it wrings suspense out of the prosaic details of middle-class family life, as revealed by a narrative speaker determined to keep his anxieties hidden from himself. Thus, the particular way that suspense is expressed in this novel is aesthetically valuable because of its contribution to the novel's unique formal structure. For Kant, the concreteness of aesthetic evaluation distinguishes it from moral evaluation, which measures every action by the same general standard of fairness.

An aesthetic judgment is *disinterested* in the sense that it is not – although it may accompany – the experience of pleasure. Thus, a tragedy can impress me as great while overwhelming me with sadness; by contrast, a formulaic potboiler might give me just what I want, without impressing me at all. In *Something Happened*, the reader's eager curiosity is an integral formal element, but so is the reader's dread and discomfort. Particular pleasures may be necessary means to achieve particular aesthetic effects, but the value of such an effect is not reducible to the pleasure producing it. Finally, according to Kant's conception, an aesthetic judgment is a judgment of *intrinsic* rather than instrumental value. A work of art is not beautiful or great because it causes pleasure, or any other good consequence. It might teach moral virtues, or give insight into human psychology, but such beneficial consequences are distinct from its aesthetic value.

Aesthetic judgment plays a role in artistic expression and in the appreciation and criticism of artistic works. Just as the creation of art cannot be reduced to a formula, art criticism does not apply general standards of value given in advance of the act of aesthetic judgment. Instead, it informs experience of the object of aesthetic judgment, in such a way as to create a shared or reproducible experience. To the extent that the shared experience made available by a critical interpretation impresses its audience as intrinsically valuable, it becomes possible to derive criteria of value from that shared experience. Aesthetic criticism identifies values expressed by human creations and judges those values on the basis of the shared experience of those creations. Thus, aesthetic criticism is less concerned with applying evaluative standards than with identifying, developing, and assessing values.

Aesthetic judgment can play a role in other kinds of evaluative decisionmaking as well. It is relevant whenever a decisionmaker has a measure of discretion, yet is not simply gratifying her own desires. Typically, this sort of evaluative decision will arise in collective action, which often requires interpreting norms or representing others' interests. Thus, when acting for an organization with an indefinite purpose or multiple purposes, a decisionmaker has to construct the organization's mission in order to serve it. Particularly if the organization depends on the voluntary cooperation of its agents, the decisionmaker must act in a way that will be accepted by others as a coherent interpretation of the organization's past practices and of the participants' community of interest. One who acts for another as a fiduciary rather than an agent often has discretion to interpret the beneficiary's interests, but cannot simply replace those interests with her own. In these situations of interpretation and representation, choice involves judgment rather than preference, and that judgment is partly aesthetic (Simon, 1978; Luban, 1988).

Ronald Dworkin has noted a similarly constructive element inherent in applying customary norms such as courtesy that require adapting conventions to changing social circumstances. Dworkin views this kind of "constructive interpretation" of an existing social practice as an exercise of aesthetic judgment (Dworkin, 1986). Pierre Bourdieu has identified an analogous combination of discretion and constrained judgment in the related social practice of gift-exchange. A well-chosen gift should express something about the giver and the receiver; it should differ from the receiver's past gifts to the giver, and yet symbolically equal or requite them (Bourdieu, 1990). The expression of courtesy is an aesthetic effect, but that does not mean it is merely ornamental. Tact facilitates trust, enabling strangers or rivals to achieve the mutual benefits of otherwise "irrational" cooperation. A British diplomat assigned to the Coalition Provisional Authority in occupied Iraq learned that "a cup of coffee delivered in the right way could win more friends than a new high school, and no amount of money could wipe clean an insult." The relationships with tribal leaders he built on this sort of courtesy enabled him "to secure the release of a British businessman, ... handed back to him as a 'present' from the uncle of the kidnapper" (Skidelsky, 2006, p. 12).

Aesthetic judgment is also required in making decisions about the cultivation of tastes, whether for one's self or another. When parents choose educational environments for a child they are acting as fiduciaries. Hopefully they are acting in the "best" interests of the child rather than simply gratifying their own preferences by unreflectively reproducing themselves or compensating for their own disappointments. Nor would we expect them merely to gratify the current preferences of the child (to do nothing but watch TV for example), who is not yet competent to formulate her own purposes without assistance. The parents are acting in part to *determine* the preferences and interests of the child by developing her character (Margulies, 1996, p. 1475). The interests that are "best" for this particular child in the long run, in the judgment of those who love and care for her, are interests she does not yet have and perhaps never would develop if raised by different parents with different capabilities and interests. Exercising such judgment is a profoundly serious responsibility, but it is nevertheless at least in part, an aesthetic choice: subjective, disinterested, informed by judgments of intrinsic worth ("best"), but also highly contingent and concrete (what are *this* child and *these* parents capable of under *these* circumstances?).

Similarly, when a young adult makes important decisions with long-term consequences for herself – going to Antioch, entering the military or holy orders, emigrating, getting married, having a child – she is not gratifying her future preferences because those future preferences depend, in large part, on her choices. These kinds of identity-altering choices are better seen as self-expressive or self-fashioning than as self-gratifying. Such choices about what kind of person one would like to become are aesthetic choices in so far as they reflect judgment of what available or achievable roles, interests, and desires are most worthy, or will best realize one's particular potential. The problem of character development that preoccupies modern fiction, drama, and lyric poetry is the problem that confronts us individually and collectively in a liberal society where we are free to define and develop our own virtues, free to – in Nietzsche's telling phrase – "give style" to our characters (Nietzsche, 1974, pp. 185–186; Nehamas, 1985). Imaginative literature engages our aesthetic judgment in this problem, and trains it; but planning the development of character is a problem we face in "real" life.

Following Kant, many thinkers have explored the role of these kinds of aesthetic judgments in politics and law. The poet Friedrich Schiller argued in his *Letters on the Aesthetic Education of Man* that aesthetic experience was essential preparation for exercising the moral and civic obligations associated with freedom in the new democratic state. Deliberating about and cooperating to achieve the public good required training in empathetic imagination and disinterested evaluation. What would it feel like to be somebody else? What would society be like to live in after this or that legislative change? For Schiller, aesthetic appreciation was also a kind of motivation necessary for compliance with moral and civic obligation. The creation of a good society, like the creation of art, could become a gratifying calling (Schiller, 1967). Hannah Arendt, in her lectures on Kant's *Critique of Judgment*, agreed that political persuasion among equals necessarily involves an aesthetic appeal. Democratic politics, for Arendt, is deliberative and transformative: if participants are unwilling to examine and alter their own preferences and identify with collective projects they are merely engaged in bargaining, not politics. Thus a legitimate law does not represent the electorate by reflecting the preferences of a majority of individuals. Instead it constitutes a figurative representation of a collective will that can only come into existence in the deliberative process and through collective action (Arendt, 1992).

Juergen Habermas's neo-Kantian ethical theory treats a deliberative discourse of instrumental and aesthetic evaluation as an indispensable legitimating condition for any legal or political arrangement. Drawing also on pragmatic epistemology, Habermas associates modern rationality with an open-ended process of testing belief, responsive not only to new evidence, but also to new conditions and purposes. For Habermas, deliberation unrestricted by a given end, concept, or object is the condition for justifying propositions in a self-governing society of equals. Habermas sees propositions of any kind as part of an institutional practice of language rather than as copies of sensory experience. Hence their validity is always provisional, dependent on ongoing social practices of evaluation and reason-giving rather than correspondence with objects or concepts. These provisional judgments of legitimacy are partly instrumental because they permit the invocation of those social purposes and practices on which interlocutors can agree. But in so far as those purposes and practices are themselves subject to challenge, interpretation, and revision, judgments of legitimacy are also aesthetic in part. Habermas's major work on legal theory, *Between Facts and Norms*, emphasizes the interpretive character of deliberation about law. Legal institutions and rules always have an arbitrary, historically contingent character, or "facticity." We tend to accept historically received laws provisionally because by establishing a modicum of social order and peace they facilitate collective action, including the justificatory deliberation that is the condition of legitimacy. The price of this provisional acceptance is the hermeneutic character of legal deliberation, the necessarily imaginative project of making normative sense of historical contingency (Habermas, 1996).

Habermas's reflections on law's historicity or "facticity" respond to two leading post-war hermeneutic theorists of law, Hans-Georg Gadamer and Dworkin. Both argued that legal interpretation was a creative process implicating aesthetic judgment. Gadamer, in *Truth and Method*, portrayed interpretation of all kinds as a dialogue between text and interpreter in which the interpreter comes to understand herself as a participant in an enabling language and culture rather than a self-determining instrumental actor (Gadamer, 1975). The legal interpreter comes to understand the historically contingent legal text as not arbitrary for her, by developing a self-interpretation as a participant in an institutional tradition that generated the text and that enables judgments of meaning and value. Even the interpreter's capacity to criticize existing legal arrangements draws upon a language, society, and history that also gave rise to those arrangements. To protest is to presume that the legal system is at some level bound by the values the protester invokes, so that the legal discourse always contains the germ of its own creative transformation. But that transformation depends on acts of creative self-fashioning by interpreters implicated in that discourse. Dworkin, in *Law's Empire*, offers a similar account of legal reasoning and argument as engaged participation in a legal system, in which a "constructive interpreter" makes sense of received legal materials by imagining the underlying purposes and principles of justice that make the "best" of them. Dworkin calls the hermeneutic obligation to make the best of law "the aesthetic hypothesis." And he likens the interpretive process to reading a legal system's past as the actions of a fictional person and continuing the story in a way that maintains that character's "integrity" in both the aesthetic and the moral senses of that term (Dworkin, 1986).

These thinkers see aesthetic judgment as part of law and politics because they see law and politics as settings for collective self-fashioning. They see political and legal legitimacy as an aesthetic effect, a value judgment that persuades individuals to identify themselves with a particular, historically contingent set of social arrangements and to embrace purposes that are not their own. In developing a conception of law as an object of literary analysis, then, we want to emphasize the role of figurative representations in legitimating law by persuading law's subjects to identify with it, or at least to identify themselves in the terms law provides.

## 2. LEGAL INSTITUTIONS

In recent decades, social scientists in various fields have developed the concept of institutions to capture the causal role of a variety of factors left out of rational choice models of society. These include cultural meanings and values, but also routines and procedures for gathering and processing information, and for allocating decisionmaking authority. The juxtaposition of such seemingly disparate phenomena in the same category suggests surprising connections among them. Thus, for example, we can think of decisionmaking procedures as semiotic relations, in which person A is authorized to decide or act on behalf of person B or organization C; or in which facts D and E are taken as conclusive evidence of quality F. Similarly, we can conceive of virtues and value commitments as the performance of roles, such as the good Catholic, the neutral judge, or the obedient soldier. On this view, persons acting out value commitments serve as symbols, standing for something beyond their own preferences. Because institutionalism presents both substantive and procedural norms as semiotic relations involving a kind of representation, it offers a perspective that may illuminate law's literary aspect.

Drawing on the institutionalist literature, we may define institutions as social practices organizing collective action through a discourse that classifies situations as subject to rules or other normative standards. Thus defined, institutions have a normative dimension, involving rule-following; a semiotic dimension, concerned with representing situations as instances of a class; and a social dimension, involving organization for collective action. Institutions sometimes also have a political dimension, concerned with the distribution of authority to make and apply normative judgments, and the distribution of responsibility to follow norms. Thus, institutions frequently classify persons as well as situations and apply so condition the application of normative standards on particular roles or statuses (MacCormick & Weinberger, 1986; March & Olsen, 1989; North, 1990; Peters, 1999; Ruiter, 1993; Scott, 1995; Searle, 1995). Institutions include almost any socially organized activity, such as science or art. Language, which organizes collective action through conventional representations that are subject to normative standards of referential and grammatical correctness, is an institution on which most other institutions depend. Money, a system of rules for representing exchange value, that facilitates exchange and resource allocation, is also an institution.

Given a conception of an institution as a practice of using norms to organize collective action, we can define *law* as including any institution that is relatively coercive, formal, and articulate. So legal institutions involve norms of conduct understood, in principle, to be binding on persons recognized as occupying certain statuses, whether or not those individuals accept those obligations. These conduct norms are backed by sanctions, imposed by some persons at the request of others, according to norms of participation, investigative procedure, decision, and discursive justification.

Finally, the process of generating all these norms is governed by additional norms of participation, procedure, and discursive justification (Komesar, 1997; Hart, 1994). The formality of law consists in the prevalence of norms of participation and procedure in the discourse of legal justification. Most legal questions are resolved by identifying the authoritative decisionmaker, the past decisions of such an actor, or the standards authorized by such an actor, rather than by directly invoking values or goals.

To characterize law as an institution is to say that it conditions participation on the acceptance of norms and the performance of roles. Institutional roles channel action by supplying actors with a set of motives, concerns, and assumptions and a limited repertoire of behaviors. Roles render action intelligible and predictable to others (Bourdieu, 1991; Bourdieu, 1977; Binder & Weisberg, 1997). The desires to communicate to others or to be associated with certain roles can therefore motivate compliance with norms. In other words, people can comply with norms out of expressive rather than instrumental motives.

As an institutional practice, then, law commands not only or ultimately by threatening. Law orders society through the combined effects of coercive force and normative authority. Norms without force are not laws, but commands are not laws unless they are obeyed also out of a sense of obligation. Moreover, law's force and its authority are integrally connected. On the one hand, law can muster manpower and weapons only because many people agree that its commands should be obeyed. On the other hand, the availability of coercive force enhances law's authority. Because many will prefer any effective legal system, however unjust, to anarchy or violent civil conflict, force tends to generate its own legitimacy. To view law as an institution, however, is to emphasize the role of law's normative authority in inducing compliance and legitimizing state force. That authority is a cultural construct, real in so far as people believe it to be so.

The authority of many institutions is a matter of unreflective habit. We usually accept money as valuable and language as meaningful without reflecting about how and why this is so. But law is different, at least in modern liberal states. Law is an arena of contestation and legal authority depends upon a self-conscious discourse of justification. In making legal arguments, participants of course try to establish the validity of particular propositions of law. Yet in so doing they also endorse the authority of law generally, warranting the rationality of the forum in which they appear, the validity of the statutes, prior cases and principles they cite, and the legitimacy of the process that generated these sources of law.

A practical incentive to justify arises only when we need to – and can hope to – influence the behavior of others with some power to withhold cooperation. We justify actions and beliefs where contestation is possible but there are nevertheless common norms to appeal to. Thus, a discourse of justification is most likely in institutional settings characterized by a relative equality among participants, and a measure of freedom of action. Indeed, we may say that a distinctive characteristic of modern liberal societies is the proliferation of justificatory practices that presuppose this kind of freedom and equality. Justificatory discourse in such a society usually involves more than invocation of hierarchical status or tradition (Ackerman, 1980). Law, with its self-conscious discourse of justification, becomes a paradigm for other modes of institutional authority in such a society.

Let us define modernity as a discursive situation premised on the epistemological principle that all knowledge must derive from human experience or reason, rather than tradition or faith; and the meta-ethical principle that all value must derive from human will or reason, rather than tradition or faith (Patterson, 1996; Lyotard, 1984). Modernity gives rise to the practice of modernist criticism, which tests beliefs by reducing them to their foundations in sensation, will, and reason. In the field of law, such reductionist movements as utilitarianism, legal positivism, legal science, legal realism, critical legal studies, and law and economics have exemplified modernist criticism (Bentham, 1996; Austin, 1873; Williston, 1920; Cohen, 1935; Singer, 1984; Posner, 1973).

Modernity shapes justificatory discourses as responses to modernist criticism. In the face of normative disagreement, modernist justificatory discourse has a tendency to discount reason and to root values entirely in some form of will or desire. Justificatory reference to desire may be teleological (interests, utility, welfare, needs), or archaeological (consent, preferences, injuries). Reason (or "rationality") may then be accorded a subordinate role in directing action to serve desire, or in reconciling conflicting desires through deliberation or aggregation. These variants of modernist justificatory discourse share a common assumption: that practices can only be justified by correspondence to observed fact. This insistence on a foundation in fact arises from modernism's mistrust of the discourses of representation on which institutional practices depend. Modernist criticism treats the need for representation as an embarrassment. Thus, it strives to reduce these representations, or signs, to the "reality" they represent – ideas, sense impressions, desires, intentions, verbal meanings, material interests, behavior, and so forth. From this perspective, representations have meaning or value by virtue of their correspondence to some state of affairs. In short modernist criticism presumes that representation has a *mimetic* function (Patterson, 1996; Ankersmit, 1996).

In epistemology, modernist criticism asks "what is it about the world that our statements must conform to, to make them true?" In philosophy of language, it asks "what must a claim about the meaning of language correspond to, to make it true?" Philosophers' answers to these questions have generally taken the form of an intelligible essence, or some similar mental entity. Thus, rationalists held that knowledge was founded on clear and distinct ideas. Empiricists complained that these ideas were unobservable specters, and replaced them with sense impressions and mental associations. As pragmatists pointed out, however, empiricists thereby reproduced the idealism for which they had criticized the rationalists. Empiricists assumed we could only understand, use, and communicate about our environment if it came equipped with mental handles for words to grasp onto (Rorty, 1979). As argued in the preceding section, however, this idea of a direct linkage between words and features of the world mischaracterizes how we use language. Linguistic and literary structuralists have pointed out that signifieds, what words denote or connote, are linguistic constructs, no less dependent on a system of conventional signs than are their verbal signifiers (Binder & Weisberg, 2000). Pragmatic philosophers of language and literary post-structuralists have converged on the view that these signifieds are shifting webs of association rather than hard-edged concepts or categories. The meaning of any term is hostage to the evolving history of its use. Because no two occasions of use are identical, every use of language is rhetorically figurative, and every act of communication or interpretation is a speculative move in a language game (Wittgenstein, 1968; Hurley, 1989; Derrida, 1976; Binder & Weisberg, 2000). Every classificatory judgment is a normative claim within an institutional practice that may be accepted, rejected, or reinterpreted by others.

Pragmatism takes the failure of philosophy's varied attempts to translate language and thought into unmediated reality, as evidence that the task should be abandoned. Pragmatism therefore rejects the assumption that representation must stand in a relation of correspondence with the world, in order to be meaningful (Rorty, 1979). Instead, pragmatism views representations simply as tools for organizing social practices, and holds that their necessarily unstable meaning inheres in their use. Since the same utterances can be used by both speakers and hearers, by multiple authors and later by different readers, there is never any single spatial and temporal locus of meaning, no ultimate authority on what any utterance means. Representation, in the sense used here – the use of signs within an institutional practice – is never purely mimetic. It is always figurative and always offered for normative judgment.

The disagreement between modernism and pragmatism about representation extends to the special case of political representation. Political representation is a form of collective action involving (1) a division of labor that allocates power to persons acting in designated roles to promulgate or apply norms backed by coercive sanctions and (2) a justificatory discourse ascribing these exercises of power to others. Persons may be represented by particular other persons, or by organizations, within which different persons may have different roles (Ankersmit,1996; Pitkin, 1967). Political representation is a common institutional structure in modern legal systems, and the justificatory discourse of political representation is an important source of legal argument.

Just as modernist epistemology and philosophy of language have looked for a third term to explain how representations can correspond to what they represent, modernist political theory has done the same. Political theory asks what about us political institutions must represent to make their representation legitimate. The answers – preferences, interests, opinions, convictions – purport to be psychological facts about persons. But like any other signified, these objects of representation depend upon the system of signs that differentiates them from other signifieds (Ankersmit, 1996; Hurley, 1989). Thus, we need an agenda, a menu of options, in order to have an opinion. We need issues, establishing political axes, before we can locate our political positions on those axes (Pildes & Anderson, 1990; Mackie, 2003). In this sense, the political preferences electoral and legislative institutions represent are "endogenous" to those institutions (Hurley, 1989; March & Olsen, 1995; Green & Shapiro, 1994). Political representations, therefore, cannot correspond to social fact. They cannot achieve mimetic truth. They must win normative acceptance from those they represent on some other basis.

Based on its view of representation as inherently rhetorical, pragmatism also offers an account of both cognitive and evaluative justification that rejects the mimetic premise of modernism. Pragmatic justification makes the test of any action or belief the difference it makes in practice. It asks us to compare the consequences of any action or claim with the consequences of available alternative actions or claims. But unlike other consequentialist doctrines, such as utilitarian policy analysis or verificationist epistemology, pragmatism does not prescribe further criteria for comparing alternative bundles of consequences. It treats the justification of action and belief as a matter of situated practical judgment, and denies that justification must rest on a foundation of indubitable knowledge (Rorty, 1979; Patterson, 1996; Herzog, 1985; Binder, 2001).

Aesthetic judgment has a special role to play in the consequentialist evaluation required in pragmatist justification. Pragmatism asks us to evaluate consequences without the metric provided by some foundational standard of value. It is tempting to assume that this means we should simply assess consequences instrumentally, by reference to the purposes we already have. But this evades such questions as what feasible choices we have among purposes, what the consequences would be of choosing different purposes, whether those consequences would be better or worse, and from what perspective. We cannot employ instrumental reason to evaluate ends: this is a question of aesthetic judgment (Binder, 2001). Thus, in so far as legal justification is pragmatist rather than modernist, it will involve a rhetorical appeal to aesthetic judgment.

## 3. THE RHETORIC OF LEGAL JUSTIFICATION

Legal justification is a rhetoric that makes an aesthetic appeal. It combines three types of rhetorical figures. The most important of these is the political representation of subjective will. In a modern liberal state, law is seen as a human creation, designed to serve human needs (Cardozo, 1921). Accordingly, law's content is justified by reference to the utility or choice of human beings or their institutional representations. Legal argument and decision therefore involve prospective reasoning about the interests of persons, groups, populations, institutions, and polities; and retrospective reasoning about the content and competence of their choices. In other words, almost all legal argument is about the desires of legal actors, how best to measure, identify, or represent those desires, and whose desires should count (Binder & Weisberg, 1997; Binder, 2001).

These political representations of subjective will are framed by three forms of narratives: narratives of reconciliation, narratives of authorization, and narratives of legitimation. Narratives of reconciliation are the rhetorical structures used to explain how the will of each becomes the will of all. Thus, they explain how the invisible hand of the market reconciles the competing desires of consumers into efficient allocations of resources; or how political processes organize the incommensurable preferences of voters into a coherent popular will; or how wise judges rationally reconcile the competing liberty claims of litigants. In other words, narratives of reconciliation warrant particular decisionmaking procedures as methods for representing society as a whole. Narratives of authorization link a particular act to the will of all, in the form of a past authoritative decision or a future societal goal. Finally, narratives of legitimation warrant the subjective will of society itself as an authoritative source of law by linking it to some greater source of virtue in the past or future.

"Narrative" refers to the recounting of a story, a chronological sequence of causally linked events in the experience of a human or anthropomorphized subject. A narrative is a kind of rhetorical trope, a structure of meaning imposed on events by their selection, ordering, and telling. It begins in equilibrium, presenting a stable routine of behaviors and roles. This equilibrium is then disturbed by some conflict, often between the subject and forces external to it, which disrupts routines and roles, opening new possibilities. The story ends in a new state of equilibrium (Binder & Weisberg, 2000; Winter, 1989; Scholes & Kellogg, 1966; Todorov, 1971). The mediation of such a story by a teller rather than performers distinguishes narrative from drama, but both are mediations distinct from events themselves (Scholes & Kellogg, 1966). In modern culture, the activity of a narrator alerts an audience to the artifactual or subjectively constructed quality of the story, even when the resulting narrative is nonfictional (Binder & Weisberg, 2000).

Narrative, like drama, makes a sensuous appeal to an audience's judgment by creating the aesthetic quality of suspense. It evokes tension by describing disequilibrium, and suspends that tension by recounting events in a temporal order. The narrator promises to resolve that tension if only the reader will patiently continue a little longer. Thus the act of reading narrative commits the reader to a kind of contract, which invests the reader in accepting the resolution, when it comes, as appropriate and satisfying (Sussman, 1998; Brooks, 1996). Despite narrative's predictable form, it must be unpredictable in the details to achieve the necessary aesthetic qualities of suspense and surprised relief. In this sense it invites the reader to engage in the particularistic judgment characteristic of aesthetic experience generally.

Narrative has always been involved in the legitimation of normative orders (Cover, 1983; Lyotard, 1984; MacIntyre, 1985). This is obvious in preliterate societies, which can only record and transmit their norms and political institutions in the form of memorable stories. But literacy begins with the transcription of these national or tribal epics. In modern society, such epics have been replaced with more specialized discourses: narrative histories to record the origins and development of political institutions, narrative novels and memoirs to recount the interaction of character and role, and non-narrative law codes to fix norms and procedures. Yet these functionally distinct and formally disparate genres presuppose one another. Modern law tends to be seen as entrenching two large institutional structures: a more or less democratic nation state and a civil society of transacting individuals. The national history underwrites the first, by grounding an argument that law has organized a population into a political community capable of conferring its consent to governance (White, 1981; Bhaba, 1990). The novel and memoir underwrite the second, by warranting that the individual is capable of rationally and responsibly exercising the discretion inherent in legal personality (Gagnier, 1987; Gallagher, 1994; Lukacs, 1920; Lynch, 1998). At the same time, law gives these genres their subjects, organizing the polities whose careers are recounted in history, and the civil societies within which novelistic characters pursue their careers of romance, intrigue, and social climbing.

Authorization narratives play an essential role in law's justificatory discourse. The very concept of sanction involves the structure of a story, triggered by some deviation from a prescribed state of affairs, followed by an act of judgment, and a corrective response (Binder & Weisberg, 2000). The official imposing a sanction justifies it as authorized by a prior act of legislation. The legislator defining the sanction justifies it as the path to a brighter future or the restoration of a disrupted past. Both official and legislator claim authority on the basis of prior acts of appointment or election.

Legal argument generally involves one of two forms of authorization narrative, depending on where the speaker locates the current dispute along the narrative arc between equilibrium disrupted and equilibrium restored. Archaelogical argument locates the disruptive crisis in the past. Thus, applicable legal norms have emerged from the authoritative settlement of that conflict. The current dispute is an echo of that earlier conflict and has, in effect already been settled. To decide otherwise is to reopen that conflict and reproduce the problems the applicable legal norm earlier solved. Teleological argument locates the disruptive crisis in the present. Thus, the current dispute results from a defective normative order, in which the needs of some are unmet or the goals of all are unrealized. The applicable legal norm will achieve the needed change. Archaeological argument predominates in litigation and teleological argument predominates in legislation. But many legal arguments combine both archaeological and teleological elements. Thus, the current dispute is governed by an earlier normative settlement that promulgated a collective goal as yet unachieved. Both teleological and archaeological narratives derive authority from a collective will that must be constructed in the act of representation.

Teleological representation involves prospective reasoning about the public interest or the social welfare. Such teleological representation involves imagining and comparing the future histories of alternative hypothetical societies, each with not only different legal regimes, but also different populations with different values and interests. When different societies have different histories and institutional structures, they are likely to make available quite disparate social identities and roles to their members. These disparate identities and roles will encourage members of differently constituted societies to pursue different purposes and interests.

When we try to compare societies with different members, values, and interests from the standpoint of social welfare we face imponderables. Should you prefer a wealthier society in which you had a different family or personality? Should you prefer a more peaceful society in which you did not exist? The choice among such incommensurable alternatives is not the simple matter of calculating which future will be better for people because the alternatives are populated by different people. Such a decision requires us to choose among the different personal, group, institutional, and societal identities that will shape the preferences of future generations. We cannot hold their future preferences fixed and choose policies that will best realize them. Instead, the design of the future society, its membership, and its values is a necessarily expressive or aesthetic choice for us (Parfit, 1984; Binder, 2001).

We face further value choices in reasoning about the future welfare of society. We must choose distributive standards both within and across generations. We must choose a time horizon: the future is infinite, our knowledge of it finite and diminishing (Herzog, 1985). We must choose how to compare aggregate and average utility (Parfit, 1984). We must choose a geographic scope: Is each government responsible only for the welfare of the population in its territory? Even if its decisions may affect immigration and emigration? (Binder, 1993a). All these choices about how best to aggregate and compare subjectivity are themselves subjective. We cannot simply enact the preferences of future people, because we must decide which future people to consult, and what preferences they will have. These decisions inevitably depend on our value choices, not those of the future people whose welfare we would serve. Indeed, our value choices about future welfare are likely to be interpretive responses to the identities, roles, and traditions we have inherited from the past (Fish, 1989; Gadamer, 1975). We express ourselves in making these choices. We fashion a design for the future that is our best vision of how to continue a historical narrative in which we find ourselves (MacIntyre, 1985; Dworkin, 1986).

The inevitable discretion we have to shape the future preferences we would satisfy prevents teleological representation from achieving mimesis. From the standpoint of modernist criticism, teleological representation therefore seems illegitimate. In the face of the subjective, expressive, and arguably aesthetic value choices entailed in prospective policy making, it is tempting to revert to some form of archaeological representation.

Archaeological representation consists in retrospective reasoning about indicia of societal consent. The difficulty is that notions like popular consent are incoherent and instable without authoritative institutional definition, and the institutions defining popular consent can ultimately find no warrant in popular consent. Institutional authority depends upon legitimating narratives, which make a persuasive appeal for a performative response (Lyotard, 1984). To judge the persuasiveness of these legitimating narratives, we must make expressive and aesthetic choices. Just as prospective reasoning about future welfare implicates aesthetic judgment, so does retrospective reasoning about past acts of consent.

Thus, when legal decisionmakers represent society's will, they again face a number of discretionary choices. First they must decide to what extent they are going to represent society as a single democratic decisionmaker, and to what extent they will represent society as a collection of individual transactors (Binder & Weisberg, 1997). In other words, we can think of the tension between majoritarian democracy and individual liberty, or between political allocation and market allocation, as an aesthetic dilemma, a problem of representation. Each of these forms of representation reconciles conflicting preferences in a different way, and by assigning different decisions to different institutions we can represent the same individuals quite differently. Within each of these modes of representation there are further dilemmas, reflecting the indeterminacy of the ideals of majoritarian democracy, individual liberty, and allocative efficiency. The indeterminacy of these three ideals in turn reflects the opacity of the corresponding institutions of elections, legal rights, and market exchange as media for representing consent.

Majoritarian democracy is the conception of consent represented by the institution of elections. Yet as an ideal, majoritarian democracy is afflicted with the familiar problem of social choice. According to Arrow's classic demonstration, no social choice mechanism can aggregate fixed individual preference orderings of more than two alternatives into a coherent social preference ordering. A coherent social preference ordering therefore requires that individual preferences vary with and depend on the institution aggregating them into a collective choice (Arrow, 1963). The practical point of Arrow's voting paradox is not that indeterminacy is possible with three alternatives or more, but that indeterminacy is almost inevitable when the number of alternatives becomes very great. Democratic electorates must choose among an infinitely large set of alternative possible futures. If they do so through pairwise comparisons, the results are likely to depend on the order of comparison. If they try to compare all alternatives at once, different schemes for weighting preferences will yield different results (Mackie, 2003). In sum, the choice of voting procedures proves more important than voting in determining electoral choices. There is no simple fact of the matter about collective preferences for the institution of democracy to represent. The figurative replacement of individual preferences by majority will is one type of reconciliation narrative.

As a conception of consent, majoritarian democracy is also necessarily incomplete. It depends on some set of procedural conditions designed to guarantee free and equal participation – universal suffrage, secret ballots, freedom of speech and press, and so on. These procedural conditions set limits to the power of democratic majorities to legislate: they cannot disfranchise, exile, enslave or exterminate minorities, for example, without destroying the conditions for majoritarian democracy. Majoritarian democracy is therefore a self-limiting ideal, requiring a supplementary scheme of individual rights (Holmes, 1995).

Individual liberty is the conception of consent represented by the institution of legal rights, supervised by the institution of courts. Liberty offers an alternative to majoritarian democracy as an organization of consent. If political processes cannot yield demonstrably legitimate choices, it is tempting to decrease the scope of political decisionmaking as much as possible, and increase the scope for individual decisionmaking. Thus the classical liberal thought popular among American and German lawyers of the mid- to late nineteenth century, attempted to restrict the domain of collective choice by recognizing individuals as autonomous within a sphere of purely self-regarding action. Individuals, it was said, were free to act as long as their actions imposed no harm on others. Classical liberals assumed that society was so designed that individuals had a wide scope within which they could act without effecting others, and reasoned that neither the state nor other individuals should interfere with such purely self-regarding action (Gordon, 1983; Singer, 1982). This vision of an atomistic society rested on a conception of property rights as relations between persons and things, and of the objects of property rights as environments – physical spaces paradigmatically – within which individuals could act without affecting one another (Binder, 2002).

Yet such American legal realists as John Wesley Hohfeld and Walter Wheeler Cook argued persuasively that purely self-regarding action is a chimera. To use a resource is to interfere with rival potential uses, and to recognize a right of autonomy on the part of one person is to impose a duty of non-interference on the part of others. This analysis demonstrated that a property right was a social relation and that the object of property was always an arena of social interaction and conflict, rather than a peaceful private retreat (Cook, 1918; Cohen, 1927; Hohfeld, 1913; Coase, 1960; Singer, 1982). This meant in turn that the problem of collective choice cannot be solved simply by disaggregating it into a series of individual choices. Any such strategy depends on a social decision to distribute to individuals the right to exclude all others from access to certain resources. The ideal of individual liberty depends on the figurative replacement of conflicting desires with an authoritative allocation of rights. In short it depends upon the reconciliation of conflicting claims of justice, perhaps by a court. The need for such an allocation of rights simply moves the problem of social choice back to an earlier stage.

Like the ideal of majoritarian democracy, the ideal of individual liberty is self-limiting. Some sort of politics must limit each person's liberty, to insure the equal, or at least minimally adequate liberty of others. And just as the unrestricted exercise of majoritarian democracy today may destroy the conditions for its exercise tomorrow, the unrestricted exercise of individual liberty in the present may waste the requisites of individual liberty in the future. Individuals may sell or indebt themselves into slavery, addict themselves to dangerous products, or enthrall themselves to exploitative creeds. To institutionalize individual liberty, society must make a political choice about how much paternalistic protection it will provide individuals.

Allocative efficiency is the conception of consent represented by the institution of market exchange. It offers a representation of desire that is collective, and yet not aggregative. In this way, it promises to resolve some questions of resource allocation in a way that responds to individual preferences, while avoiding the paradoxes of social choice theory. By hypothesis, when a resource is exchanged it is moved to a use that is more valuable socially, but without any social decisionmaker aggregating the utilities of the transacting parties. Assuming that a transaction is uncoerced, it should make both parties at least marginally better off. And assuming there are no transaction costs, anyone else whose welfare is decreased by the transaction can attempt to prevent it by bribing the parties forgo it (Coase, 1960). So if unrestricted opportunities for costless transactions are institutionalized, society should be able to constantly reallocate resources in ways that increase the welfare of some without decreasing the welfare of any. Assuming no transaction costs or coercion, market exchange should be able to allocate resources optimally, regardless of their initial distribution. By means of the reconciliation narrative of the invisible hand, individual desire is transformed into collective utility without the need for politics. But like majoritarian democracy and individual liberty, allocative efficiency is a necessarily incomplete representation of aggregate desire.

First, efficiency depends on politics. While efficiency presumes the ideal of costless transactions, all transactions involve the cost of enforcing promises and defining and securing entitlements to the resources traded. These costly services are typically provided by government without a fee. So the transactional model of collective decisionmaking presupposes a political process of collective decisionmaking to establish the institutions of property and contract within which transactional decisions will take place (Barzel, 2002; North, 1990; Rose, 1989).

Second, efficiency depends upon individual liberty. If choices are coerced, we cannot interpret them as welfare-maximizing revelations of preferences. And since all market choices are constrained by the available goods, and the limitations of the actor's purchasing power, market choices are all coerced in varying degree (Crawford, 1997). Determining whether to deem a particular menu of options excessively coercive requires a collective, political judgment.

Third, any claim that uncoerced, costless transactions are allocatively efficient becomes circular, when combined with two premises of neo-classical economics: the behaviorist methodological assumptions that satisfaction cannot be reliably observed and that utility cannot be compared across persons (Robbins, 1938; Samuelson, 1938; Samuelson, 1950; Friedman, 1953). On these assumptions welfare must be defined behaviorally as the result of uncoerced, costless transactions; yet there is no way to determine if an actual or possible transaction meets these conditions without knowing its welfare effects. Economists recognize no independent measure of welfare by which they can determine whether coercion has caused, or transaction costs have prevented any particular transaction.

Just as an election cannot register each voter's preferences for all possible futures, a market cannot register each consumer's preferences for all possible goods and services. Consumers can only spend wealth they have, and only on the particular goods and services producers provide. Like electoral institutions and property, markets construct an arena for the exercise of choice and thereby create a medium for expressing desires choosers might not otherwise have (Anderson, 1993; Walzer, 1983).

Finally, like the ideals of majoritarian democracy and individual liberty, the ideal of allocative efficiency is self-limiting. Like voting and the exercise of property rights, market exchange can destroy its own institutional conditions. If individuals can sell themselves, or trade away the requisites of participation in market exchange, their preferences will no longer influence market allocation. The unrestricted transacting required for efficient allocation is a procedural impossibility. Politics must create and define markets, as well as spheres of individual liberty.

We have seen that each of the idioms for representing consent – majoritarian democracy, individual liberty, and allocative efficiency – is an opaque medium. Thus, each medium of archaeological representation constructs the consent that it represents. But when legal decisionmakers represent societal will they must not only choose within each idiom, they must also choose among them. In designing the institutions of electoral politics, individual rights, and market exchange, legal decisionmakers are not only influencing the particular goals and policies to which members of society consent, they are also shaping the forms of consent – democracy, liberty, or efficiency – made available to them. The design of a mix of institutions for registering consent is itself a social or political choice that cannot be justified by consent alone, without an infinite regress.

But if neither future social welfare nor past consent can legitimate legal institutions what can? Such institutions can only be rendered authoritative by means of a legitimating narrative. Legitimation narratives present particular legal institutions as their audience's proper path from virtuous origins to future well-being. They make a performative appeal, inviting an audience to identify itself with a particular institutional medium for representing desire. Such legitimating narratives are a necessary part of legal argument, because without them, legal argument cannot warrant particular archaeological and teleological representations of societal will as author-itative. A narrative of virtuous institutional origins is needed to cope with two related problems of liberal political theory, the problem of collective action and the problem of political obligation.

The collective action problem arises among individuals who are rationally self-interested, uncoerced, and well-informed. Such persons have no incentive to cooperate in producing or conserving public goods such as renewable resources, common defense, or security of entitlements. By defecting, they can receive the benefits of the public good without bearing the costs of its provision. Hence all will find it rational to defect, with the perverse result that none will enjoy the public good (Olson, 1965). And so, the argument concludes, government is needed to coerce free riders into cooperating to produce public goods. Convinced by the security of government enforcement that one's fellow citizens will cooperate in the provision of public goods, each citizen will ungrudgingly cooperate in turn.

But this willingness depends upon each citizen's faith in the stability, effectiveness, and civic responsibility of the institutions charged with enforcing cooperation. And rational self-interest maximizers will be very skeptical of promises to establish a stable and effective rule of law. For such a government is itself a public good requiring cooperation to establish. So government arguably could never come into existence among people who were uncoerced, rationally self-interested, and well-informed, even if they desired it (Rose, 1989).

The existence of an effective liberal government therefore presupposes a prior history involving coercion, altruism, or myth. Coercion can play at least two roles in establishing liberal government. A liberal government can arise as a result of the internal reform of an authoritarian state or as a result of a violent revolution, establishing military rule before building liberal institutions. Yet a revolutionary movement is also an irrationally cooperative enterprise that must be explained in terms of coercion, altruism or myth. By altruism, I mean a disposition to cooperate regardless of the defection of free riders. Altruism can play a role in establishing effective government when tribal, religious or ideological solidarity becomes a basis for civic loyalty. By myth I mean faith that others will cooperate in obeying and defending government when this has not been proven by experience. Typically, myth takes the form of an invented past characterized by heroic altruism, solidaristic cooperation, and virtuous government. A myth of national origin can support a solidaristic ideology (Binder & Weisberg, 2000; Anderson, 1983; Gellner, 1983). Historically speaking, modern liberal states arise through a combination of these processes, rather than through uncoerced contracting among rationally self-interested individuals. Indeed, we are unlikely to see rationally self-interested individuals unencumbered by solidaristic commitments or authoritarian beliefs except in a liberal state. Rationality can only be the product of liberal institutions, not their source.

In addition to solving the collective action problem, a mythic narrative of a heroic founding can solve a related problem, that of political obligation. This problem arises in consent theories of political legitimacy. If government derives its legitimacy only from the consent of the governed, it is not clear why its citizens should comply with laws they do not personally agree to. Nor is it clear why anyone born into such a society (rather than joining it voluntarily) should respect its laws. Revolutionary origins symbolize the moral basis of many modern states in the consent of the governed, yet they also illustrate the fragility of such a foundation. Every legal system must account for its origins in an act of transgression against a preexisting legal order (Cover, 1983). So a state's revolutionary origin poses the problem of political obligation, unless it provides some additional basis of legitimacy beyond consent. That is why a myth of revolutionary heroism is particular important: a reputation for extraordinary virtue is needed to explain why the founding generation had a right to revolt, but their successors do not.

The liberal state cannot induce cooperation and provide public goods unless it is stable. But it cannot promise stability if it holds that citizens are only bound to obey law as long as they consent to do so. The disenchanted liberal individual, loyal only to his own property, cannot by himself sustain the polity that protects it. Thus the authority of the liberal state can never be explained by reference to consent alone. To solve the problem of political obligation, the narrative mythology of the liberal state must offer a reason why the consent of the founders binds their successors. To distinguish the founding exercise of will from future defections, it must be remembered as virtuous, motivated by altruism rather than selfishness. The popular "consent" which legitimates new laws is not purely a matter of will: it is a matter of keeping faith with virtues that a patriotic mythology ascribes to a political founding. When we make law, we do not simply reveal preference: we exercise the authority of office. Our consent can only authorize law, if we have first characterized ourselves as authoritative, in an act of literary imagination (Vining, 1988; Derrida, 1986).

Thus the claim that a legal system makes to legitimacy is not simply a claim about ethics, or about political fact. It is a performative appeal that offers each citizen recognition as a member of a particular political community. It must offer not only just and efficacious institutions, but an identity which each citizen will perceive as appealing to all, and so which may plausibly promise to bind each citizen to those institutions. It demands of each citizen a performative response, identifying with a political community and thereby recognizing other citizens as members. To thus identify herself with a political community and its other members, is to make an expressive choice (Ankersmit, 1996). And such an expressive choice depends on at least two kinds of judgment that can fairly be characterized as aesthetic. First, in choosing an identity for herself and others she chooses purposes. Second, in choosing an identity to share with others, she must interpret a collective project. Such judgments are too subjective and historically contingent to count as moral, yet they are aimed at self-constitution rather than merely self-gratification.

# 4. CONCLUSION: THE AESTHETIC PREDICAMENT OF LEGAL CRITICISM

In liberal states legal arguments depend on representations of human will, taking the form of judgments about future social welfare or past popular consent. Yet these representations are not simply mimetic, because social welfare and popular will are constituted in the very act of representing them. The process by which we represent our society's will and welfare in the medium of law is an imaginative and expressive one, narrating the path from a virtuous past to a decent future, and informed by aesthetic judgment as well as instrumental reason. In so far as law involves the presentation of rhetoric for aesthetic judgment it is a literary practice.

Recognizing the constitutively aesthetic basis of legal justification in the liberal state should induce us to revise the practice of modernist criticism of law. Much contemporary critical scholarship accepts the modernist premise that law should mirror the desires of society's members and takes law to task for failing to do so with perfect accuracy. Such mimetic criticism is subject to two pathologies: skepticism and sentimentalism

Skepticism is the disposition to see every practice as illegitimate unless it can be shown to rest on some indubitable foundation independent of the practice (Binder & Weisberg, 2000). Mimetic criticism becomes skeptical when it tries, and fails, to turn societal will into such a foundation for law. The skeptical form of mimetic criticism tends to begin with the proposition that political representation always involves an agency problem, a potential conflict between the interests of the represented and the interests of those who represent them. Accordingly, skeptical criticism deems representation legitimate only if the medium of representation is transparent: that is, only if it can simply copy the represented, without involving any discretionary choices. But as we have seen, political representation cannot be transparent in this sense. The teleological representation of welfare and the archaeological representation of consent are both inevitably discretionary acts of imaginative construction.

Mimetic critics tend to treat each of the paradoxes and limitations of majoritarian democracy, individual liberty, and allocative efficiency separately. Thus, one points to the problems of social choice theory in arguing that we can represent society more accurately by shifting decisionmaking authority from state to market (Riker, 1982; Riker & Ordeshook, 1973). Or, one points to the legal rights problem, and the indeterminacy of allocative efficiency in arguing that we can represent society more accurately in shifting decisionmaking authority from individuals and markets to the state (Sunstein, 1986). Each argument is based on the fallacious premise that a more accurate, less discretionary, depiction of society is possible, or even desirable. The mimetic critic appears to be saying something constructive about which institutions should have the leading role in governing society, but he is merely bearing witness to the opacity inherent in any institutional representation of society.

Skeptical variants of mimetic criticism recognize the opacity of both state and market as representative institutions, but nevertheless insist that legitimate law must stand on a foundation of actual consent, warranted by law's mimetic resemblance to society. Skeptical criticism reasons that since law must be a transparent medium of representation, and legal decisionmakers necessarily have discretion as to how they represent society, these decisionmakers rule society rather than taking instruction from society (Tushnet, 1988; Levinson, 1988). One response to this skeptical conclusion is a flight to the formalist ideal of the rule of law. According to this view, law must constrain legal decisionmakers with rules, to prevent them from ruling oppressively. The skeptic will likely respond that since any such scheme of rules is subject to discretionary interpretation, no such scheme can prevent the oppressive exercise of discretion (Tushnet, 1988). But rule formalism has also provoked a second and equally pathological form of mimetic criticism: sentimentalist criticism.

Sentimentality is the experience of pleasure in emotion. By sentimentalism I mean a sanctimonious insistence on insulating this pleasure from the threat of critical reflection (Binder & Weisberg, 2000). Mimetic criticism becomes sentimentalist when it venerates individual or group subjectivity as the occasion for sentimental experience, and so tries to protect it from the representative mediation necessary to any institutional order. Sentimental criticism of law argues that formal rules designed to constrain official discretion are arbitrary and inflexible. The result is that decision according to rule will not yield outcomes the represented would choose. It follows that such legal rules cannot express the true subjectivity of those whom law represents, and the rule of law therefore demeans those subject to it (Abrams, 1991; Getman, 1988; Weisberg, 1984, 1992; White, 1990). The sentimentalist complaint is not that the rule of law oppresses, but that it fails to recognize, express, and empathize with the personality of the legal subject. The demand is not that law should construct some serviceable representation of the will of those subject to it, but that it should represent their authentic feelings and identities.

But the demand that law represent its subject authentically misunder-stands what political representation is. It is not an effort to copy a preexisting fact about the public good, but an effort to construct the public good. At an early stage in the development of the liberal state, Hegel offered an analysis of the problem of legitimacy as a challenge to universalize recognition and civic dignity in a dynamically competitive economic environment. Hegel saw that recognition in a dynamic society had to be dialectical rather than mimetic. The state had to enable the citizen's self-conscious transformation and development rather than preserve the conditions for a static identity. For example, to enable the individual to participate in the dignity of collective self-governance, the liberal state had to encourage cooperation by fostering the institutions of civil society (Hegel, 1942; Binder, 1993b).

Both skeptical and sentimental variants of mimetic criticism set unrealistically high standards of accuracy and fidelity in representation. Skeptical criticism demands that knowledge of social will rest on indubitable epistemological foundations, even though pragmatism demands only that beliefs be justified by comparing their consequences to those of available alternatives. Sentimental criticism demands that representations capture the full particularity and intrinsic worth of each individual, even when reductive generalization may serve as a useful tool of practical reason. Sentimental criticism requires that law treat its subjects with all the tenderness and insight appropriate to an intimate interpersonal relationship, providing a kind of civic substitute for love.

Yet law has the more modest ambitions of keeping the peace and organizing collective action. And if it is to realize these more prosaic ambitions, law will inevitably require institutions with arbitrary decision-making procedures and coercive power, a division of labor with attendant agency problems, and trade-offs among competing values. In particular, representative democracy, contract, some sort of property, and the rule of law have all proven themselves necessary components of productive, peaceful, and politically responsive societies. Skeptical and sentimental criticisms do not offer practical alternatives to the institutions they criticize. This suggests that from the pragmatic standpoint, aesthetic standards such as social decency are more germane in evaluating law than mimetic standards such as representative accuracy or faithful agency (Binder, 2001).

Mimetic criticism is useless to normative practice because it searches obsessively for a foundation that cannot possibly exist. Mimetic criticism misconceives the nature of law's representation of society. As we have seen, there is no fixed fact of the matter about individual subjectivity that law can represent in the process of organizing collective action. The individual preferences measured, aggregated, and represented by institutions such as elections and markets are endogenous to those institutions. Individual preferences depend on the social settings for the development and expression of choice. Collective preferences depend on the methods by which institutions identify them. The current freedom of individuals and collectivities to choose is at odds with their future freedom, and the future welfare of society depends on how we choose to constitute that society and measure its will. In sum, individual and societal will and welfare are not facts which exist independent of law. Legal concepts such as public interest, contractual consent, and legislative intent are institutional constructs, not independent facts about society. This means that the mimetic conception of law's representation of society is premised on a fallacy. Apart from law, society has no determinate features for law to represent.

Because law does not – and cannot – mimic the will of society or of legal actors, critical scholarship about law should no longer be organized by a mimetic conception of law. Mimetic criticism should be replaced by aesthetic criticism, premised on a pragmatist model of justification and an institutionalist conception of law. Such aesthetic criticism presumes that law ascribes intentions and preferences, conditions choice, and organizes institutional settings for the discursive development of interests and goals. This means that law represents legal persons in something like the way a novel represents characters, and law represents legal interests and values the way a novel represents themes.

Aesthetic criticism sees law as an arena of cultural contestation and tries to understand it from the standpoint of legal actors for whom it is an expressive as well as a strategic practice. Thus, the strategic interests legal actors pursue are given by identities and roles – which are shaped in part by law. In particular, the legal activities of disputing, transacting, and decisionmaking provide opportunities to claim, perform, and define identities and roles. In so doing actors reproduce and reshape the law and thereby affect the expressive resources available to themselves and others. Aesthetic criticism must recognize that our legal institutions, our social identities and our individual interests are mutually constitutive elements of culture. It is this entire culture that is the proper object of critique, not legal institutions taken in isolation. In helping to fashion such a culture, law of course influences the interests we will define and pursue. But perhaps more importantly, law helps determine our identities and most fundamental values (Binder & Weisberg, 1997). In evaluating alternative futures, we should be more concerned with what passions will fire our souls, than with how efficiently society will gratify those passions.

To evaluate, critique, and improve law, we must give up the comforting assumption that there is any fact of the matter about society's purposes for law to replicate. Society constructs its purposes along with its institutional organization. The choices society must make in thus creating itself are aesthetic choices. In a democratic polity, these choices must be made reflectively, as a result of a public discourse of aesthetic criticism.

# REFERENCES

Abrams, K. (1991). Hearing the call of stories. *California Law Review, 79*, p. 973.

Ackerman, B. (1980). *Social justice in the liberal state.* New Haven: Yale University Press.

Anderson, B. (1983). *Imagined communities: Reflections on the origins and spread of nationalism.* London: Verso.

Anderson, E. (1993). *Value in ethics and economics.* Cambridge: Harvard University Press.

Ankersmit, F. R. (1996). *Aesthetic politics.* Stanford: Stanford University Press.

Arendt, H. (1992). *Lectures on Kant's political philosophy.* Chicago: University of Chicago Press.

Arrow, K. (1963). *Social choice and individual values.* New York: Wiley.

Austin, J. (1873). *Lectures on jurisprudence.* London: J. Murray.

Barzel, Y. (2002). *A theory of the state.* Cambridge: Cambridge University Press.

Bentham, J. (1996). *An introduction to the principles of morals and legislation.* Cambridge: Cambridge University Press.

Bhaba, H. (1990). DissemiNation: Time, narrative and the margins of the modern nation. In: H. Bhaba (Ed.), *Nation and narration* (pp. 291–321). London: Routledge.

Binder, G. (1993a). The case for self-determination. *Stanford Journal of International Law, 29*, p. 223.

Binder, G. (1993b). Post-totalitarian politics. *Michigan Law Review, 91*, p. 1491.

Binder, G. (2001). The poetics of the pragmatic. *Stanford Law Review, 53*, p. 1509.

Binder, G. (2002). Twentieth century legal metaphors for self and society. In: A. Sarat, B. Garth & R. Kagan (Eds), *Looking back at law's century* (pp. 151–183). Ithaca: Cornell University Press.

Binder, G., & Weisberg, R. (1997). Cultural criticism of law. *Stanford Law Review, 49*, p. 1149.

Binder, G., & Weisberg, R. (2000). *Literary criticisms of law.* Princeton: Princeton University Press.

Bourdieu, P. (1977). *Outline of a theory of practice* (Richard Nice, Trans.). New York: Cambridge University Press.

Bourdieu, P. (1990). *The logic of practice* (Richard Nice, Trans.). Stanford: Stanford University Press.

Bourdieu, P. (1991). *Language and symbolic power* (Gino Raymond and Matthew Adamson, Trans.). Cambridge: Harvard University Press.

Brooks, P. (1996). Reading for the plot. In: M. J. Hoffman & P. D. Murphy (Eds), *Essentials of the theory of fiction* (p. 327). Durham: Duke University Press.

Cardozo, B. (1921). *The nature of the judicial process.* New Haven: Yale University Press.

Coase, R. (1960). The problem of social cost. *Journal of Law and Economics, 1.*

Cohen, F. (1935).Transcendental nonsense and the functional approach. *Columbia Law Review*,
      p. 809.
Cohen, M. (1927). Property and sovereignty. *Cornell Law Quarterly, 1.*
Cook, W. W. (1918). The privileges of labor unions in the struggle for life. *Yale Law Journal, 27,*
      p. 779.
Cover, R. (1983). The Supreme Court, 1982 term – foreword: Nomos and narrative. *Harvard
      Law Review, 97,* p. 4.
Crawford, P. (1997). The utility of the efficiency/equity dichotomy in tax policy analysis.
      *Virginia Tax Review, 16,* p. 501.
Culler, J. (1975). *Structuralist poetics.* New York: Cornell University Press.
Culler, J. (1983). *On deconstruction.* New York: Cornell University Press.
Derrida, J. (1976). *Of grammatology.* Baltimore: Johns Hopkins University Press.
Derrida, J. (1986). Declarations of independence. *New Political Science, 15,* p. 9.
Dworkin, R. (1986). *Law's empire.* Cambridge: Harvard University Press.
Fish, S. (1989). *Doing what comes naturally: Change, rhetoric and the practice of theory in
      literary and legal studies.* Durham: Duke University Press.
Friedman, M. (1953). *The methodology of positive economics.* In *Essays in Positive Economics*
      (Vol. 3). Chicago: University of Chicago Press.
Gadamer, H.-G. (1975). *Truth and method.* New York: The Seabury Press.
Gagnier, R. (1987). Social atoms, working class autobiography, subjectivity and gender.
      *Victorian Studies, 30,* p. 335.
Gallagher, C. (1994). *Nobody's story: The vanishing acts of women writers in the marketplace,
      1670–1820.* Berkeley: University of California Press.
Gellner, E. (1983). *Nations and nationalism.* Ithaca: Cornell University Press.
Getman, J. J. (1988). Voices. *Texas Law Review, 66,* p. 577.
Gordon, R. (1983). Legal thought and legal practice in the age of American enterprise,
      1870–1920. In: G. Geison (Ed.), *Professions and professional ideologies in America.*
      Chapel Hill: UNC Press.
Green, D., & Shapiro, I. (1994). *Pathologies of rational choice theory.* New Haven: Yale
      University Press.
Habermas, J. (1996). *Between facts and norms: Contributions to a discourse theory of law and
      democracy* (William Rehg, Trans.). Cambridge: MIT Press.
Hart, H. L. A. (1994). *The concept of law.* Oxford: Clarendon.
Hegel, G.W.F. (1942). *The Philosophy of Right* (T. M. Knox, Trans.). Oxford: Clarendon.
Herzog, D. (1985). *Without foundations: Justification in political theory.* Ithaca: Cornell
      University Press.
Hohfeld, W. (1913). Some fundamental legal conceptions as applied in judicial reasoning. *Yale
      Law Journal, 23,* p. 16.
Holmes, S. (1995). *Passions and constraint: On the theory of liberal democracy.* Chicago:
      University of Chicago Press.
Hurley, S. L. (1989). *Natural reasons.* Oxford: Oxford University Press.
Kant, I. (1986). *The Critique of Judgment* (James Creed Meredith, Trans.). Oxford: Oxford
      University Press.
Komesar, N. (1997). *Imperfect alternatives; choosing institutions in law, economics and public
      policy.* Chicago: University of Chicago Press.
Levinson, S. (1988). Law as literature. In: S. Levinson & S. Mailloux (Eds), *Interpreting law and
      literature: A hermeneutic reader* (pp. 155–175). Evanston: Northwestern University Press.

Lieber, F. (1839). *Legal and political hermeneutics*. Boston: Little, Brown.
Llewellyn, K. (1960). *The common law tradition*. Boston: Little, Brown.
Luban, D. (1988). *Lawyers and justice: An ethical study*. Princeton: Princeton University Press.
Lukacs, G. (1920). *The theory of the novel*. Cambridge: MIT Press.
Lynch, D. S. (1998). *The economy of character: Novels, market culture and the business of inner meaning*. Chicago: University of Chicago Press.
Lyotard, F. (1984). *The postmodern condition: A report on knowledge*. Minneapolis: University of Minnesota Press.
MacCormick, N., & Weinberger, O. (1986). *An institutional theory of law*. Boston: D. Reidel Publishing Company.
MacIntyre, A. (1985). *After virtue: A study in moral theory*. South Bend: University Notre Dame Press.
Mackie, G. (2003). *Democracy defended*. Cambridge: Cambridge University Press.
March, J., & Olsen, J. (1989). *Rediscovering institutions*. New York: Free Press.
March, J., & Olsen, J. (1995). *Democratic governance*. New York City: The Free Press.
Margulies, P. (1996). The lawyer as caregiver: Child client's competence in context. *Fordham Law Review, 64*, p. 1473.
Nehamas, A. (1985). *Nietzsche: Life and literature*. Cambridge: Harvard University Press.
Nietzsche, F. (1974). *The gay science*. (Walter Kaufman, Trans.). New York: Random House.
North, D. (1990). *Institutions, institutional change and economic performance*. Cambridge: Cambridge University Press.
Olson, M. (1965). *The logic of collective action: Public goods and the theory of groups*. Cambridge: Harvard University Press.
Parfit, D. (1984). *Reasons and persons*. Oxford: Oxford University Press.
Patterson, D. (1996). *Law and truth*. New York: Oxford University Press.
Peirce, C. S. (1931–1935). *Collected Papers* (Vol. 5). Cambridge, MA: Harvard University Press.
Peters, G. (1999). *Institutional theory in political science*. New York City: Pinter.
Pildes, R., & Anderson, E. (1990). Slinging arrows at democracy. *Columbia Law Review, 90*, p. 2121.
Pitkin, H. (1967). *The concept of representation*. Berkley: University of California Press, Ltd.
Posner, R. (1973). *Economic analysis of law*. Boston: Little, Brown.
Quine, W. V. O. (1963). *From a logical point of view*. New York: Harper & Row.
Riker, W. (1982). *Liberalism against populism*. Prospect Heights: Waveland Press.
Riker, W., & Ordeshook, P. (1973). *An introduction to positive political theory*. Englewood Cliffs: Prentice-Hall.
Robbins, L. (1938). Interpersonal comparisons of utility: A comment. *Economic Journal, 48*, p. 635.
Rorty, R. (1979). *Philosophy and the mirror of nature*. Princeton: Princeton University Press.
Rose, C. (1989). Property as storytelling. *Yale Journal of Law & the Humanities, 2*, p. 37.
Ruiter, D. (1993). *Institutional legal facts*. Boston: Kluwer Academic Publishers.
Samuelson, P. (1938). A note on the pure theory of consumer behavior. *Economica, 5*, p. 61.
Samuelson, P. (1950). The problem of integrability in utility theory. *Economica, 17*, p. 355.
de Saussure, F. (1959). General course of linguistics. In: W. Baskin (Trans.). New York: McGraw-Hill.
Schiller, F. (1967). *Letters on the aesthetic education of man*. (Ed. and Trans., E. M. Wilkinson and L.A. Willoughby). Oxford: Clarendon.
Scholes, R., & Kellogg, R. (1966). *The nature of narrative*. New York: Oxford University Press.

Scott, R. (1995). *Institutions and organizations*. Thousand Oaks: Sage Publications.

Searle, J. (1995). *The construction of social reality*. New York City: The Free Press.

Simon, W. (1978). The ideology of advocacy: Procedural justice and professional ethics. *Wisconsin Law Review*, p. 29.

Singer, J. (1982). The legal rights debate from Bentham to Hohfeld. *Wisconsin Law Review*, p. 975.

Singer, J. (1984). The player & the cards: Nihilism and legal theory. *Yale Law Journal, 94*, p. 1.

Skidelsky, R. (2006). Drawing a dog in Iraq. *New York Review of Books*, October 6.

Sunstein, C. (1986). Legal interference with private preferences. *University of Chicago Law Review, 53*, p. 1125.

Sussman, H. (1998). *The aesthetic contract: Statutes of art and intellectual work in modernity*. Stanford: Stanford University Press.

Todorov, T. (1971). *The poetics of prose* (Richard Howard, Trans.). Ithaca: Cornell University Press.

Tushnet, M. (1988). *Red, white and blue: A critical analysis of constitutional law*. Cambridge, MA: Harvard University Press.

Vining, J. (1988). *The authoritative and the authoritarian*. Chicago: University of Chicago Press.

Walzer, M. (1983). *Spheres of justice*. New York City: Basic Books.

Weisberg, R. (1984). *The failure of the word*. New Haven: Yale University Press.

Weisberg, R. (1988). The law-literature enterprise. *Yale Journal of Law & the Humanities, 1*, p. 1.

Weisberg, R. (1992). *Poethics and other strategies of law and literature*. New York: Columbia University Press.

White, H. (1981). The value of narrative in the representation of reality. In: W. J. T. Mitchell (Ed.), *On narrative*. Chicago: University of Chicago Press.

White, L. (1990). Subordination, rhetorical survival skills, and sunday shoes: Notes on the hearing of Mrs. G.. *Buffalo Law Review, A38*, p. 1.

Williston, S. (1920). *The law of contracts*. New York: Baker, Voorhis.

Winter, S. (1989). The cognitive dimension of the agon between legal power and narrative meaning. *Michigan Law Review, 87*, p. 2225.

Wittgenstein, L. (1968). *Philosophical investigations*. New York: Macmillan.

# TEXTUAL PROPERTIES: THE LIMIT OF LAW AND LITERATURE – TOWARDS A GOTHIC JURISPRUDENCE

Susan Chaplin

Law and Literature scholarship appears in recent times to have come up against a limit or, perhaps more optimistically, a threshold. It is lucidly defined by Costas Douzinas and Adam Greary in terms of the movement's 'restricted sense of the literary', its tendency thus far to avoid 'the darker, problematic elements of the literary, the philosophical problem with literature itself' (Douzinas & Greary, 2005, p. 337). This article seeks to address 'the problem with literature' from a philosophical and historical perspective that prioritises the extent to which 'the literary' is implicated in and disruptive of a law that 'shares the conditions of its possibility with the literary object' (Derrida, 1992, p. 191). Literature is fundamentally the law's problem. This essay considers the 'darker elements' of the literary (which might be understood as the symptoms of the law's literary dis-ease) in an attempt to re-appraise the relation between literature and law. In particular, it suggests an engagement with one of the most contested, undisciplined and margin-alised of modern literary forms – the Gothic – as a means of opening up a point of passage beyond a somewhat bounded sense of the literary that seems partially to have stifled the promise of law and literature jurisprudence thus far.

Special Issue: Law and Literature Reconsidered
Studies in Law, Politics, and Society, Volume 43, 113–131
Copyright © 2008 by Emerald Group Publishing Limited
All rights of reproduction in any form reserved
ISSN: 1059-4337/doi:10.1016/S1059-4337(07)00605-9

The essay re-visits first of all the philosophical status of 'writing' within the Western tradition, drawing particularly upon Derrida's account of the impossible relation between textuality and truth within this tradition. I seek initially to establish the paper's theoretical orientation through an analysis of Derrida's playful reading of a text that he terms a 'handbook of literature', a text that, significantly for my argument here, concerns the staging of a crime: Mallarmé's *Mimique* (Derrida, 2000a, p. 223). This aberrant, yet *exemplary* literary work[1] introduces one of this chapter's central concerns: the juridical and literary significance of the narration of 'crimes' that appear in some sense spectral, half-hidden, always just outside of the proper scene of representation.

This conceptualisation of literature's 'darker elements' and their place within/beyond the law will then be brought to bear upon the emergence in the early modern period of the literary Gothic – a genre that contests the very notion of 'genre' and that from the moment of its inception embodied and articulated the dis-ease that marks the modern philosophical and ideological relation between literature and law. In the eighteenth century, literature was brought decisively before the law; it was defined in juridical terms and subjected to processes of generic and historical systemisation that had the aim of categorising and disciplining newly emerging modes of textual production. This project of literary systemisation can be compared to efforts jurisprudentially to formulate a rigorous 'discipline' of English law through the rationalisation of juridical textuality: to both of these developments, the emergence of a deeply ambivalent English Gothicism was the key.[2] The Gothic enters into legal and literary discourse in the modern period as an aberrant, yet exemplary narrativity that simultaneously guarantees and repudiates the possibility of authentic juridical and literary 'truth'. This chapter considers the Gothic as a literary and juridical 'category' that 'challenges the concept of category' and that may thus be deemed, as Punter puts it, 'the paradigm of textuality' per se (Punter, 1998, p. 1). The modern Gothic also becomes, I will argue, increasingly implicated in the law's uncanny relation to spectrality and death as it presents/effaces its crime scenes, spectres and monsters.

This leads in the final part of this essay to a consideration of two early Gothic novels that set various ambivalent precedents in terms of literary Gothicism and that I take to be exemplary of 'the literary' as such: they function, in terms of my argument, as 'handbooks of literature'. They are Horace Walpole's (1764/1996) *The castle of Otranto* and Mary Shelley's (1818/1996) *Frankenstein*. Each of these texts privileges a certain transgressive textuality *and* a strangely spectral criminality: central to each work is the *appearance* of a crime scene. Each text also forms a part of an unfolding tradition of Gothic writing that existed, and that has continued to exist very much in the shadows of 'legitimate' literary discourse, even as it throws that very discourse into dispute.[3] The Gothic is that which cannot be controlled by an order of representation for which 'the literary' per se is a problem. It is a maddening, transgressive 'literature' that opens up the possibility of a more contested, less limiting, darker conceptualisation of what 'literature' is to the law.

## *MIMESIS* – THE SCENE OF A CRIME

Textuality within the Western tradition has functioned in Derrida's analysis as the essential, yet disavowed supplement of a *logos* that perpetually sets itself against the necessary interventions of writing. Derrida compares textuality to a *pharmakon*, an ambivalent substance that has the capacity to act as both poison and cure. The 'cure' that textuality offers to the law pertains to the law's inability to establish its own permanence, or presence, without some literary intervention: only once it is 'put into writing' does the law remain 'on record', its permanence 'ensured [by the text] with the vigilance of a guardian' (Derrida, 2000b, p. 113). At the same time, however, textuality could be said to commit a kind of crime against the *logos*: it improperly appropriates the 'presence' of the law, steals it and substitutes itself for it. Writing is, as Maurice Blanchot puts it, 'the enemy of all relationships of presence, of all legality' (Blanchot, 1987, p. 156). The law's 'presence' nevertheless depends upon this criminal narrativity. In particular, the emergence of law requires the emergence of a narrative capable of resolving the trauma that attends the inception of communal and individual subjectivity: the law acquires its 'presence' only after a certain violent communal fantasy has established a vital untruth about the law's origins. The founding moment of Western law is a representation of a fictive transgression that serves to account for the terrifying, symbolically *unrepresentable* rupture that separates the individual and the community from the pre-symbolic void. In order for the law to take its place, it is necessary to stage a 'crime' and then to re-present it as the law's sure foundation. This crime is parricide and Derrida links it explicitly to the advent of narrativity as the law's uncanny, necessary condition of being:

> [...] this quasi-event bears the marks of fictive narrativity (fiction *of* narration as well as fiction as narration: fictive narration as the simulacrum of narration and not only as the

narration of an imaginary history). It is the origin of literature as well as the origin of
law – like the dead father, a story told, a spreading rumour, without author or end, but
an ineluctable and unforgettable story. (Derrida, 1992, p. 199)

The question of the law's origin thus becomes a question of *mimesis*: a
quasi-event, a murder, is staged just outside of the order of representation it
is said to institute and it is narrated thereafter as the 'legitimate' origin of
law and literature.

In Derrida's (2000a) essay on Mallarmé (The Double Session), he
addresses the question: 'What is literature?' This question, he contends, can
be answered only at the interface between 'literature' and 'truth', and this
relation has been defined within the Western tradition by means of a 'certain
interpretation of mimesis' (Derrida, 2000a, p. 183). The 'logic' of mimesis
according to this interpretation operates thus: mimesis produces a double of
some original to which the double is inferior. More than this, the double is
posited as 'worth nothing in itself'; whatever value it might have comes only
from its model, such that the copy 'is in itself negative' (p. 187). Nevertheless,
this double can still be seen to 'exist', if only in terms of its resemblance to its
original, and thus it has a subversive form of inauthentic 'being'. It is on
account of the untruthful existence of the double generated by mimesis that
mimesis ultimately becomes 'an evil' within this order of representation. To
imitate 'is bad in itself', and this *in itself* is vital. The very 'being' of mimesis is
untruth and its 'evil' lies not in the fact that it doubles a more authentic
original that remains apart from it, but in its re-presentation of the original
*as* untruth and the eventual effacement of the original *with* untruth. Mimesis
sets in motion a chain of 'repetition, resemblance, doubling, duplication'
according to which the copy substitutes for the original, disseminates it and
finally, necessarily, displaces it (p. 188). The original requires the intervention
of mimesis to 'ensure its permanence', to put it 'on record', and yet this
essential intervention is always already a *supervention* of the 'truth' it
purports to 'copy': '[the] image *supervenes* upon reality, the representation
upon the present in presentation, the imitation upon the thing, the imitator
upon the imitated' (p. 191). The order of mimesis becomes 'the order of all
appearances. It is the order of truth' (p. 192). It is thus also the order of 'the
literary', since the question of literature turns upon the relation between
literature and a 'truth' that achieves its only possible presence through
mimesis. Mimesis is the abject ordering principle of literature and law; it is
'the philosophical problem', or the limit, or threshold, of literature and law.

To reiterate, this threshold, the law's 'origin', exists only through the
fabrication of a crime – a parricide that has relevance to Derrida's
theorisation of an outlawed textuality. The pure 'being', or 'life', of the

*logos* – the immediate self-presence that is presumed to exist *before* the intervention of narrative – is negated by a textuality that is consequently aligned with death: 'Pure repetition, absolute self-repetition, repetition of a self that is already reference and repetition, repetition of the signifier, repetition that is null or annulling, repetition of death – it's all one. Writing is not the living repetition of the living' (p. 136). By an extension of this argument, the order of mimesis (which is the very 'order of truth') is also an order of death that is founded upon parricide: 'Writing is parricidal' since the 'being-there' that writing negates 'is always a property of paternal speech' (p. 146). The origin of law is a crime scene. This is a 'crime', though, that must be staged just outside of the order of representation it institutes; it takes place as an absence, an abyssal re-presentation of death that reproduces the law as a copy of the authority of an imaginary, murdered father. In Mallarmé's *Mimique*, a murder is simulated by the mime, Pierrot. Conventional readings of this work (which proceed according to that 'interpretation of mimesis' which Derrida critiques) tend to emphasise the apparent tension in the narrative between 'representation' and 'reality', between the mime show and the 'authentic' event. These readings have been seen to be authorised, as it were, by Mallarmé's own intervention into the narrative: he inserts into the text a quotation – 'The scene illustrates but an idea, not any actual action' (p. 194). The twist, as Derrida points out, is that this 'quotation' is in fact fictive and Derrida's own approach to the text resists the Platonic Idealist interpretation that this fake 'quotation' appears to demand. Derrida reads *Mimique* according to 'the specular process and play of reflections' that mimesis initiates (p. 188). The 'crime', or 'idea', that the text reproduces emerges for Derrida not merely as an absence, but as a series of absences endlessly deferred by the aberrant textuality of Mallarmé's work. *Mimique* challenges that interpretation of mimesis which places representation secondary to a 'presence' that supposedly precedes and authorises the image (and, subversively, the text calls attention to the very philosophy it repudiates by means of that inauthentic citation placed at the very centre of the narrative). Mallarmé's ghostly Pierrot silently reproduces a 'crime' that has no existence beyond the ambiguous moment in which it is recited by the gestures of the mime, and by the text of *Mimique*, and by the mysterious 'original' narrative upon which Mallarmé purports to base his fiction, 'the suggestive and truly rare booklet that opens in my hands' (p. 198). The 'crime', the 'idea' (which is not to be confused with 'any actual action'), takes place only through these multiple stagings of it, and through these abyssal re-presentations of no actual *event* it assumes (as Mallarmé puts it) 'the false appearance of a presence' (p. 200).

As has been noted, Derrida refers to *Mimique* as a 'handbook of literature'. I would argue that it can also be read as an example of *Gothic* textuality, where this is understood to signify (as I will explain in the following section) an abyssal, inauthentic narrativity that paradoxically constitutes narrative in its 'truest' (most spectral, most monstrous) form. One could argue further that this 'Gothic' text brings before the law the 'philosophical problem of literature', the problem of a mimesis that simultaneously sets the law in place (copying it, disseminating it) and effaces its claim to original presence. The law here (the 'idea' that Mimique alludes to, one might say) is the *logos* as a copy derived from the staging of an imaginary point of origin – a 'crime' that is always already a fiction.

## LITERATURE BEFORE THE LAW

The law is necessarily and uncannily dependent upon its relation to death, textuality and *spectrality* – a relation that Derrida theorises more completely (and, one could say, more 'Gothically') in *Specters of Marx*. I will return to this Gothic turn in Derrida's analysis of law below. In this section, I aim to place the philosophical question of 'literature' within the historical context of an emerging capitalist modernity, a context within which new formulations of 'the literary' begin to unfold alongside the disruptive entrance of the Gothic into literary and juridical discourse. The question of mimesis, first of all, assumed a certain urgency for literary critics and authors in the eighteenth century as expanding categories of 'literature' (the novel, the short story, the quasi-fictional 'biography' and so on) came increasingly to be judged in terms of their ability to represent 'life'. Verisimilitude became an essential textual property, the defining quality of legitimate fictional narrative and Samuel Johnson's mid-eighteenth century writings in particular reveal a privileging of literary realism which sets the Platonic interpretation of mimesis within a new historical context.[4] For Johnson, literature is 'proper' only to the extent that it furnishes what he terms a 'pleasing dress' for 'Truth'.[5] Literature has no existence independent of its supplemental relation to a 'Truth' that precedes and authorises it: it has its only authentic origin in the model which it mimics. Implicit in Johnson's argument, furthermore, is the assumption that there is in every act of mimesis an earlier, interior moment of representation that occurs within the mind of the artist, and it is in fact *this* mental model of 'life' which legitimises the artistic work. In his discussion in *The Rambler 4* of the ethics and epistemology of the newly emerging realist novel, Johnson observes that 'it is necessary [for the writer] to distinguish those parts of nature, which are the most proper for imitation'. Before the artistic copy appears, then, the 'original' model has already been replicated within the consciousness of the artist and, as Plato's *Phaedrus* had already contended, this moment of primary representation is essential to *all* discourse. Indeed, it constitutes the only 'unquestionably legitimate' mode of representation:

> Socrates: But now tell me, is there another sort of discourse, that is brother to the written speech, but of unquestioned legitimacy? Can we see how it originates, and how much better and more effective it is than the other?
>
> Phaedrus: What sort of discourse have you now in mind, and what is its origin?
>
> Socrates: The sort that goes together with knowledge and is written in the soul of the learner, that can defend itself, and knows to whom it should speak and to whom it should say nothing.
>
> Phaedrus: Do you mean the discourse of a man who really knows, which is living and animate? Would it be fair to call the written discourse only a kind of ghost of it?
>
> Socrates: Precisely.[6]

The knowledge that is 'written in the soul of the learner' is posited here as authentic, originary discourse: all other discourses that mimic it are 'deformed at birth' (p. 147). Writing is set against this 'living and animate' representation of truth as 'a kind of ghost of it'. Textuality emerges as 'traitor, infidel, simulacrum' (p. 147); from the moment of its inception, it is a crime, a spectre, a fraud.

Johnsonian literary criticism evinces a general philosophical hostility towards fictional narrative even as it tries to appraise, authorise and discipline its multiple modern forms. At this historical moment, this unease with the very question of 'literature' takes the form of various anxieties concerning the properties of certain specific modes of literary writing – the Gothic novel in particular. What is more, juridical and economic developments in this period served further to complicate the conventional philosophical understanding (re-iterated with considerable ideological force by Johnson and his circle in the mid-eighteenth century)[7] of the relation between literature and 'Truth'. In the late- seventeenth and eighteenth centuries, the literary text came to be defined, first and foremost, as a juridical entity. As Derrida contends, 'the relatively modern specificity of literature as such retains a close and essential rapport to a period in legal history[...]. Only under the conditions of law does the [literary] work have an existence and a substance, and it becomes 'literature' only at a certain period of the law that regulates problems involving property rights over works, the identity of corpora, the value of signatures, the difference between creating, producing and reproducing, and so on (Derrida, 1992, p. 215). The ownership of the text – or, rather, of the original *idea* expressed within it – came to depend, as in the case of chattels or real estate, upon the existence of proper legal title, and proper legal title depends in this instance upon the unequivocal association of a given author (an authentic 'signature', as Derrida puts it) with an original work – with an unplagiarised, unique idea. Intellectual originality (the perceived presence within a text of an *uncopied* idea) thus generated a form of intellectual property that was – following the acrimonious copyright disputes of the mid-eighteenth century – capable of increasingly unfettered economic alienation and exchange.

These new laws of literature, then, created an economy in which it was not the literary text as a material entity that was the subject of property rights, but the idea expressed therein: it was this 'commodity' that was now to be conceived of as alienable. The very contents of consciousness thus seemed to acquire the status of commercially exchangeable chattels, a development which, whilst commercially useful, potentially undermined the very foundation of subjectivity and truth as conventionally understood.[8] The law attributed to *ideas* the common material quality of 'other Articles, that usually compose a Taylor and Butcher's Bill'.[9] The 'knowledge that is written in the soul of the learner', and that constitutes the only legitimate authority for texts that purport to copy and disseminate that knowledge, begins itself to participate as an object of exchange in an economy of production and reproduction that appears increasingly perverse in its ability to proliferate new and intangible forms of property. This new marketplace of ideas, moreover, opened up the possibility of new forms of fraud, of the theft or corruption of ideas by readers parasitic upon the original works of others. The law's intervention into the textual domain thus helped create a modern literary economy in which authors and readers became producers and consumers of commodified ideas alienated from their point of origin in consciousness. The 'living' knowledge, the paternal 'being-there' which precedes a deathly, parricidal textuality, threatens within this economy to become 'a kind of ghost' of itself.

## SPECTRES OF LAW AND LITERATURE – 'GOTHIC DEVILISM'[10]

It was Gothic fiction – in terms of its form, its content and its modes of textual production and circulation – that emerged in the mid-eighteenth century to contest and, paradoxically, to *consolidate* this model of juridically defined 'literature'. At this particular historical moment, Gothic fiction comes to exemplify (as does textuality per se within the broader Western philosophical tradition) the tensions inherent within 'a certain interpretation of mimesis'. In its aesthetically privileged form, 'literature' came in the eighteenth century to exist as a representation of 'truth' and a manifestation of original genius (the 'Idea' that guarantees the authenticity of art, in so far as it can ever be guaranteed). Gothic fiction, on the other hand, thrived on fakery; its sensationalistic, emotive, unreal and often plagiarised narratives were produced and reproduced without any apparent regard for standards of artistic and philosophical integrity. It was therefore not properly 'literary'. Simultaneously, however, Gothic fiction developed as the 'literary' commodity *par excellence*. At the very moment when 'literary' works were re-defined to facilitate their participation within a free market of texts and ideas, Gothic fiction emerged as the most economically successful mode of writing. It satisfied a seemingly insatiable desire on the part of the reading public for sensationalistic, emotive, unreal narratives; it also had the philosophically disquieting (though also, at this historical moment, a juridically and economically *legitimate*) capacity to render itself entirely alienable. Circulating promiscuously within the new textual economy of production and distribution, beyond categorisation and control, Gothic fiction became the purest and the most obscene literary commodity.

Horace Walpole's *The Castle of Otranto* is judged to be the originary text of the Gothic literary tradition: it is an exemplary, precedent text which has functioned (within a modern literary economy that demands generic stability in order to conceptualise and control 'the literary') to legitimise subsequent reiterations of 'Gothicism'. This novel was initially published under a pseudonym. Moreover, it was prefaced by an 'editor's' note presenting the text as a Gothic 'original' – a medieval manuscript from Southern Italy found by the 'editor' in a library in the north of England. Walpole thus effaced the text's authorial origin, distancing himself from a fantastical supernatural narrative that defied contemporary expectations of what a 'proper' literary work should be. It was a huge popular success, however, in spite of its mixed critical reception, and Walpole consequently re-published it with a second preface admitting his authorship and justifying the work now in terms of its originality (it was posited as a radical experiment in literary form and psychological realism). These authorial interventions, however, far from stabilising the origin and generic status of the work, can be seen significantly to subvert what Derrida terms the 'legality' of the modern literary text – its status as a juridical entity capable of attracting certain legal rights premised upon proper origin and ownership. On the one hand, in admitting his authorship of *The Castle of Otranto* in 1764, Walpole could be said to be asserting his *title* to the text, positioning himself within an economy of artistic production which places authors and their texts/ commodities before new laws of literature. At the same time, though, *The Castle of Otranto*, and the Gothic imitations it initiated, contested developing juridical notions of 'the literary'. At the moment of its original publication – at the moment of its inception as a 'literary' commodity (and a highly successful one at that) – the text was a fake. There was thus a sense in which, according to Derrida's analysis, such a fiction did not count as 'literature' at all: it conformed instead, albeit fraudulently, to a more medieval model of textual production whereby institutions 'had quite a different way of regulating the identity of works, which were more readily delivered to the transformative initiatives of *copyists* or other "guardians", to the graftings practiced by inheritors or other "authors" (whether anonymous or not, whether masked by pseudonyms or not, or whether more-or-less identifiable individuals or groups)' (Derrida, 1992, p. 187).

From the moment of its dubious 'origin', then, Gothic has tended to problematise an emerging ideological relation between literature and law. Walpole's faked 'Gothic', argues Robert Miles, 'exposes the bad faith of literary forgery in the manner Kristeva allots to aesthetic abjection: [Walpole] turns aside, misleads, corrupts a "prohibition", or "rule"; he is a "trickster who draws attention to the fragility of law"' (Miles, 2001, p. 61). Gothic textuality is a peculiarly abject textuality, a perverse mode of writing that can be seen to function, in David Punter's terms, as 'the paradigm of all fiction, all textuality' (Punter, 1998, p. 1). Gothic writing is *exemplary* writing. What is more, it is a literary form that has found the most inventive and transgressive means of bringing before the law the 'disavowed ghosts' that haunt the public domain of power (Žižek, 2000, p. 3). Walpole's originary Gothic text, for example, turns upon the commission of a hidden crime – the murder of the legitimate prince of Otranto and the usurpation of his throne. The work has been read as Walpole's personal and political negotiation of the constitutional violence of the late-seventeenth and early-eighteenth centuries. It may also be interpreted as a more general symbolic engagement with the hidden trauma that founds the law and that is covered over by a juridical fantasy of parricide. The novel stages the murder of the originary father *outside* of its own economy of representation: it repeats the law's own authenticating gesture, generating a narrative of 'proper' origin that is (like the 'crime' in Mallarmé's text) purely fictive, the 'false appearance of a presence'. In *Otranto*, however, the originary father returns to the scene of representation that his 'death' has instituted. Appearing initially through a variety of bizarre spectral interventions (a giant helmet crashing into a courtyard, a bleeding statue, disembodied body parts), the ghost of the usurped prince eventually returns in gargantuan form partially to destroy the castle at the very moment that its 'legitimate' heir is announced. The spectre of this absent father confronts the law with the inauthenticity of its origin and prevents any straightforward re-assertion of the principle of patrilineal succession. The Gothic castle of Otranto – the material site of the power of the genealogy of law – ends in ruins.

*Otranto* was published only 10 years after William Blackstone had famously figured English law as a 'Gothic castle' in need of only a modicum of modernisation to render it compatible with the contemporary juridical landscape, as it were. In averring to the 'Gothicism' of English law, Blackstone drew upon and consolidated an alternative, *juridical* meaning of the Gothic in the mid-eighteenth century. The notion of the English constitution's ancient, Germanic Gothic origin created a potent myth of historical and political continuity that served to separate the English body politic from the constitutional traumas of the seventeenth century and from the hostile legal systems of Catholic Europe. The contemporaneous emergence of the literary Gothic supplemented this national myth-making project, moreover, in spite of the deep philosophical and literary unease provoked by the perceived irrationality, indiscipline and immorality of Gothic fictions. The romanticisation of a (faked) national 'history' in the *Ossian* poems of James Macpherson, for example, and the Gothic fiction of Clara Reeve (termed 'patriot Gothic' by the critic James Watt)[11] contributed to the nation's sense of itself as a historically and juridically privileged community. At the same time, however, the Gothic could not escape the charge of 'barbarism', of 'devilism', even in its most conservative juridical and literary manifestations.[12] By the 1790s, the Gothic, as a deeply unstable signifier of national and political unity, had become implicated in and subversive of shifting and fissured representations of power. The Marquis de Sade attributed the unprecedented growth of Gothic fiction in this decade to the traumatic effects of the French revolution, an event that was itself often figured in distinctly Gothic terms. It was in the aftermath of the revolution, moreover, that the Gothic began to shape itself into the multiple hybrid forms that came later to be associated with a genre so fluid and diverse as to be almost incapable of proper determination (Punter, 1998; Wolfreys, 2002). Gothic textuality came also in this period to be subject to a degree of censure so diverse that this in itself could be said to reveal the shape-shifting, mercurial quality of the modern Gothic. For radicals opposed, in particular, to Edmund Burke's narration and theorisation of the events of 1789, conservative evocations of constitutional Gothicism were held responsible for generating in uneducated minds a misplaced passion for corrupt government; the Gothic romance of English legal history was seen by writers such as Paine and Godwin to cloak the force of law in a legitimising mystique. For conservatives, on the other hand, Gothic literary 'terrorism'[13] could easily be aligned with inflammatory, revolutionary rhetoric in terms of its capacity to derange the individual and disorder the community.[14] From various political perspectives, then, the Gothic becomes at this moment a signifier of the political and ontological insecurity of law.

Moreover, in so far as there *is* a common element within Gothic fiction during the early years of its development, it could be said to exist as an almost obsessive concern with the resurrection of the dead. Gothic fictions symbolise the law's persistent and necessary evocation of the dead. The principle of succession is a mechanism for raising the dead; its genealogical fictions ensure that juridical power is dependent upon a calling up of spectres that disrupts the law's claim to a pure, eternal 'Presence' beyond death. As Derrida's *Specters of Marx* contends, the law must insist upon the uncanny 'presence' of spectres; they are its dreadful, paradoxical condition of Being – the essential supplement to the law's 'Spirit' (Derrida, 1994, p. 135). The ontology of law thus becomes, in Derrida's analysis, a *hauntology* that reveals precisely what Gothic fictions begin to symbolise in the modern period: that the sacred space of law is also a tomb, or crypt, haunted by the 'ghostly echo' of a trauma that the law's narratives of 'proper' origin can never fully efface (Jameson, 1999, p. 38). As this essay has contended, moreover, spectrality is related within the Western symbolic order to a parricidal *textuality*, to the institution of an (im)proper mimesis that is (like the Gothic fictions that emerge in the early modern period) always already a 'crime' against the logos.

# MONSTER/TEXT/*PHARMAKON* – MARY SHELLEY'S *FRANKESTEIN*

There is something about *Frankenstein* that tends to confuse, or even to frustrate modern readers who approach this text for the first time. I would suggest that it is the failure of the novel to conform to the extraordinary number of twentieth- and twenty-first-century cultural representations of the novel, its protagonist and his monster. Most modern readers will come to

Shelley's novel through one or more of the adaptations of it that persist within Western culture. Read through its adaptations, through its paratexts, as it were, the text appears uncannily at odds with itself: students reading the text for the first time are often wont to comment that, 'this is not *Frankenstein*! This is not what happens in *Frankenstein*!', as if their knowledge of subsequent interpretations and representations of the text is somehow more authoritative than the 'original' work. I would suggest further that what is most striking about the novel's lack of resemblance to the tradition it initiates is its absence of a crime scene. The one iconic image that *Frankenstein* has bequeathed to modern and post-modern culture is that of Victor engaged directly in his appalling, criminal act of creation – he throws the lever and the monster jerks into life. Nowhere is this scene present within Shelley's text, however. The novel builds up to this moment of transgression only to efface it. There is probably no other moment of 'representation' within literature that has so thoroughly assumed 'the false appearance of a presence'.

The extraordinary textual afterlife of *Frankenstein* has thus twisted modern perceptions of the 'precedent' text. This is a work, though, which (like Walpole's Gothic 'original') contests from the very moment of its inception any proper conceptualisation of 'precedent' and 'origin'. For this very reason, it may be understood as *exemplary* of that perverse textuality that characterises Gothicism from its own dubious beginnings in an 'abject fake'. Gothic fictions possess the uncanny ability to produce copious imitations of themselves, defying literary laws that seek to insist upon a certain order of precedence. The Gothic reproduces itself outside of the 'archive' that produces and enforces the law. It can be imaginatively innovative to the point of fantastical excess, or derivative to the point of plagiarism. Or, when it purports to 'copy', it can so defy hermeneutic discipline that, as in the case of *Frankenstein*, the very notion of a precedent that might properly authorise a generic tradition collapses. *Frankenstein* resists interpretation, slipping out of bounds from horror, to high camp, to blaxploitation movie, to parody and beyond.[15] To invoke Derrida's theory of the *parergon* in this context (Derrida, 1987), it could be argued that *Frankenstein's* various 'adaptations' function as *parerga* to some 'absent Idea' – the 'Idea' being the impossible notion of *any* text serving as the clear, unmediated point of origin of a literary, philosophical or juridical tradition. The textual afterlife of *Frankenstein* – that deeply unstable chain of Gothic signification – thus uncannily mimics a Western juridical discourse that has no origin in any Idea outside its own spectral, abject textuality.

*Frankenstein* is, moreover, a work that foregrounds the relation of an unstable principle of power to aberrant forms of textuality. The monster that Victor brings out of the crypt is related to a deviant narrativity that places and displaces meaning within and beyond the law. One contemporary review of *Frankenstein* hints at the perverse textual practices which the novel embodies and transmits through its observations on Victor Frankenstein's unorthodox reading practices: his destructive ambition, the review suggests, is in part the consequence of his immersion in 'marvellous writings'.[16] Victor is a protagonist whose desires are provoked and corrupted by an abject tradition of writings (alchemy, romance, and Gothic) that shadows and doubles a 'legitimate' literary and philosophical tradition. What is more, the reading practices of the monster himself signify an uncanny relation between subjectivity, (im)proper textuality and the law. The first text that the monster reads is Victor's account of the monster's creation. It is after he has read this narrative of his own abject origin that the monster discovers the three 'classics' (Plutarch, Goethe, and Milton) that then educate him so adeptly in rhetoric. These texts re-form the monster into a dangerously eloquent speaking subject – a seductive subject whose capacity, as it were, to incorporate the Western archive into himself collapses the opposition bet-ween 'archive' and 'crypt' (Derrida, 1995). To see the monster and to hear him speak is to confront the fictivity of the demarcation between the 'sacred' and the 'abject', and this is why the monster occasions such wholesale trauma within the text: his existence as an abject speaking subject – as a monstrous subject of the law – is an absolute 'social scandal' that goes beyond Victor's personal drama of desire and loss (Reider, 2003, p. 8).

The monster misappropriates and manipulates the authorised texts of the Western tradition; he is the abjected 'other' who suddenly demands a hearing, speaking and subverting the law's language. In so doing, the monster reveals the fundamental (il)legality of writing. Textuality guarantees the law a certain permanence, but also opens it up to the possibility of supplementation and mutation; the law is severed from its (fictive) 'origin' in the self-present, spoken Word of the *logos*. The monster (who likewise lacks any proper point of origin) similarly preserves and perverts the 'truth' of the texts that he reads and recites. Now, in this regard, there is one minor textual and sartorial detail pertaining to Victor's monster that I think is particularly illuminating: the monster carries his four texts around with him in the pocket of his coat. In Plato's *Phaedrus*, Socrates and Phaedrus are about to discuss a speech by Lysias ('the ablest writer of our day') when Socrates asks his companion to remove whatever it is he has concealed in his cloak (Derrida, 2000b, pp. 71–72). Phaedrus has hidden there a copy of Lysias's speech; he needs it 'because he has not learned the speech by heart' (p. 72). He is uneasy at the relation between his speech and the written record that he must give an account of, and he guiltily keeps the text close by him in order that he might, if necessary, supplement his spoken, memorised recitation of Lysias's argument. Socrates compares the text to a drug – a *pharmakon*. Derrida reads this moment of anxiety concerning the supplemental writings Phaedrus conceals about him thus:

> This *pharmakon*, this medicine, this filter, which acts as both remedy and poison, already introduces itself into the body of the discourse with all its ambivalence. This charm, this spell-binding virtue, this power of fascination, can be – alternately or simultaneously – beneficent or maleficent. The *pharmakon* would be a substance – with all that that term can connote in terms of matter with occult virtues, cryptic depths refusing to submit their ambivalence to analysis, already paving the way for alchemy – if we didn't have eventually to come to recognise its anti-substance itself: that which resists any philosopheme, infinitely exceeding its bounds as non-identity, nonessence, nonsubstance; granting philosophy by that very fact the inexhaustible adversity of what funds it and the infinite absence of what founds it.

> Operating through seduction, the *pharmakon* makes one stray from one's general, natural, habitual paths and laws [...] (p. 70).

The *pharmakon* is a monstrous substance – matter 'with occult virtues'; it evokes abject corporeality as well as the possibility of mutation and magic. It carries perverse connotations of the sacred, for it is also an 'anti-substance' that is nevertheless *not* Spirit; the *pharmakon* does not partake of any immaterial 'truth'. The *pharmakon* is a spectral substance, one might say; it exceeds categorisation as 'presence' or 'absence'; it is beyond symbolic fictions of the sacred and the abject. It reveals (as Derrida puts it in *Specters of Marx*) the abyssal *differance* that characterises the essential, supplemental relationship of spectrality to Spirit. It evokes the *differance* that is the abject 'origin' of law, bringing to philosophy the dreadful 'inexhaustible adversity that funds it, the infinite absence that grounds it'. Victor seeks to exploit 'matter with occult virtues' and in so doing he creates the living/dead *pharmakon* which embodies and defeats his desire: he becomes consequently outcast from 'natural, habitual paths and laws'. On the very border between the living and the dead, the monster meanwhile seeks to exploit an alchemic textuality that has the potential to transform *him* into a proper, speaking subject. He carries his texts with him. They only succeed, however, in making him more monstrous, in alienating him further from the 'habitual paths and laws' that his traumatised victims call 'home'.

## CONCLUSION: "TAKE PRECISELY THIS EXAMPLE"

Lawyers seek to prove a point always with reference to examples of a principle that is meant to transcend the point at issue; in this fashion, they make their case. This essay has invoked throughout the principle of exemplarity and, in seeking to make a case for the critical significance to literature and law of the relation between the Gothic and the rule of law, it has cited various 'examples' of the Gothic (including its 'originating' text, *The Castle of Otranto*) in order to show the extent to which the Gothic is implicated in the modern rule of law – how it consolidates and contests 'lawfulness'. I have ended by following many critics in citing *Frankenstein* as possibly the most exemplary of all Gothic texts – a text in respect of which there must surely exist a generic 'truth' about the Gothic. The principle of exemplarity, however, relies upon what Derrida terms the 'performative fiction' that there *is* an 'Idea' beyond the example, a 'truth' outside of the chains of citations that are meant simply to point towards, and invoke, and clarify the concept, law or genre that lies beyond them. According to this analysis, the principle of 'genre' depends upon the fiction that there is a 'mark' of genre that somehow stands outside of any specific instance of generic categorisation (Derrida, 1992, p. 230). The 'mark' of genre, the 'distinctive trait' that might define 'the Gothic', cannot be properly accounted for, however: it exists beyond categorisation, 'within and without the work, along its boundary' (pp. 230–231). The mark of genre is akin to the *Pharmakon* that brings to philosophy 'the infinite absence of what founds it'; it evokes the *differance* that 'brings forth to the light of day' the fiction of the law as *logos* (Derrida, 2000b, p. 70). More than any other literary form, the Gothic – and 'within' the Gothic, the unruly signifier that is *Frankenstein* – reveals the impossibility of proper literary taxonomy. It also exposes the impossibility of coherent juridical narratives. The Gothic 'brings to the light of day' the trauma that attends the 'origin' of law.

In its engagement with 'the literary', law and literature scholarship has tended to neglect the *example* of Gothicism. This is perhaps understandable if one considers the extent to which literary jurisprudence has been wont to insist upon 'a notion of a fit between the manner of representation and the object represented [...] between "style and substance"' (Douzinas & Greary, 2005, p. 337). This 'fit' is precisely what the Gothic has contested from the moment of its dubious origin in a literary fraud. Gothic fictions defy literary 'laws' that have sought to insist upon a certain order of precedence and upon a certain relation between mimesis and truth. The Gothic is fantastical and fake. It reproduces itself outside of the literary and juridical traditions that produce and enforce the law. Its unruly precedents subvert the modern notion of 'literature' as grounded in artistic originality and stable literary tradition. Even when it purports to mark out an authentic generic space for itself – a 'Gothic' tradition – it slips so easily out of generic bounds that, as in the case of *Frankenstein*, the very notion of an 'original' that might authorise an orderly, properly disciplined scheme of representation begins to disintegrate. Indeed, the Gothic has emerged as one of the most *knowing*, one of the most self-referential, self-disruptive and self-mocking forms of contemporary cultural representation: it is hyper-aware (in the manner of Mallarmé's *Mimique*) of its own problematic relation to representation and reality. The Gothic, however, does not simply *play games* with 'truth'. The exemplary texts discussed here offer, in their various ways, a deeply serious interrogation of the hidden criminality that constructs notions of 'lawful' origin and authority. From the work of Walpole and Shelley through to the novels of Joyce Carol Oates, Toni Morrison, Stephen King and the films of Michael Haneke, David Cronenberg and David Lynch, diverse and hybrid forms of Gothic have developed what Richard Devetek (2005) has termed an 'aesthetics of unease' (p. 621) with significant political implications for a Western culture in which 'terror' has once more become 'the order of the day'.[17] With its liminal, aberrant representations of terror and power (from the spectral interventions of *Otranto* to the uncanny evocations of personal and political violence in Haneke's *Hidden*), the Gothic places before the law its 'disavowed ghosts', its demonised others, outlawed victims and hidden crimes. To law and literature scholarship, this neglected yet exemplary textuality offers perhaps an opening – a means to move beyond the limits of a certain Western interpretation of mimesis.

# NOTES

1. Derrida's interpretation of 'exemplarity' as a subversive *supplementarity* that has a particular bearing upon 'the literary' (and, I argue, upon the literary Gothic) will be considered more fully later in the chapter. See Derrida (1995, pp. 20–31).

2. See Chaplin (2007), Chapter 2.

3. See Wolfreys (2002), Punter (1998), Williams (1995), and Miles (1993).

4. The ideological significance of the privileging of literary Realism in the eighteenth century is expertly analysed in Mckeon (2002).

5. See Samuel Johnson, *Rambler* 4 and *Rambler* 96.

6. *Phaedrus*, quoted in Derrida (2000a, 2000b, p. 148).

7. Clara Reeve's *Progress of Romance* (1785) is one of the period's most influential attempts to discipline the contemporary novel according to Johnsonian principles; it displays considerable anxiety concerning the epistemological and ethical propriety of

emerging forms of prose fiction. See also the prefaces to Samuel Richardson's novels *Pamela* (1740) and *Clarissa* (1748).

8. See Susan Eilenberg, 'Copyright Rhetoric and the Problem of Analogy in the Eighteenth-Century Debates', *Romantic Circles Praxis Series* (University of Maryland, 1999). On the relation between the law and the emerging discourse of the novel, see Davis (1996), Chapter V, and Polloczek (1999).

9. William Warburton, *An Enquiry into the Nature and Origin of Literary Property* (1762), quoted in Eilenberg (1999).

10. The appraisal of Walpole's Gothic romance given in the *Monthly Review* (1765), see Sabor (1987, p. 71).

11. See Watt (1999).

12. Ann Radcliffe's first Gothic romance, *The Castles of Athlin and Dunbayne* (1789), is an example of the conservative form of the eighteenth-century Gothic novel that Watt terms 'patriot Gothic'. Nevertheless, it received mixed reviews from the conservative press: *The British Critic* condemned its 'disgustful' fantastical excesses, even though, by the standards of the contemporary Gothic, it was exceptionally restrained in its evocation of the fantastical elements that characterise *The Castle of Otranto*, for example.

13. Thomas Mathias, *The Pursuit of Literature* (1797), in Norton (2000). Mathias terms Gothic fiction 'terrorist novel writing'.

14. See Steven Blakemore (1997) and John Barrell (2000).

15. *The Rocky Horror Picture Show* (1975) features the transvestite Dr Frank N. Furter; *Blackenstein* (1973) features a black monster. The most famous adaptation is probably still that directed by James Whale in 1931 starring Karloff as the monster. Whale's sequel, *Bride of Frankenstein* (1935), has also been hugely influential. Other less reverent adaptations have included *I was a Teenage Frankenstein* (1957), *Jesse James Meets Frankenstein's Daughter* (1966) and the Mel Brooks and Gene Wilder parody, *Young Frankenstein* (1974). One of the most recent adaptations, the 2004 *Van Helsing*, is unusual in naming the monster Frankenstein and in portraying him very sympathetically.

16. *Bell's Court*, March 1818, p. 149.

17. Thomas Mathias in 1790 condemned the capacity of Gothic fiction to 'make terror the order of the day' within a turbulent, post-revolutionary political context. See Sage (1990, p. 59).

# REFERENCES

Barrell, J. (2000). *Imagining the King's death: Figurative treason, fantasies of regicide, 1793–1796*. Oxford: Oxford University Press.

Blakemore, S. (1997). *Intertextual war: Edmund Burke and the French Revolution in the writings of Mary Wollstonecraft, Thomas Paine and James Mackintosh*. London: Associated University Press.

Blanchot, M. (1987). *The gaze of Orpheus*. New York: Station Hill.

Chaplin, S. (2007). *The Gothic and the rule of law*. London: Palgrave.

Davis, L. (1996). *Factual fictions: The origins of the English novel*. Philidelphia: University of Pennsylvania Press.

Derrida, J. (1987). *The truth in painting*. Chicago: Chicago University Press.
Derrida, J. (1992). Before the law. In: D. Attridge (Ed.), *Acts of literature*. London: Routledge.
Derrida, J. (1994). *Specters of Marx*. London: Routledge.
Derrida, J. (1995). Passion. In: D. Thomas (Ed.), *On the name*. Stanford: Stanford University Press.
Derrida, J. (2000a). The double session. In: J. Barbara (Ed.), *Dissemination*. London: Athlone Press.
Derrida, J. (2000b). Plato's pharmacy. In: J. Barbara (Ed.), *Dissemination*. London: Athlone Press.
Devetak, R. (2005). The Gothic scene of international relations: Ghosts, monsters, terror and the sublime after September 11th. *Review of International Studies, 31*(4), 621–643.
Douzinas, C., & Greary, A. (Eds). (2005). *Critical jurisprudence: The political philosophy of justice*. Oxford: Hart Publishing.
Eilenberg, S. (1999). Copyright rhetoric and the problem of analogy in the eighteenth-century debates. In: M. Micovski (Ed.), *Romantic circles*, March 1999. Also available on http://www.rc.umd.edu/law/eilenberg
Jameson, F. (1999). Marx's purloined letter. In: M. Sprinker (Ed.), *Ghostly demarcations: A symposium on Jacquesderrida's specters of Marx*. London: Verso.
McKeon, M. (2002). *The origins of the English novel, 1600–1740*. Baltimore: Johns Hopkins University Press.
Miles, R. (1993). *Gothic writing 1750–1820: A genealogy*. London: Routledge.
Miles, R. (2001). Abjection, Nationalism and the Gothic. In: F. Botting (Ed.), *The Gothic: Essays and studies*. Cambridge: English Press.
Norton, R. (2000). *Gothic readings: 1764–1840*. London and New York: Leicester University Press.
Polloczek, D. P. (1999). *Literature and legal discourse: Equity and ethics from Sterne to Conrad*. Cambridge: Cambridge University Press.
Punter, D. (1998). *Gothic pathologies: The text, the body and the law*. London: Macmillan.
Reider, J. (2003). Frankenstein's dream: Patriarchal fantasy and fecal child in Mary Shelley's Frankensetin and its adaptations. In: J. E. Hogle (Ed.), *Romantic circles*, Also available on http://www.rc.umd.edu/frankenstein/reider/reider.html
Sabor, P. (Ed.) (1987). *Horace Walpole: The critical heritage*. London: Routledge.
Sage, V. (1990). *The Gothick novel: A casebook*. London: Macmillan.
Shelley, M. (1818/1996). *Frankenstein*. London: Norton.
Walpole, H. (1764/1996). *The castle of Otranto*. Oxford: Oxford University Press.
Watt, J. (1999). *Contesting the Gothic: Fiction, genre and cultural conflict, 1764–1832*. Cambridge: Cambridge University Press.
Williams, A. (1995). *Art of darkness: A poetics of the Gothic*. Chicago: Chicago University Press.
Wolfreys, J. (2002). *Victorian hauntings: Spectrality, Gothic, the uncanny and literature*. London: Palgrave.
Žižek, S. (2000). *The fragile absolute*. London: Verso.

# "READING AS IF FOR LIFE": LAW AND LITERATURE IS MORE IMPORTANT THAN EVER

Teresa Godwin Phelps

## ABSTRACT

*Over the past few decades, the law and literature movement has fragmented, expanded, and evolved to include fields as diverse as hermeneutics and narrative theory. This chapter discusses the developments in and contributions of these two strains of the law and literature movement and argues that each respectively provides us with important ways of seeing acts of interpretation and the use of stories in the legal culture. Hermeneutics provides an understanding of the phenomenon of interpretation that avoids the trap of choosing originalism or postmodernism as the accepted method of interpreting legal texts. Narrative theory provides tools for understanding and critiquing the burgeoning use of stories in the law.*

Early in Charles Dickens' novel *David Copperfield*, David, trapped in the "gloomy theology of the Murdstones [which] made all children out to be a swarm of little vipers," and which, not surprisingly, made David's life

---

Special Issue: Law and Literature Reconsidered
Studies in Law, Politics, and Society, Volume 43, 133–152
Copyright © 2008 by Emerald Group Publishing Limited
All rights of reproduction in any form reserved
ISSN: 1059-4337/doi:10.1016/S1059-4337(07)00606-0

miserable, finds some solace in his late father's small library. "From that blessed room," David (as Dickens' first person narrator) relates,

> Roderick Random, Peregrine Pickle, Humphrey Clinker, Tom Jones, the Vicar of Wakefield, Don Quixote, Gil Blas, and Robinson Crusoe, came out, a glorious host, to keep me company. They kept alive my fancy, and my hope of something beyond that place and time … . This was my only and my constant comfort. When I think of it, the picture always rises in my mind, of a summer evening, the boys at play in the churchyard, and I, sitting on my bed, reading as if for life. (Charles Dickens, 1981, pp. 51–52)

"The gloomy theology of the Murdstones," alas, has reappeared, if indeed it ever went away. And like David we may seek solace, and useful insights, in literature. In the legal culture, in particular, the insights of the law and literature movement have become more important than ever, offering indispensable counterpoints to some of law's gloomy "theologies." Each of us, unhappily, could choose a particular favorite from among the many absolutisms (theologies) that characterize the legal community of the early twenty-first century. In this chapter, I focus on two that I find particularly troubling: first, sanctimonious pronouncements about the nature of "The Law" and its interpretation and, second, ongoing, unspeakable, human rights violations, often perpetrated within the confines of the law. What we Americans have learned in the past few years, if we did not learn it from the terrible history of the Holocaust, is that the law can justify anything. Seen as abstract philosophical discourse divorced from the realities of life, the law and its interpretation can be manipulated at will. It can justify exterminations, disappearances, and torture.

So what has literature to do with this? How can literature possibly offer a remedy to the malignities of the current legal culture? The law and literature discipline to which I was introduced as a fledgling legal academic several decades ago was largely constructed of looking at lawyer characters in works of literature: the nobility of Atticus Finch in *To Kill a Mockingbird*, the tricky advocacy of Portia in *The Merchant of Venice*, the problematic ethics of multiple lawyers in the stories of Louis Auchincloss. Left at that, the discipline would have remained merely a piece of fluff in the law school curriculum – a welcome break for former English majors who were tired of reading cases. But legal scholars did not leave it at that. Instead, the discipline deepened and fragmented into what is really a series of related disciplines: fields as diverse as legal hermeneutics, narrative theory, and linguistics. The developments in the law and literature movement over the past few decades have been stunning in their complexity, their originality, and their imaginative transfer of the many tools of the literary enterprise into the legal enterprise. From its promising renaissance in 1973, in the minds of many of us, in James Boyd White's breakthrough text, *The Legal Imagination*, which he described as a "study of what lawyers and judges do with words," (White, 1973, p. 9) to more recent work that includes complex and sophisticated analyses of legal documents, especially of Supreme Court opinions, and discussions of the power dynamics inherent in the use of language and its interpretation,[1] the law and literature movement has more than lived up to its initial promise. It has provided us with crucial new ways of seeing, understanding, and even transforming the law.

My own work has focused on interpretive theory (hermeneutics) and narrative theory, and, somewhat to my surprise, both areas have become widely discussed in the legal academic community. Or perhaps not surprisingly, as both areas offer ways of seeing that are unavailable in law uninformed by the insights of literature and its related disciplines. In this chapter, I trace some of the developments in each of these branches of law and literature – hermeneutics and narrative theory – and offer an appraisal of their respective contributions to our understandings of the law and the legal culture.

## HERMENEUTICS AND THE LEGAL CULTURE

Despite the fact that judges have "done hermeneutics" since time immemorial, the term itself is rarely used. During his Supreme Court confirmation hearings, now Chief Justice John Roberts likened the role of a judge to that of an umpire in baseball. He said, "Judges and justices are servants of the law, not the other way around. Judges are like umpires. Umpires don't make the rules; they apply them." Shortly afterwards, he personalized the metaphor:

> I have no agenda, but I do have a commitment. If I am confirmed, I will confront every case with an open mind. I will fully and fairly analyze the legal arguments that are presented. I will be open to the considered views of my colleagues on the bench. And I will decide every case based on the record, according to the rule of law, without fear or favor, to the best of my ability. And I will remember that it's my job to call balls and strikes and not to pitch or bat. (Hearing, 2005, pp. 55–56)

In so describing the role of a judge and his own aspirations, Roberts joined a line of jurists and legal philosophers who lay claim to the possibility of complete objectivity in interpreting neutral laws. For the French philosopher Montesquieu, who was the "most cited European author in America at the time of the Constitution's framing" (Carrese, 2003, p. 52), judges are "but the mouth that pronounces the words of the law" (Montesquieu, 1748, pp. 11.6, 404, quoted in Carrese, 2003, p. 52).[2] For the unconfirmed Robert Bork, we have lost our way since the founding, judges in general have gone wild, and "the nations of the West are increasingly governed not by law or elected representatives, but by unelected, unrepresentative, unaccountable committees of lawyers applying no law other than their own will" (Bork, 2003, p. 9). This phenomenon is resulting in serious inroads against our freedom as we succumb to rule by appointed magistrates. Similarly, for the easily confirmed Antonin Scalia, "it is up to the judge to say what the Constitution provided, even if what was provided is not the best answer, even if you think it should be amended. If that's what it says, that's what is" (Scalia, 2005). A judge's position on hermeneutics – that is, how he or she will interpret legal texts, in particular the Constitution – has become a political litmus test by which a judge's nomination to the bench may succeed or fail. Differing positions on interpretation tend to go undiscussed, at least in public, and mainstream legal scholarship, uninformed by the insights of the hermeneutical strain of law and literature, has few tools with which to unpack theories of interpretation, and to evaluate and critique what those who will shape our laws are claiming.

Although the word never came up in the hearings, Chief Justice Roberts was doing hermeneutics[3]: he was offering a theory of interpretation. He identified with the "foundationalist" school of interpretive theory[4] that holds that the proper meaning of a text is found in the text itself. The text to be interpreted is just there, over the plate and between the chest and the knees (to extend Roberts' metaphor) or not. The neutral judge/umpire sees it and calls it as it is. Its counterpart, the "antifoundationalist"[5] school, includes those who harbor a deep skepticism about the possibility of both a neutral observer and an objective text. At its extreme, the antifoundationalist view holds that a text is open to virtually *any* interpretation; it all depends on who is doing the interpreting.[6]

When the possibilities of interpreting a text are stated that baldly, setting up a polarity between the Roberts et al.'s view that a discoverable, true meaning resides in the text and the fearful specter of bands of unfettered judges interpreting as they will and, worse, imposing their own values upon a hapless citizenry, the foundationalists win hands down. And in the political arena, that is the way the conversation goes. Justice Scalia, who has become the cheerleader for the foundationalist position, speaks of the arrogance of judges being able to "make up the moral values of America" unless judges restrict themselves to "what it [the Constitution] meant, what was understood by the society to mean when it was adopted" (Scalia, 2005). He mocks phrases like "evolving standards of decency" (Scalia, 2005). From a most visible bully pulpit on the Supreme Court bench, Justice Scalia has managed to make "textualism," his word for an originalist, interpretive method that accords primacy to the words of the text itself and the meaning of those words as they were understood by those who wrote them,[7] the accepted method of interpretation. He has also managed to insert his view of interpretation into popular discourse, championing it whenever he speaks, easily conquering the straw man who would argue the opposite opinion. Ronald Dworkin laments that "we are all originalists now" (Dworkin, quoted in Rossum, 2006, p. 2), in that Scalia's persuasive arguments have reached so wide an audience that few are brave enough to openly espouse another interpretive method.

Those of us who believe that the drafters of the Constitution created a document that did not, nor was it designed to, protect groups such as African-Americans and women, find adhering to the original meaning of the text problematic. Those who believe that society has changed since 1789, that there are indeed evolving standards of decency that now abhor slavery, racism, and sexism, and that the meaning of the Constitution has changed with society, have little with which to argue. We seek a more nuanced position than the absolutist rhetoric that either version of popular interpretive theory allows us.

The hermeneutics strain of the law and literature movement, however, does give us tools with which to question the authoritativeness of the foundationalists without having to embrace the seeming chaos of the antifoundationalist view. Phenomenological hermeneutics, in particular, helps us to get beyond these basic claims and examine what actually occurs when someone – a judge, for example – interprets a text. In *Truth and Method*, Hans-Georg Gadamer sets forth a theory of interpretation by which we can refute the absolutisms of Roberts and Scalia without having to embrace an utter lack of foundations. What it does do, however, is require of us a certain humility, lacking in both camps, about the act of interpretation.

In *Truth and Method* (perhaps better entitled *Truth or Method*), Gadamer does not focus on the proper method for interpreting a text, as do the foundationalists (look to the original meaning) and the antifoundationalists (look to the evolving standards of society). Instead of what interpreters *should* do, Gadamer examines what actually occurs in the act of interpretation, the phenomenon of interpreting. He puts aside, and in fact questions, the idea of a *valid* interpretation, and instead examines how one can act while interpreting so that the truth of the text shines through. Adhering to a particular method for interpreting (original meaning or evolving societal standards) impedes finding the truth; one finds only that for which the method allows, the truth implicit in the method itself: original meaning or societal standards, but not the truth of the text. Instead of choosing a method of interpretation, an interpreter should go openly to the text, engaging in a dialectic with the text. Truth is thus revealed – dialectically, not methodically.

Because my point here is not a full explication of phenomenological hermeneutics, but instead to make the point that the hermeneutical strain of law and literature contains insights that cut through the current super-ficiality of discussions about constitutional interpretation, let me over-simplify the theory. Picture two circles: one circle is the text and the other is the interpreter. The interpreter does not have a subject–object relationship with the text; both exist in their full subjectivity. Within the circle of the text are all the things that the text itself offers, including the plain meaning of the words,[8] the historical meaning of the words, the intent of its drafters,[9] its institutionalized purpose, and the moment in time in which it was written. Within the circle of the interpreter are all the things that an interpreter brings to a text, including her method, her prejudices and presuppositions, the paradigms she uses,[10] the moment of time in which she is interpreting, her understanding of her role as a judge, her sense of the consequences of her interpretation, and the community of interpretation in which she resides.[11] An interpreter can no more shed these things than shed a skin; to achieve a true interpretation, an interpreter must acknowledge that he brings all this to the text. In addition, an interpreter must acknowledge the unbroken line of tradition, including court decisions, that connects the world of the text (its "horizons") with the world of the interpreter (the interpreter's horizons).

What occurs in an act of interpretation that yields the truth, then, is that the interpreter enters into a dialectic with the text, going openly to the text with unfettered questions. The interpreter immerses himself in a paradoxical union of timelessness and history, using the language and horizons of the text itself as the medium through which understanding can occur. The interpreter does not seek some objective meaning, but instead attempts to mediate the text into the present. She asks, "What do these words mean for us today, on this occasion, with these facts in front of us, in this act of being a judge?" When this open probing occurs, the worlds of the text and the interpreter begin to merge and in the overlapping area, the truth – the meaning of the text – is revealed. Fig. 1 provides an image of the interaction

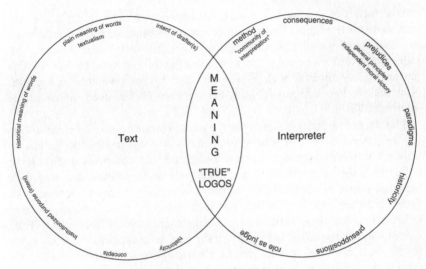

*Fig. 1.* The Interaction of Text and Interpreter.

of text and interpreter. Importantly, the truth does not merely emerge; it results from an open, active probing of the text. Neither the text nor the interpreter is dominant.

Gadamer takes this understanding of the phenomenon of interpretation a step further explicitly into the realm of legal interpretation. For him, legal hermeneutics provides a model for what occurs during all interpretation: "When a judge regards himself as entitled to supplement the original meaning of the text of a law, he is doing exactly what takes place in all other understanding" (Gadamer, 1975, p. 305). He describes what ideally occurs when a judge interprets a law:

> [F]or purely legal reasons it was necessary for an awareness of the historical change to develop, which involved a divergence between the original meaning of a law and that [meaning] applied in current legal practice. It is true that the jurist is always concerned with the law itself, but its normative content is to be determined in regard to the given case in which it is to be applied. (Gadamer, 1975, p. 291)

In the law, interpretation serves a practical purpose: there is a given case that gives rise to the necessity of the interpretation. Naturally, a fundamental and critical difference exists in an act of interpreting a literary text, in which there is no specific application in mind, and an act of interpreting a law.[12] Yet contrary to popular political discourse, the judge's interpretation of the law is not a choice between an arbitrary reinterpretation that is a boundless imposition of her own values *or* a strict adherence to some meaning indelibly inscribed in the words of the text. Instead, she rediscovers and recognizes the true meaning of the text for us, in this particular case, bound both by the text and by her own role as a judge. Nonetheless, her full personhood, her horizons, is involved in the act of interpretation.

This deeper understanding of the act of interpreting a text, of what judges do, helps us to see the disingenuousness in comparisons of judges to umpires, however quotable the mass media find such analogies. Judges serve us better if they are willing to acknowledge that they come to a text with their full personhood, with all that they have experienced and believe: with their sex, their religious beliefs (or lack thereof), their education, their upbringing, their neighborhood, their experience, their understanding of the role of a judge, as well as the details in the case at hand. Justice Scalia comes to the text, a federal statute or the Constitution, as Antonin Scalia. He cannot do otherwise. Judges cannot shed their personhood. Instead they should take into account that they have positions (horizons) and nonetheless attempt to mediate the meaning of the text into the present. At the same time, the text itself is not endlessly fungible. It has its own horizons, including the original meaning, the intent of the drafters, the plain meaning of the words, the historical moment in which it was written, the reason it was written and so on. The merging of the richness of the text and the richness of the interpreter reveals true meaning.

If we think about phenomenological hermeneutics as a practical matter, that is, what does all this theory mean to, say, a trial judge, deciding whether to grant a motion, we can see that there is no single "judge horizon" through which all judges peer at the law they must interpret. A trial judge's horizons include the restraints of her position as a trial judge: she operates under the constraints of the jurisdiction in which she sits. An appellate judge is bound by precedent. Even a Supreme Court justice operates under the constraint of stare decisis. But each act of interpretation, in each case, is a new one. There is no "one size fits all" for judging. Interpreting a text (a law) involves everything about the text and the judge; it is no simple matter.

Absent these critical insights into the phenomenon of interpretation, insights made available to legal scholars by the hermeneutics strain of the law and literature movement, the discussion about the "valid" method of interpretation remains a superficial shouting match of claims and counterclaims. Law and literature not only provides insights; as a practical and political matter, it also equips us with a vocabulary and theory that allow us to enter and keep open the conversation about what it means to interpret the laws that both provide us with our freedoms and restrict us from practicing them.

## NARRATIVE AND THE LAW

In the film "Rabbit-Proof Fence," Constable Riggs (Jason Clarke) comes to a village in northern Australia to take three girls away from their mother. He is acting on the orders of A. O. Neville (Kenneth Branaugh), the Chief Protector of Aboriginals, who was the legal guardian of every Aboriginal in the State of Western Australia. Neville has the power to remove any half-caste child from the child's family anywhere within the state. As soon as Riggs shows up, the girls and their mother start to run away, screaming. As he forcibly snatches the girls from their frantic mother's grasp, he says, pointing to a piece of paper "It's the law, Maud. I've got the papers."

"Rabbit-Proof Fence" is based on a non-fiction book, *Follow the Rabbit-Proof Fence*, written by the daughter, Doris Pilkington, of one of the girls, Molly Craig, who was part of the infamous "stolen generation" of aboriginals (Pilkington, 1996). The film itself, and particularly this scene, sets up the dichotomy between what the law *says* and what happens when the law is applied – the stories told by its victims. It also sets up a counter-authority, the authority of the personal story of a person victimized by the law. The three girls are captured and transported across the country to the Moore River Native Settlement where half-caste children are educated to become more integrated into white society. Led by Molly (Everlyn Sampi), the oldest and most experienced of the three girls, the girls escape and trek back, following for 2000 km the rabbit-proof fence built by the government to keep rodents out of farm land.

Thus, the story that the law tells and on which it is based – that it is best for half-caste aboriginals to leave their aboriginal families and become integrated into white society so that the "pollution" of being aboriginal can be wiped out of them – is undercut and replaced by the story of love for one's family. The legal narrative is told compellingly in the film by A. O Neville (Kenneth Branagh), a man who genuinely believed that he was doing the right thing – that the white race was so unquestionably superior that it was just and beneficent for the state to remove and "civilize" half-caste children. But the competing narrative is also told and vividly portrayed: girls taken from their loving yet powerless mother and sent away to be subject to an education that will make them suitable servants for the white upper class.

The narrative theory branch of the law and literature movement has increasingly revealed that the legal culture is chock-full of such competing stories, some of which become encoded in the official law and some of which become suppressed.

The law and literature movement has spawned this increased interest in narrative theory as a way both of understanding the law and of undermining its authority. Narrative theory, like hermeneutics, grew out of a wedding of philosophy and literary studies, in which the definition of "literature" and narrative was broadened to include all kinds of documents, including legal and quasi-legal texts. Philosophers of language, such as Paul Ricoeur and Hayden White, in their studies of narrative and history, paved the way for the inevitable, it now seems, entry of the study of narrative into legal studies. The law, after all, is based upon and is developed by a series of interlocking stories.[13] In 1983, Robert Cover wrote that "[n]o set of legal institutions or prescriptions exists apart from the narratives that locate it and give it meaning. For every constitution there is an epic, for each decalogue a scripture" (Cover, 1983, pp. 4–5). He urged his readers to look beneath the laws to the narratives that the laws buttress and those that they suppress; to acknowledge that "[a] legal tradition is ... part and parcel of a complex normative world ... [that] includes not only a corpus juris, but also a language and a mythos" (Cover, 1983, p. 9). As the law embraces and furthers some narratives, it simultaneously does violence to others.

Law and literature scholars, consciously influenced by Cover or not, have acted with this cognizance and narrative theory has entered multiple areas of the law, informing trial practice, human rights practice, analyses of opinions, even the teaching of legal writing. It has argued for an awareness of the competing narratives that exist in any legal story and has encouraged a healthy skepticism about blindly accepting the hegemonic narrative. Competing narratives are not only found in films like "Rabbit-Proof Fence"; they permeate the legal culture. It has become commonplace, for example, for legal writing teachers to use the majority opinion and the dissent in *Walker v. Birmingham*[14] to demonstrate to students that no narration of the facts is "neutral" or "true."[15] Instead, there are multiple versions of the facts; the true story can be told in many ways. An opinion supports a certain story and uses it to legitimate its holding; at the same time it ignores, suppresses, does violence to others.

In *Walker*, the majority writes a sanitized, "neutral" version of the events that occurred in Birmingham, Alabama prior to Good Friday in 1963, events made famous by the media and by Martin Luther King, Jr.'s *Letter from Birmingham Jail.* The Court's holding, that those who violated the injunction, even if it was unconstitutional, broke the law, requires a watering down of the racism and violence that led up to the injunction. Instead of allowing the civil rights activists to be the heroes of the story (as indeed they were by the time the case reached the Supreme Court in 1967), the majority takes as its rhetorical hero the law itself, the injunction. The supporting cast includes "officials," "bill," "infractions," "conduct calculated to provoke breaches of the peace," "writ." To justify its Creon-like conclusion – "This Court cannot hold that the petitioners were constitutionally free to ignore all the procedures of law and carry their battle into the streets. One may sympathize with the petitioners' impatient commitment to their cause. But respect for judicial process is a small price to pay for the civilizing hand of law, which alone can give abiding meaning to constitutional freedom"[16] – the Court must depersonalize the conflict that occurred in the streets of Birmingham and tell a story in which the law itself emerges as heroic.

The two dissents tell a different story, a story about people rather than about the law. The narrative of the facts in the first dissent begins – "Petitioners are Negro ministers who sought to express their concern about racial discrimination in Birmingham, Alabama, by holding peaceful protest demonstrations in that city on Good Friday and Easter Sunday 1963."[17] It then tells how one of the petitioners' representatives sought a permit from the Public Safety Commissioner Bull Connor, who told her twice that he would "picket you over to the City Jail."[18]

Leaving aside the merits of the Court's decision, legal writing teachers, informed by narrative theory borrowed from their law and literature colleagues, enable students to see through their naive misconception that there is one true version of the facts. Facts are in service to the legal conclusion and the different narratives duel for primacy.[19]

Those who teach trial advocacy as well as trial attorneys and their consultants have also turned to narrative theory to explain and articulate the means, for good or ill, by which a jury may be influenced. In *Nothing but the Truth: Why Trial Lawyers Don't, Can't, and Shouldn't Have to tell the Whole Truth*, Steven Lubet argues that the best lawyers are storytellers who take raw and direct observations of witnesses and transform them into coherent and persuasive narratives. These narratives, Lubet maintains, do not hide the truth but enhance it: "A fully developed and well-conceived 'trial story' may result in an account that is actually 'truer' in many respects than the client's uncounseled version of events, even though the narrative was adroitly structured with courtroom victory in mind" (Lubet, 2001, p. 1). While Lubet admits that this story-shaping device can be misused, he maintains throughout the book that what he calls the "lawyer's art" of storytelling is quite the opposite of unprincipled: "A conscientious attorney fashions a story not to hide or distort the truth, but rather to enable a client to come closer to the truth" (Lubet, 2001, p. 2). He also points out that not only do different narratives compete for the truth in a trial, but also narratives themselves struggle to be heard against the rules of evidence that seeks to constrain stories (Lubet, 2001, p. 186).[20] While lawyers may have intuitively and instinctively used storytelling in trials for centuries, the practice was undertheorized until law and literature scholars turned their attention to narrative theory and its use in the day-to-day practice of law. With the insights of law and literature scholars, we can analyze and critique what lawyers do. We have acquired a sophisticated vocabulary by which we can evaluate the practices and ethics of day-to-day law practice.

In the area of human rights law, the study of narratives has become increasingly important as the phenomenon of truth reports, composed in part of victims' stories, have come to dominate the international political scene. So commonplace has the practice of gathering victims' stories become that a country emerging from a period of internal violence would be seen as remiss if it did not embark on the process. "Tell me a story." Perhaps one of the most basic of human impulses: to be immersed in a world of stories, telling them and listening to them. To shape the messy events of a life into a narrative with a beginning – "I was born in ... .", a middle, and a temporary end. "Homo narrans" some call humankind, or "homo fabula," as if our impulse to tell stories was as characteristic as our walking upright.

In the second half of the twentieth century, this storytelling impulse has exploded into politics and into the international legal culture with the emergence of this new phenomenon of truth reports. When a country emerges from a violent past, generally caused by internal political upheaval, the new president, legislature, or some other political organ appoints a truth commission. This commission hears, collects, and publishes stories from victims (and sometimes perpetrators) of the problematic political past. "Tell us your story," the commissions asks, and, for the most part, the victims eagerly comply. The establishing of a truth commission has become the democratic bona fides of nearly every newly minted leader, and it would be peculiar to find a transitional democracy that did not launch a truth commission. And if one is not initiated, as in Bangladesh and Spain, some citizens may clamor, even decades later, for a truth report so that victims may have a chance to speak out and so that perpetrators and collaborators may be unmasked.

In my own recent work, in an effort to understand better the phenomenon of truth reports, I used narrative theory to delineate seven ways in which narratives work in our lives and in our legal systems. The first way, and the foundational one, is that making stories of our lives in what we humans do. The others: (2) that being encouraged and able to tell one's own story can, in part, help to balance harm done by violence; (3) that truth about what occurred can be uncovered; (4) that stories can communicate the experience of suffering and pain among groups that normally do not understand each other; (5) that the stories (akin to Bakhtin's sense of *carnival*) can help to disrupt an oppressive social order; (6) that remembering by means of storytelling can be a sacramental act that helps to put dismembered societies back together; and (7) that the truth reports themselves, with their salient personal stories, tell history in a radically new way and become constituent documents for the renewed or emerging nation (Phelps, 2004, pp. 53–73). I wanted to step back, look at the reports as stories, and think about the ways that stories operate in our lives and our legal systems. I used narrative theory to illuminate a pressing legal question: can, and should, these truth reports be allowed to substitute for more traditional retributive state action? My object was to provide a foundation by which we can analyze whether the burgeoning international practice of writing truth reports has a positive effect on the countries in which they are written.

Narrative theory enables us to look at the making of these reports as a literary enterprise as well as a legal and political one. It enables us to see the positive worth of the storytelling and the resultant truth reports and helps to lay bare some of the possible negatives of the endeavor. At the very least, the storytelling that a truth report encourages satisfies a basic human instinct to shape an experience, even a tragically violent one, into a narrative. At the same time, because stories have beginning, middles, and ends, the shaping of a time of violence into a story can tempt us to a reassuring, and utterly false, sense of closure.

This kind of public storytelling after a traumatic event had its paradigm, if not its beginning, following World War II when Holocaust victims began telling their personal stories in a variety of public settings, at the Nuremberg trials, in essays, in novels, in movies, even in comic books. From Nuremberg to *Maus*, the variety and quantity of victims' stories has given a lie to any suggestion that the singular horror of the Holocaust might result in silence. While it is widely acknowledged that Nuremberg initiated a culture of international human rights, it is less widely recognized that Nuremberg also initiated a culture of storytelling. When the language of the law fails or falters, the language of narrative fills the void.

Perhaps sensing the failure of legal language to capture the enormity of the horror of the Holocaust and that the Nuremberg trials, while giving a reasonably accurate historical picture of the events, marginalized the experiences of the victims, Hartley Shawcross, the British chief prosecutor, dedicated much of his summation to personalizing the catastrophe. He quoted from the affidavit of Hermann Gräbe, a German engineer who had headed a construction firm working in the Ukraine and had witnessed an *Aktionen* against the Jewish people. Shawcross read what Gräbe had seen:

> Without screaming or weeping these people undressed, stood around in family groups, kissed each other, said farewells, and waited for a sign from another SS man, who stood near the pit, also with a whip in hand. During the 15 minutes that I stood near I heard no complaint or plea for mercy. I watched a family of about eight persons ... . An old woman with snow-white hair was holding the one-year-old child in her arms and singing to it and tickling it. The child was cooing with delight. The couple was looking on with tears in their eyes. The father was holding the hand of a boy about 10 years old and speaking to him softly; the boy was fighting his tears. The father pointed to the sky, stroked his head, and seemed to explain something to him. At that moment the SS man shouted something to his colleague. The latter counted off about 20 persons and instructed them to go behind the earth mound. Among them was the family I have mentioned. (Quoted in Douglas, 2001, p. 93)

This story, with the backdrop of the enormity of the Holocaust with its staggering numbers and statistics, is a small and insignificant event. Yet, somehow the simple stories of a single father pointing to the sky, a single grandmother singing to and tickling her doomed grandchild, capture the horror more profoundly than any numbers. The philosopher of language Paul Ricoeur, looking at the phenomenon of the Holocaust, wrote, "Either one counts the cadavers or one tells the stories of the victims" (Ricoeur, 1984, p. 188). Some harms so push the boundaries of our understanding that perhaps the best we can do by way of understanding is listen to stories about and by the victims.

In the years since World War II, the phenomenon of victim storytelling has blossomed into an observable, and perhaps unstoppable, international practice. Subsequent Holocaust trials (Eichman, Barbie, etc.) were heavily characterized by redundant and extralegal storytelling. It has become increasingly apparent that at the intersection of law and literature, a deeper understanding of both the law and the past can occur. Consequently, significant questions have arisen for the legal culture. Is it appropriate to use victims' stories in a legal proceeding? The prosecution at Nuremberg had over 100,000 captured German documents with which to make its case. Why did Shawcross feel that he had to tell that story? What if its details were not entirely true? What, indeed, about the victims themselves and their families – was their privacy violated? What are the (legal) ethics of such use of victims' stories? And what if a story is fabricated, such as Binjamin Wilkomirski's *Fragments* or Rigoberto Menchu's *I, Rigoberto Menchu*? Is the entire storytelling enterprise undermined if some stories are untrue?

Aside from the problems inherent in the use of narratives in formal legal proceedings, what about the use of narratives in documents such as truth reports? Are such practices capitalizing on victims' need to tell their stories in order to circumvent more commonplace (and appropriate) legal practices, such as investigations, prosecutions, trials, and punishment? The legal questions are fully intertwined with questions about narrative theory and its relationship to the law and to justice; they are questions that only law *and* literature can address. In providing a foundation for this theorizing and by providing a vocabulary with which we can ask and even perhaps begin to answer these questions, law and literature has partnered with anthropology, psychology, sociology, political science, and other disciplines. Instead of remaining static and self-absorbed, the law and literature movement has opened the way for even more interdisciplinarity, which in turn has opened the way for a deeper understanding of the problems that beset the legal culture of the twenty-first century. Many of these troubling questions about the use of stories remain unanswered, yet the task of working toward answers falls squarely within the venue of law and literature scholars.

Yet, narrative theory does not only illuminate legal problem and injustices, it also can point the way to solutions in that, as we have seen, stories, properly told, can contribute to the making of justice. In the area of human rights, narrative theory coupled with legal action has become a powerful tool for change. Narratives have epistomological, constitutive, and political dimensions; they also have two important virtues: they reveal the truth, which has sometimes been hidden, and in so doing unsettle power (think of "Rabbit-Proof Fence"). Human rights activists, many of them lawyers, have recognized this and embraced storytelling as a means by which the law can be criticized and changed.

Let me diverge momentarily from the international legal scene to American law to provide an example of how stories were used to change the law and achieve rights – in the area of domestic violence. Domestic violence (or "wife beating," as it was called) has probably always been with us, but it has been shrouded in silence and myth. The mythology (or the master narrative controlled by those in power, those with the microphone) went this way: if a woman was beaten, it was her own fault. She had failed in some way – she was not a good cook, or an attentive spouse, or a firm disciplinarian with the children. And it was a husband's right, even responsibility, to "discipline" his wife. Or, if abuse did happen, it happened to "other people," not people "like us." Besides, even if it did occur, even repeatedly, it was a wife's duty to keep silent and protect both her husband and her family. Because this multilayered story held sway, the law did very little to protect victims of domestic violence, and women who were victims were too ashamed to voice any counter-narrative.

Then in the 1970s, two important books appeared, one in England and one in the United States, in which numbers of women who were victims of domestic violence finally told their own stories. The first of these, *Scream Quietly Or the Neighbours Will Hear*, was published in England in 1974 and was the first book ever in which women of domestic violence told their stories. The book's compiler, Erin Pizzey, became the founder of the shelter movement for victims of domestic violence (Pizzey, 1974). The second, Lenore Walker's *Battered Woman*, published five years later, launched a similar movement in the United States (Walker, 1979). There is a direct and traceable line connecting the telling of the stories and the changes that occurred in society's treatment of and regard for battered women. Because of these women's stories, the mythology was dismantled and the laws began to change. Activists who had been trying with little success to change the discourse and the laws surrounding domestic violence were now armed with a powerful weapon: the victims' personal stories. As these stories became known, others with similar experiences were emboldened to break their silence, to speak out against their tormentors, and to insist that the state hear and respond to their stories. As a result, there are now protective orders, police procedures, prosecutorial guidelines, and new laws on the books that protect the basic rights of victims, both women and men, of domestic violence.

In the international legal community, belated justice is sought using stories as a powerful tool for breaking silence and dismantling unjust laws. At the intersection of law and story (literature), transformation of an unjust system can occur. Many "life narratives" that are being told around the world reveal human rights abuses that have been carefully hidden by a legal system.

> Victims of abuse around the world have testified to their experience in an outpouring of oral and written narratives .... As people meet together and tell stories, or read stories across cultures, they begin to voice, recognize, and bear witness to a diversity of values, experiences, and way of imagining a just social world and of responding to injustice, inequality, and human suffering. (Schaffer & Smith, 2004, p. 1)

Examples of this transformative storytelling include the ongoing public storytelling of the Mothers of the Plaza de Mayo in Argentina (who have been instrumental in forcing legal change in that country), the narratives of the Stolen Generation in Australia (as in "Rabbit-Proof Fence"), stories told by former "comfort women," stories from Chinese political dissidents, stories from ethnic Turks in Germany, and coming-out stories from gays in the United States (Schaffer & Smith, 2004, pp. 1–2). And, alas, stories from detainees at Guantanamo and prisoners at Abu Ghraib. The list goes on and on.

These stories of injustice and marginalization by the law demand our attention. These stories, brought to our attention in part by law and literature scholars, are instrumental in effecting change in the law. The law and literature movement's emphasis on the dynamics of storytelling puts pressure on static, unjust laws and those responsible for them. Yet, narrative theory offers even more: it alone (as far as I can tell) gives us a way of thinking about the problems inherent in using personal stories to understand the law and to solve legal problems. It informs us that the truth can be heteroglossic and multi-faceted. For the enterprise of law, which in large part operates on an assumption of a single discoverable truth, such a disclosure can seem problematic, even contradictory to the entire project of doing law. The law and literature movement, because it integrates law and literature, does not undercut the foundations of the law; it broadens them to include the life of the imagination. David Copperfield may be "reading as if for life," but as we know from the rest of the novel, David does not remain trapped in the Murdstones' house or in their gloomy version of life's possibilities. David's imagination, enriched by stories, equips him to live life better and to thrive. Likewise, we who do the law – judges, lawyers, and human rights activists – may better live lives in the law because the law and literature movement has furnished us with new ways of understanding what we do. It has taught us to "read as if for life."

# NOTES

1. See, e.g., LaRue (1995) and White (2003).
2. A caveat is in order here. While Montesquieu did write these much-quoted words, he was using them to refer to citizen-jurors, whose decisions were reviewable by an "upper house" whose members had much more discretion in interpreting the law. See, Carrese (2003, p. 52).
3. In the mid-1980s when I was beginning to research legal hermeneutics, trying to make a link between my former discipline of literary theory and my new one of legal theory, I found no articles in law reviews that used the word "hermeneutics." Recently, when I searched the word "hermeneutics" in a legal database, I was

advised (electronically) to narrow my search as the word had turned up thousands of documents. When I narrowed the search to the last three years, 284 documents turned up.

4. All of the terms used to identify the various schools tend to be slippery, even sometimes used interchangeably. See, Crisey (1998, p. 849). The foundationalist theory is also called "originalism," "textualism," and "plain meaning" interpretation. See, Teresa Godwin Phelps and Jenny Ann Pitts (1985, p. 370).

5. Also variously called "non-interpretivists," "deconstructionists," and "critical legal theorists."

6. See, e.g., Michael Perry (1982).

7. Textualism differs from intentionalism in that Justice Scalia does not give a fig for the intent of the drafters, which he believes is impossible to deduce anyway. But he does care about what the words themselves meant at the time of the drafting.

8. Justice Scalia's version of what a text means.

9. Perhaps the leading proponent of intent of the drafters as the real meaning of a text is Raoul Berger (*Government by Judiciary: The Transformation of the Amendment*, 1977; *Death Penalties: The Supreme Court's Obstacle Course*, 1982; *Federalism: The Founder's Design*, 1987).

10. E.g., Natural law, rights, utility (law and economics).

11. See, e.g., Stanley Fish (1980).

12. See, Robin West (1988, p. 129).

13. See, Stanley Fish (1982, p. 551).

14. 388 U.S. 307 (1967).

15. See, Shaun B. Spencer (2004, pp. 209–223).

16. 388 U.S. 307, 321.

17. 388 U.S. 307, 324–5.

18. 388 U.S. 307, 325.

19. Examples of these kinds of dueling narratives can be seen in many opinions. One of my personal favorites comes from the majority and dissent in *DeShaney v. Winnebago County Dept. of Social Services*, 489 U.S. 189 (1989). The majority holds that the state is not responsible for the actions of the Department of Social Services that, forewarned of abuse, placed Joshua DeShaney with his father, who beat him into retardation. The facts are sparsely stated: "Petitioner is a boy who was beaten and permanently injured by his father with whom he lived." (191). The dissent writes the facts far more expansively and emotionally: "Poor Joshua! Victim of repeated attacks by an irresponsible, bullying, cowardly, and intemperate father and abandoned by respondents who placed him in a dangerous predicament and who knew and learned what was going on and yet did essentially nothing." (212).

20. I have also made this point in analyzing the trials of those who have practiced civil disobedience. See, Teresa Godwin Phelps (1991, p. 123).

# REFERENCES

Berger, R. (1977). *Government by judiciary: The transformation of the fourteenth amendment.* Cambridge, MA: Harvard University Press.

Berger, R. (1982). *Death penalties: The Supreme Court's obstacle course.* Cambridge, MA: Harvard University Press.

Berger, R. (1987). *Federalism: The founder's design.* Norman, OK: University of Oklahoma Press.

Bork, R. H. (2003). *Coercing virtue: The worldwide rule of judges.* Washington, DC: The AEI Press.

Carrese, P. O. (2003). *The cloaking of power: Montesquieu, Blackstone, and the rise of judicial activism.* Chicago: University of Chicago Press.

Cover, R. (1983). The Supreme Court 1982 term – foreword: *Nomos* and narrative. *Harvard Law Review, 97*, 4–69.

Crisey, I. (1998). Note: Worlds in stone: Gadamer, Heidegger, and originalism. *Texas Law Review, 76*, 849–867.

Dickens, C. (1981). *David Copperfield.* New York: Bantam.

Douglas, L. (2001). *The memory of judgment: Making law and history in the trials of the holocaust.* New Haven, CT: Yale University Press.

Fish, S. (1980). *Is there a text in this class? The authority of interpretive communities.* Cambridge, MA: Harvard University Press.

Fish, S. (1982). Working on the chain gang: Interpretation in law and literature. *Texas Law Review, 60*, 551–606.

Gadamer, H. G. (1975). *Truth and method.* New York: Seabury Press.

Hearing of the Senate Judiciary Committee: Confirmation Hearing for Judge John G. Roberts to be Chief Justice of the United States, September 14, 2005 (The Federal News Service, Inc. 2005) (Lexis–Nexis, 2006).

LaRue, L. H. (1995). *Constitution law as fiction: Narrative in the rhetoric of authority.* University Park, PA: Pennsylvania State University Press.

Lubet, S. (2001). *Nothing but the truth: Why trial lawyers don't, can't and shouldn't have to tell the whole truth.* New York: New York University Press.

Montesquieu, C. S. (1748). *The spirit of the laws.* Cambridge: Cambridge University Press.

Perry, M. (1982). *The constitution, the courts, and human rights.* New Haven: Yale University Press.

Phelps, T. G., & Pitts, J. A. (1985). Questioning the text: The significance of phenomenological hermeneutics for legal interpretation. *Saint Louis University Law Journal, 29*, 353–382.

Phelps, T. G. (1991). No place to go, no story to tell: The missing narratives of the sanctuary movement. *Washington and Lee Law Review, 48*, 123–138.

Phelps, T. G. (2004). *Shattered voices: Language, violence, and the work of truth commissions.* Philadelphia: University of Pennsylvania Press.

Pilkington, D. (1996). *Follow the Rabbit-Proof Fence.* St. Lucia: University of Queensland Press.

Pizzey, E. (1974). *Scream quietly so the neighbours don't hear.* London: Penguin.

Ricoeur, P. (1984). *Time and narrative* (Vol. 3) (K. McLaughlin & D. Pellauer, Trans.). Chicago: University of Chicago Press.

Rossum, R. A. (2006). *Antonin Scalia's jurisprudence: Text and tradition.* Lawrence, KS: University of Kansas Press.

Scalia, J. A. (2005). *Discussion on the constitutional relevance of foreign court decisions.* Forum at American University, Washington College of Law, January 13.

Schaffer, K., & Smith, S. (2004). *Human rights and narrated lives: The ethics of recognition.* New York: Palgrave MacMillan.

Spencer, S. B. (2004). Dr. King, Bull Connor, and persuasive narratives. *Journal of the Association of Legal Writing Directors*, 2, 209–223.

Walker, L. E. (1979). *Battered woman*. New York: Harper & Row.

West, R. (1988). Communities, texts, and law: Reflections on the law and literature movement. *Yale Journal of Law and Humanities*, 1, 129–156.

White, J. B. (1973). *The legal imagination: Studies in the nature of legal thought and expression*. Chicago: University of Chicago Press.

White, J. B. (2003). *The edge of meaning*. Chicago: University of Chicago Press.

# AFRICAN AMERICAN LITERATURE AND THE LAW

## Jon-Christian Suggs

### ABSTRACT

*Reading African American literature through the lens of American legal history broadly construed and reading American legal history through the lens of African American literature reshapes both texts of American experience and provides new readings of the literature and new perspectives on the law. Consequences for the understanding of each socially constructed "text" of reality proceed from examining their common narratival practices, specifically calling for a new periodization and taxonomy of African American literature and for a new "romantic" history of American law.*

The writer of this chapter begins from the assumption that the reader, having opened this volume, has some sense of the fundamental positions that can be taken in a consideration of the relationships between literature and the law: literature in law; law in literature; law as literature.[1] Case has been put for and against the efficacies of each of these as an enterprise and most of those arguments will be examined, surely, in the essays which accompany this one.

The purpose of this chapter is to examine an additional or alternative relationship between one particular body of literature, African American literature as represented by fiction in a specific period, and "law" if "law" is

Special Issue: Law and Literature Reconsidered
Studies in Law, Politics, and Society, Volume 43, 153–172
Copyright © 2008 by Emerald Group Publishing Limited
All rights of reproduction in any form reserved
ISSN: 1059-4337/doi:10.1016/S1059-4337(07)00607-2

understood not only as legislation and litigation, but as legal philosophy, legal history, legal scholarship, and legal education. One claim of the chapter is that African American literature, especially the classical African American narrative that emerges in the 1840s and begins to merge into the larger body of American literature written by Euro-Americans in the 1950s, has as its central concern matters of American law and that African American literature of the nineteenth and twentieth centuries can be profitably, indeed perhaps "best," read through lenses ground out of American law. Corollary to that claim is the claim that using lenses ground of African American narrative a reader can begin to see the outlines of an alternative text of American legal history.

There are several reasons I am moved to make these claims. Some are grounded in the more general observation that both literature and law are narrative systems. As such, each is informed by conventions of representation the elements of which are often closely analogous if not coterminous. So, for example, each privileges some speech and some speakers while excluding others; each drives toward closure; each is self-referential; each must manage, through some authorized process of editing, the narrative elements of character, setting, and action. This familiar list of essentialized characteristics, while incomplete, stands well enough as the base for some observations. One is that these narrative systems are not only alike in that they are systematic sets for making meaning and both produce not only narratives but narratives about narratives, but that they complement and compete with one another as and for authority as social texts. The competition exists not only because they share conventions of representation but because they share a common subject, human relationships within social contexts played out in actions.

More specifically, in the case under consideration here, that of African American literature and American law, both take as their subjects the existence under the law of Africans in America and create two compelling, if often contradictory, narrative records. There are both obvious and more obscured elements of this problem of the creation of these texts, in the creation of contradiction from commonality. In the first instance, for example, African American literature exhibits a consistency in its attention to relationships that are also scrutinized by American law: property, contract, identity, citizenship, crime, tort, regulation, federalism, constitutional law and civil rights, taxation, commerce, environment, family relations and estates, military law, petit and high treason, and corporations. For over a century, the legal framework for defining and allocating the problems, rights, privileges, and penalties attendant to these issues is the undergirding frame for literary narrative as they are played out among African Americans and between African Americans and whites. There is not a moment in which African American literature as it is considered here is not assuming the primacy of law in and representing both a description of the effects of law on African American life and a moral and intellectual history of those effects that are alternative to those accounts written by whites. To read African American literature of this period otherwise, without reading for its obsession with American law, reduces that literature to a random collection of texts sharing little in common but the racial identity of their authors and a recurring litany of wrongs.

On the other hand, American law has been, since its first colonial inscriptions, a narrative record of the presence of Africans in North America. That presence is not only a matter of record but the centrality of the fact of that presence to all American law is quantitatively evident. There is not an arena of the law in which the African American presence is not implicated, as property or propertied, contracted for or contracted with, citizen or subject, criminal or victim, petitioner or respondent. Laws have been passed to control the African American and to free him and then her from control, to enfranchise and to disenfranchise; laws have been repealed for the same reasons, precedents set and overturned. The impact of these interventions on African American life, as understood by African Americans, is observable almost exclusively in the literature written by African Americans. While there were comparatively few African American novelists, essayists, poets, and dramatists between the 1840s and the 1950s, there were fewer still black lawyers and historians.[2]

The ubiquity of these concerns in the two narrative systems, law in the literature and lives in the law, is in itself a good reason to examine *what* the two systems have to say. Another matter is that of *how* they say whatever it is they are going to say. If by "how" we mean not only the technical devices of literary and legal literacies but also the nominal presumptions from which each defines reality, then we move to the last level of claims in this chapter. As narrative systems, African American literature and American law make meaning by way of conventions (rules for order/ing) and suppositions that appear natural, universal, timeless; what Peter Sloterdijk (2006) identifies as the "*nomotop*."[3] Their accounts of experience present themselves not only as specific representations of relationships at a moment in time but claim a transcendence over the definitive ground of that moment to all such ground as far as those relationships are concerned. In addition, each of these narrative systems carries an argument for the timeless universality of its own conventions and assumptions, which it also imparts to each particular representation.

That assumed, the penultimate claim I want to make is that by reading America's legal narrative intertextually through or with African American literary narrative, we glimpse the fundamental romanticism of American law, its nomotopic grounding in typologies of self, imagination, community, property, privacy, individualism, authenticity, innocence, and irony that emerge in American consciousness after Independence and become the unspoken premises from which white Americans reasoned toward their understanding of the social body of the United States throughout the nineteenth century. This understanding not only shaped white American attitudes toward property and citizenship in general but as a consequence of the assumptions behind those attitudes excluded African Americans from citizenship in both the legal and imagined American community and acted to suppress the expression of African American desire for any and all aspects of human intercourse whites defined as natural, including life, liberty, and the pursuit of happiness.

In the America so premised, matters of law are tied not only to matters of race but of property. Race in America is and has always been a narrative of property, as the racialized other lived among whites as property and then as potentially propertied. Once black Americans could have rather than be property, racial identity itself took on the status of property as both civil and cultural citizenship in post-Reconstruction America became once again the property of those having the properties of romanticized white essentialism. Thus, through the almost limitless recuperative power of the law as social text in the United States between the formal cessation of the slave trade and passage of the Civil Rights Act of 1964, romantic ideas of self, property, place, desire, and identity defined the national being such that the fundamental assumptions on which constitutional protections are based peremptorily excluded African Americans from those protections. It is, after all, unlikely that the law, as one of the two primary texts of American life (literature being the other) in the nineteenth century, would fail to exhibit characteristics of romanticism, the dominant cultural paradigm of American life in the nineteenth century. A romantic history of American law itself would be necessary to capture that evidence. As we wait for that history to be written, it would be useful to read the law through the literature with which it competes and which itself was shaped by the imperatives of the same romantic assumptions.

This then is the final claim posited in the chapter: that African American literature, in reaction to the romantic configuration of African American identity and the legal consequences of that identity within the American social compact eschewed poetry for fictional prose in general and specifically adapted formal practices and conventions of literary realism and naturalism in fiction that defined that literature much longer than similar conventions and practices dominated the literature of whites. The lag of three decades between the appearance of literary modernism in Euro-American literature and its appearance in African American literature is directly attributable to the normative power of American romantic law over the formulation of African American social identity.

The study of African American literature of the nineteenth century and well into the twentieth is a study of prose fiction and other prose writing because African American poetry was, until the 1920s, a poetry of imitation of European and Euro-American versification. There are more than one reasons for this, including the autodidactic nature of most nineteenth-century black experience with poetry, the absence of formal training in belles lettres, the absence of texts of any but the most inoffensive and digestible poets of religiosity and sentimentality in black communities. But most of all there was the evident fact that only prose narrative could capture and address the problematic that African American literature emerged to serve, that of the legal condition of Africans in bondage and in what passed for freedom prior to and after the Civil War.

Whether one is reading *Our Nig*, Wilson (1859/2004) or *Clotel, Blake* or *The Garies and their Friends*, Webb (1857/1969), one encounters the novel form as adapted by African American writers to interrogate the effects of American law on African life in America. Whether the "law" under interrogation is slave law in the antebellum South, proto-Jim Crow practices in antebellum New England, the Fugitive Slave act of 1850 or Chief Justice Taney's opinion in *Scott v. Sandford*, African American fiction sought to argue for a common realization of African American humanity. But that humanist vision was often as not as secular as spiritual. African American literature did not share with African American religiosity the annealing functions of Christian forbearance and resignation. Rather, it confronted the romantic arguments of white America, that only white males possessed the property of being propertied and the qualities of authentic desire and personal will which marked their capacity for stewardship and the right to privacy, including the right to the privacy of their own property against the common weal on their own grounds. These arguments of white male romantic identity, of the monadic entity whose liberty resided in his very properties of self and will, were played out in the daily life of the nation against the absence of just those properties in the bodies of enslaved Africans, entities who had no desire, only appetite; no will, only subjection, no property except that of being property.

As a consequence, the arguments of antebellum African American literature were narrativized through representations of Africans whose thoughts and actions denied every tenet of American laws of property and citizenship of the day. Heroes were as magnificent as Deerslayer, as noble as Washington, as impassioned as Paine. The applications of antebellum law, whether local or national, to these characters revealed the law for the perversion of the founding impulses of the nation that it was. Antebellum black writers and their readers were devoted to the natural law bases of the Declaration of Independence and valued that document above the Constitution. Liberty was a *natural* right, not a negotiated one.

After the Civil War, after Emancipation and the ratification of the post-war amendments and the passage of the enabling legislation to enforce their imperatives, African American writing suddenly and irrevocably began to valorize the Constitution as the document to which all black Americans could turn for succor if need be. The possibilities of positive law were, for a brief moment during Reconstruction, both visible and tangible. But post-Reconstruction attacks and the series of federal court actions which culminated in *Plessy v. Ferguson*, while not altering African American faith in the Constitution, disabused them of any thoughts that whites in the aggregate saw the document as they did. As a consequence, African American fiction took on new attitudes toward the law: the Constitution was a sacred document but it had been betrayed, suborned by whites who had perverted its intent so that it had become an instrument of oppression perhaps far more deadly than it had been before the war. The difference was that having seen the promise of the law after the war, African Americans continued to embrace it and to turn their scorn not on the document but on those who betrayed it.

This assumption of the moral superiority of African Americans, held by African American writers and public intellectuals at the end of the nineteenth century, can only be understood against the backdrop of the charges levied against the race by the legalization of their inferiority in the Taney opinion. These commentators, Frederick Douglass, Frances E. W. Harper, Pauline Hopkins, Charles W. Chesnutt, Sutton E. Griggs, T. Thomas Fortune, T. McCants Stewart, Gertrude Mossell, Booker T. Washington, and W. E. B. Du Bois among others lesser known, insisted that blacks' moral superiority resided in their devotion to and reliance on the rule of law and that whites' moral perfidy lay exactly on the ground of their betrayal of both the natural law imperatives of the Declaration of Independence and the positive law guarantees of liberty through due process made possible by the Constitution and made explicit in the post-bellum Reconstruction statutes.

Two characteristics of African American literature emerged from this transition in the last two decades of the nineteenth century: (1) an intensification of argumentation against the finding of Taney in *Scott v. Sandford* that had begun as early as Martin Delanys *Blake*, such that almost no novel written by an African American between 1880 and 1952 failed to contain a counter argument to either Taney's premises or his conclusions and (2) an adaptation of literary realism and naturalism to the tasks of depicting African American life under the weight of white perfidy.

The first title of this chapter was something like "African American Literature and American Law: The Centrality of Dred Scott in American Literature." 2007 marks the 150th anniversary of the decision and so this seemed like a good time to go back to the books. When I did, I found that at first Dred Scott seemed not central to American literature and not to African American literature. One possible explanation of this "present absence," as literary theorists like to call these gaps, is suggested by J. M. Balkin and Sanford Levinson (1998) in their *Harvard Law Review* essay, "The Canons of Constitutional Law." In pursuit of their argument that extra-legal texts should be part of legal pedagogy, especially in this instance Frederick Douglass's 1860 Glasgow address, the authors put case for the proposition that "as a matter of cultural literacy, students of the Constitution (and of the Supreme Court) should know something about *Dred Scott v. Sandford* – a case that helped precipitate a civil war. This is so even though *Dred Scott* is almost completely irrelevant to contemporary constitutional litigation. Similarly, many cases and materials that are valuable for the purpose of cultural literacy are not necessarily crucial for any serious academic theory to explain. Few constitutional scholars believe that the principles or the holding of *Dred Scott* are important for modern constitutional theory (except perhaps as a symbol continually to be vilified)" (p. 976). A similar condition may well hold for the impact of the case on American and particularly African American literature. While the story itself is never recapitulated, the consequences of its absent presence reverberate through the texts.

One might expect to find traces of *Dred Scott* in American cultural production in several ways. The man Dred Scott or members of his family could appear as themselves as named in novels, poetry, or drama. Characters based on them or figuring in conflicts modeled on theirs could appear in such texts. The case and/or its principals could be referred to or invoked in such texts. In fact, none of this happens. No "Dred Scott" appears, no fictionalized litigant plods through years of quotidian labor while enduring seemingly endless rounds of argumentation and appeal. This is not *Bleak*

*House.* Instead, African American narrative after 1857 engages published legal opinion by drawing on definitions or representations of identity, personhood, citizenship, or standing made visible by Taney's decision in the creation of characters and conflicts as well as in the "wallpaper" of an imagined world within the text, that is, the general cultural and political assumptions as well as the historic consequences against the backdrop of which characters premise their actions and responses.

In the following short passage from Charles Chesnutt's *The House Behind the Cedars*, a white lawyer attempts to convince a young mulatto that he has no chance of becoming a lawyer and cites the case in point:

> Did you ever hear of the Dred Scott decision, delivered by the great, wise, and learned Judge Taney?"
>
> "No, sir," answered the boy.
>
> "It is too long to read," rejoined the judge, taking up the pamphlet he had laid down upon the lad's entrance, "but it says in substance, as quoted by this author, that negroes are beings 'of an inferior order, and altogether unfit to associate with the white race, either in social or political relations; in fact, so inferior that they have no rights which the white man is bound to respect, and that the negro may justly and lawfully be reduced to slavery for his benefit.' That is the law of this nation, and that is the reason why you cannot be a lawyer."
>
> "It may all be true," replied the boy, "but it don't apply to me. It says 'the negro.' A negro is black; I am white, and not black." (p. 152)

In the novel, Chesnutt reveals how deeply and ironically, even tragically, wrong the young man is. He leaves home, "passes" for white, studies law and after the Civil War marries the widow of a Confederate officer. His life is charmed but even he knows that it is because he is assumed white. When his sister arrives and is also taken for white, she attracts a suitor. His response on discovering her racial identity is a condemnation of her "betrayal" expressed as though her act were outside the law. Earlier, she had anticipated just such a discovery:

> But would her lover still love her if he knew all? She had read some of the novels in the bookcase in her mother's hall, and others at boarding school. She had read that love was a conqueror, that neither life nor death, nor creed nor caste, could stay his triumphant course. Her secret was no legal bar to their union. If Rena could forget the secret, and Tryon should never know it, it would be no obstacle to their happiness. But Rena felt with a sinking of the heart, that happiness was not a matter of law or of fact, but entirely within the domain of sentiment. (p. 69)

Of course, the domain of sentiment was always already corrupted by the narrative of law, in this case Taney's dictum that the Negro had no standing before the law. The implication of the Taney opinion as the climax for *Scott v. Sandford* is revealed when the reader realizes that Tryon and Rena live too soon after slavery to be free of the weight of its former power, as evidenced in the opinion, to define social as well as "legal" reality. The power of romance, of the novels in the bookcase in Rowena's mother's hallway, of the culture of the beloved in love's conquering tale are nothing against the power of the image of the despised as legal narrative, even when that narrative has been formally superseded, as *Scott v. Sandford* had been by the Fourteenth Amendment:

> A Negro girl had been foisted upon [Tryon] for a white woman, and he had almost committed the unpardonable sin against his race of marrying her. Such a step, he felt, would have been criminal at any time; it would have been the most odious treachery at this epoch, when his people had been subjugated and humiliated by the Northern invaders, who had preached Negro equality and abolished the wholesome laws decreeing the separation of the races. (p. 130)

Over time, despite *Scott v. Sandford*, the most consistently recognizable position taken by these black writers is a passion for and trust in the efficacy of law as a matter of principle. This belief in the face of the historical record was to be taken as a concrete argument against the Taney opinion. Its corollary is a profound mistrust of white Americans' ability or willingness to abjure the perversion of the law, beginning with the immediate aftermath of the decision itself, before the war.

Here, for example, is a passage from Blake, *or, The Huts of America*, by Martin R. Delany, written somewhere between 1859 and 1861:

> How about the Compromise measures, Judge? Stand up to the thing all through, and no flinching.

> My opinion, sir, is a matter of record, being the first judge before whom a case was tested, which resulted in favor of the South. And I go further than this; I hold as a just construction of the law, that not only has the slaveholder a right to reclaim his slave when and wherever found, but by its provision every free black in the country, North and South, are [*sic*] liable to enslavement by any white person. They are freemen by sufferance or slaves-at-large, whom any white man may claim at discretion. It was a just decision of the Supreme Court – though I was in advance of it by action – that persons of African descent have no rights that white men are bound to respect!

> Judge Ballard, with this answer, I am satisfied; indeed as a Southern man I would say, that you've conceded all that I could ask, and more than we expected. But this is a legal disquisition; what is your private opinion respecting the justice of the measures?

I think them right, sir, according to our system of government. (p. 61)

Four decades later, with *Imperium in Imperio*, Sutton E. Griggs (1899/1992) and with *The Colonel's Dream*, Charles Chesnutt (1905/1968) expose yet again the moral failure of the law in the hands of whites to protect the interests of people of color:

"Your state may disenfranchise you with or without law, may mob you; but my hands are so tied that I can't help you at all, although I shall force you to defend my sovereignty with your lives. If you are beset by Ku Klux, White Cappers, Bulldozers, Lynchers, do not turn your dying eyes on me for I am unable to help you." Such is what the federal Government has to say to the Negro. (*Imperium*, pp. 181–182)

An ambitious politician in a neighbouring [southern] State had led a successful campaign on the issue of Negro disenfranchisement. Plainly unconstitutional, it was declared to be as plainly necessary for the preservation of the white race and white civilization. ... No Negro had held a State office for twenty years. In Clarendon they had even ceased to be summoned as jurors, and when a Negro met a white man, he gave him the wall, even if it were necessary to take the gutter to do so. But this was not enough; this supremacy must be made permanent. Negroes must be taught that they need never look for any different state of things. New definitions were given to old words, new pictures set in old frames, new wine poured in old bottles. (*Dream*, pp. 192–193)

Sometimes the consequences of the denial of African American personhood as objectified in Taney's opinion are attacks on the physical black person, bringing forth clear moments of moral rectitude. Chesnutt's *The Marrow of Tradition* is a case in point. Not long before the physical climax of the narrative, the doomed working class black rebel, Josh Green, responds to advice about forgiving his white enemies just given by the young black doctor who is the book's protagonist:

Yas, suh, I've larn't all dat in Sunday-school an' I've heared de preachers say it time an' time ag'in. But it 'pears ter me dat dis fergitfulniss and fergivniss is mighty one-sided. De w'ite folks don' fergive nothin' de niggers does. Dey got up de Ku-Klux, dey said, on 'count er de kyarpit-baggers. Dey be'n talking 'bout de kyarpit-baggers ever sence, an' dey 'pears ter fergot all 'bout de Ku-Klux. But I ain' fergot. De niggers is be'n train' ter fergivniss; an' fer fear dey might fergit how ter fergive, de w'ite folks gives 'em somethin' new ev'y now an' den, ter practice on. A w'ite man kin do what he wants ter a nigger, but de minute de nigger gist back at 'imp, up goes de nigger, an' don' come down tell somebody cuts 'imp down. If a nigger gets a' office, er de race 'pears ter be prosperin' too much, de w'ite folks up an' kills a few, so dat de res' kin keep on fergivin' an' bein' thankful day dey're lef' alive. (p. 113)

Sure enough, at the novel's moral climax, the doctor, mourning the death of his young son killed in a race riot, is called to operate on the invalid child of the white man who fomented the riot. At first he refuses, but is prevailed upon by his wife. He saves the life of the white child in the very wake of his own loss. I have always felt that Chesnutt's determination to carry forward the countertextual response to Taney, four decades later, undermined his artistic sense. By forcing his protagonist to assume the burden of moral paragon, Chesnutt takes sides in the emerging confrontation over the color line. Dr. Miller's decision to save the white child's life can only be understood as the author's imperative, not that of the character. Chesnutt was resolute in each of his three published novels to present the face of African American moral superiority to a national reading public. His argument, like that of Du Bois, is that the indices of inferiority are not indicative and have never been so. Yet, like Booker T. Washington, Chesnutt seems to want to say that the performance of rectitude will shame white Americans into recognition of this fact. He was, of course, wrong.

The most poignant appropriation of *Scott v. Sandford* is Sutton Griggs' insertion of John H. Van Evrie's *White Supremacy and Negro Subordination; or, Negroes a Subordinate Race*, ... an 1868 reworking of his 1861 polemic, *Negroes and Negro "Slavery": The First an Inferior Race, The Latter its Normal Condition*, into his novel of black nationalism at the end of Reconstruction. In 1859, Van Evrie had written an analysis of the case, *The Dred Scott Decision*. In that and in the later work he argues that the presence of a naturally inferior and subordinate race ensures white male liberty. The presence of that subordinate race is threatened by miscegenation as the "dominant" white "blood" eliminates all trace of the Negro.

Whatever Van Evrie's unease about the effects of miscegenation on the "natural" balance of things, the eventual disappearance of the Negro race through intermarriage posing a threat to the status hierarchy that established and preserves liberty in America, and however bad the science is behind his analysis, in Griggs' novel, Viola, fiancée of protagonist Bernard Belgrave, reads Van Evries' book and takes its argument as her own. Her opposition to miscegenation does not lie in its threat to the bases of white supremacy but in its promise of the death of her race. If the races cannot be kept separate, she believes, but equally free and fully enfranchised, then one must withdraw. Until then she cannot betray her "weaker' but, as we come to realize, morally superior race, through marriage to the octoroon, Belgrave. She loves him too much to deny him her body if they marry but she loves her race too much to betray it by injecting more white blood into its veins. Loving the heroic but virtually white Belgrave, but loving her race more, she kills herself rather than betray it in the embrace of even its most noble champion.

Belgrave goes on to form the Imperium and to plot the secession of an all-black nation from the corrupt United States. In a late chapter, before the

plot is exposed, Belgrave presents this picture of post-Reconstruction
America under law, a testimony to the long life of Taney's argument:

> Colored men are excluded from the jury box; colored lawyers are discriminated against
> at the bar; and negroes with the highest legal attainments are not allowed to even dream
> of mounting the seat of a judge.

> Before a court that has been lifted into power by the very hands of prejudice, justice need
> not be expected. The creature will, presumably, serve its creator; this much the creator
> demands ...

> If a negro murders an Anglo-Saxon, however justifiably, let him tremble for his life if he
> is to be tried in our courts. On the other hand, if an Anglo-Saxon murders a negro in
> cold blood, without the slightest provocation, he will, if left to the pleasure of our courts,
> die of old age and go down to his grave in perfect peace ...

> The courts of the land are the facile instruments of the Anglo-Saxon race. They register
> its will as faithfully as the thermometer does the slightest caprice of the weather. (p. 215)

The speaker who follows him continues in the same vein:

> As for the courts of justice, I have not one word to say in palliation of the way in which
> they pander to the prejudices of the people. If the courts be corrupt; if the arbitrator
> between man and man be unjust; if the wretched victim of persecution is to be stabbed to
> death in the house of refuge; then indeed, has moral man sunk to the lowest level ...

> ... The Supreme Court of the United states, it seems, may be relied upon to sustain any
> law born of prejudice against the negro, and to demolish any law constructed in his
> interest. Witness the Dred Scott decision, and in keeping with this, the decision on the
> Civil Rights Bill and Separate Coach Law.

> If this court, commonly accepted as being constituted with our friends, sets such a
> terrible example of injustice, it is not surprising that its filthy waters corrupt the various
> streams of justice in all their ramifications. (pp. 236–237)

How these texts and others represent these conflicts, contradictions, and
moral triumphs is as problematic and complex as the subject matter itself. In
general, one way to understand the formal relationship of African American
literature and American law is to think of the literature as "signifying" on the
law. According to Henry Louis Gates Jr. (1988) signifying is to comment on
and through another's discourse with your own more empowered one.[4] An
example is Josh Green's speech as given above. Green comments on white
use of the laws of racial subordination to enforce psychological submission
on blacks. Now this definition does not capture either the spirit or the
complexity of the act of signifying, but it is nicely literary and it restates and
complicates my original observation that these two texts are in competition
with each other but the results are intertextual. African American literature

does not only speak to American law, it speaks through it, penetrating it, strikes through its nomotopic mask as a function of testimony and imagination. Or, seen another way, the literature we are examining is a palimpsest. American law is overwritten but not erased by African American literature, superseded as truth but not removed from its stipulations. As an example take the passage from *Imperium in Imperio* above. Griggs' story of a shadow black government which seeks to critique and eventually wrest control of an African American homeland from the federal government ends in betrayal and defeat. The actual supercession of the law is foiled but by writing the critique (and it permeates the novel) Griggs super-inscribes a different legal order on black imagination. Whichever of these metaphors you like, they each give us access to a significant observation necessary for the study of African American literature and the law, that law and literature are mutually and inextricably responsible for writing the larger texts of social reality that define any given moment and place in American life. It is in reading these as texts of social reality that I turn to consider the problem of literary realism and naturalism.

Just as American law and African American literature of the antebellum period were shaped by the nomotop of romanticism, both African American literature and American law were influenced through the closing of the nineteenth century and well into the twentieth by various formulations of "realism." For reasons of length and because the argument is clearer in relationship to the literature, I will omit any extensive discussion of legal modernism and its evolution into legal realism by the 1930s and will only note here the increasing influence of the social sciences in general and the sense that the post natural-law jurisprudence and scholarship of the late nineteenth century had begun to suggest that law could not be essentialized and discovered where it lay but was always being made, formed by forces acting on it.[5] The situation in American literature in general and in African American literature specifically was analogous. The dominant mode of literary representation in American fiction at the close of the nineteenth century was realism. By this it was meant that the central property of fictional representation was plausibility. It was not that one's story was merely possible, nor that it was determinedly probable, but that, given an assumed character and setting, the narrative would unfold in such a way that the reader would say to herself, "Yes, of course. Had I been there, that is what I would most likely have done under the circumstances, were I such a person as Ethan Frome." In the realistic novel, setting and character are everything. The plot can be manipulated and the ending contrived, but with sufficient setting and characterization, everything will seem real. This needs to be contrasted to the traditional conventions of the romance, which list excludes in no uncertain terms verisimilitude. Instead, romance evades causality.

In romance, "natural" laws are set aside for the primary characters and logic is associative, linking essential qualities, rather than syllogistic, linking contingencies. Heroes of high romance have supra-natural qualities or prostheses, invulnerability or a magic sword. Law stands aside in romance. So, too, in the romantic conception of the Republican citizen of the early nineteenth century. He is a white male endowed with the capacity, *liberty*, to alienate and own the properties of things, to sweep aside law that seeks to constrain his right to private productive property, to own it and to dispose of it as he sees fit, without regard for any social contract that might argue to regulate any such action. So Americans, white Americans, are always looking for the door when liberty is constrained, always seeking the frontier beyond the law when the law tells him he cannot own this, sell that, even when the this and that are human beings. Thus the question of the westward expansion of slavery, the Compromise of 1820, and once again, *Scott v. Sandford*.

The literature of white America's romance with the western frontier is among its richest, but its enthrallment to matters of property and the right to property is exposed by the simple observation that there is no African American literature of the west, no infatuation with the frontier until the twentieth century, until after Jim Crow, after legal segregation. There is no westward impulse in African American literature as long as there is de jure or de facto slavery. The impulse to tell the story of flight from the law was to tell the story of the flight from slave law or from its post-war sequel, the Taney-inspired incarceration of black civic identity, Jim Crow. That flight was not west but north, from the land of being property, not to some romantic land of limitless property to be had.

For the African American novel of the 1890s, realism was the perfect mode for its agenda, the representation of African Americans as the proof of the invalidity of Taney's opinion. This was the case in the novels of Frances E. W. Harper (*Iola Leroy*, 1892/1988), Pauline Hopkins (*Contending Forces*, 1900/1988, *Of One Blood*, 1901–1902, 2004), Sutton Griggs (*Imperium In Imperio*, 1899/1992, *The Hindered* Hand, 1905/1969), and Charles W. Chesnutt (*The House behind the Cedars*, 1900, *The Marrow of Tradition*, 1901/1969, *The Colonel's Dream*, 1905/1968). In each of these, the presenting problem of how the African American character is to be understood presages the formulation by W. E. B. Du Bois of the problem of double consciousness. In these novelistic variants of the problem, personal identity, how one knows and understands oneself as a moral, loving human, is always occluded by legal identity, how one is understood under the law and how one's formal and informal identity as civil and cultural citizen is determined not by your internal qualities but those assigned to you by your racial identity under the law. So the protagonists are always maintaining internal moral identities which inform and buttress them against the consequences of their legal identities. The depiction of this contest is always realized through the exposition of character, the centerpiece of realistic technique. These novels are clearly didactic. The lives under consideration in them are those of the black bourgeoisie, for the most part. Hopkins and her contemporaries are out to salvage the reputation of a race by creating realistic episodes in the lives of morally superior and intellectually gifted heroes and heroines. If such people exist, how could Taney be right? That the arguments were to no avail is clear enough. *Plessy v. Ferguson* rides in on the Fourteenth Amendment but rides out on *Scott v. Sandford*.

The period from *Plessy* to the end of the First World War is known in African American studies as "the Nadir." Black folks were worse off than under slavery, most people felt. The black peasant class gradually moved first to southern cities and then to the industrial north. The black middle-class of Harper's and Hopkins' novels were joined in the cities by poor, uneducated, African Americans. Realism needed some help. Naturalism is the representation of "reality" through the imagined application of laws of nature, whether those be physical or social laws. In the theory of the naturalistic or "experimental" novel, as Zola called it, the proposition was that one would create a character, position her in society and simply record what the laws of biology, heredity, sociology, and psychology (and here the psychology was pre-Freudian or what we would now call "behavioristic") would cause her to do. As African American literature changed to reflect the characteristics of life under Jim Crow, it became more harshly realistic and, by the mid-1930s more naturalistic. From Paul Laurence Dunbar's (1902/1969) *Sport of the Gods* to Chester Himes' (1945) *If He Hollers Let Him Go*, social forces represented by the law combined with atomized urban anomie to create ever increasingly victimized and devastated black protagonists. What sets African American "naturalism" apart from most European and Euro-American uses of the term is that the shaping external force was almost always the law specifically and always the law or some legalization of external stimuli from which whites would have been protected by the law.

But what is as important as the change in characterization here in terms of the law's effect on black literature is what did not happen. Because the problem of African American identity in everyday life was first a foremost a problem of legal identity, African American writers never moved their

investigation of the shaping forces of personal conflict from the external to
the internal. Thus, while European and Euro-American writers from Joyce to
Faulkner were experimenting with the Freudian psychoanalytic subject of
literary modernism, African American writers such as Jesse Fauset, Wallace
Thurman, Walter White, Claude McKay, Richard Wright, Dorothy West,
Zora Neale Hurston, Himes, Ann Petry, and Willard Motley were spinning
their characters through version after versions of pre-Freudian Pavlovian
stimuli and response, always framed by the assumptions of laws shaped a
century ago, driven to answer an opinion written by a man some 70 years
earlier. All character was essential and fixed until it encountered the law or
some stimulus protected by or undergirded by the law, usually a racist
practice or the denial of police protection from racial hatred. Laws that
enabled white capital to exploit black workers warped the sensibilities of
Matt, Melody, and Chinatown, three half-brothers destroyed in the steel
mills of 1918 Pennsylvania in William Attaway's 1941 novel, *Blood on the
Forge*. Only Chester Himes, in *The Lonely Crusade* (1947/1986) came close to
imagining an interiority so complex that the question of identity could be
located there and destroyed from there.

African American fiction's only concession to modernism was to accept
the isolation of the individual from communal support as a grounding
supposition. After the "nadir," the African-American family saga, the tale of
generations, begins to disappear from African American fiction and the
individual is left increasingly alone to struggle against the implications of his
legal identity, isolated from traditional sources of moral and ethical identity
in the hyper-Victorian black bourgeois community of the clear-sighted and
virtuous. Left so alone, he and she falter and flail against the external forces
that drive them.

The last response to Taney coincides with a benchmark in American legal
history but never quite escapes the determinism of American law. By the time
Ralph Ellison's *Invisible Man* appeared (1952), the NAACP had been
planning its challenge to school segregation for two decades. Even more than
*Brown v. Board of Education* (1853/1969) "reversed" *Plessy*, it freed African
Americans from *Scott v. Sandford* and freed African American literature
from its thralldom to the law. Similarly, every episode in Ellison's novel
counters the romantic nomotop of race, will, and desire. Ellison's answer to
the stranglehold American law had held on the definition of black American
identity was decidedly modern: one just steps outside of history. The
protagonist refuses to be defined by the external forces that act on him. He
abandons the object role and assumes that of the subject. That he does so by
plunging into a hole in the ground to await another day, and calls that

freedom, is a marker of his modernity and is a performance of one of the qualities of African Americans that whites had never understood, the capacity for irony.

Irony is almost always outside the law and is one of the conventions of literature not available to the law as narrative. While the law comments on itself, it never does so ironically. An observer may make an ironic observation at this decision or that acquittal, but the law seems always oblivious to its own ironic condition. The introduction of irony into African American interrogation of the law[6] is what characterizes the relationship from Ellison to the present. There are exceptions to that observation, such as Toni Morrison's *Beloved* (1987) a romance and a meditation on the law, and the theater pieces of Suzan Lori Parks. But African American fiction, film, music, and even the graphic novels of the past quarter century at least are deeply ironicized in their approaches to the place of law in African American life. As Randall Kennedy has pointed out in his study of race and justice, one irony of African American life and the law is that while the historical battle was to secure the protection of the law to black Americans as part of their rights as citizens, that protection brought with it increased scrutiny by the criminal justice system and the weight of that scrutiny is often problematic.[7] Notice, too, that while the primary issues of law in nineteenth century African American literature were civil or constitutional and had to do with status and property, in the twenty-first century the issues are of criminality and state oppression. Of course, H. Bruce Franklin has argued that all African American literature is prison literature and his argument is a cogent one.[8]

In sum, the relationship between African American literature and American law should provoke questions about the general standing of inquiries into such relationships. Can one assume always an equivalent degree of intertextuality? Might the connections be even closer than this chapter has time or space to suggest? Are the interactions between the two narrative systems not only intertextual but dialectic? If so, in what way does the literature shape the third text that would arise? We can see that reading African American literature through its responsiveness to American law gives us a new realm of potentialities, for literary history and for specific reading of specific texts. But where is literature's intervention? One possible space is in that of legal history. If we were to read nineteenth-century American literature as a primary text of American legal history, how would we understand that history? Or is it that reading the literary text invites us to apply some criteria to the history of law that has slipped by us? Can there be a "romantic" history of the law? There certainly can be an African American one.

# NOTES

1. Numerous approaches to these and other considerations, but not of those in this chapter, can be found in Richard A. Posner's (1998) *Law and Literature*; Stanley Fish (1989), *Doing what Comes Naturally: Change, Rhetoric, and the Practice of Theory in Literary and Legal Studies*; *Interpreting Law and Literature, A Hermeneutic Reader*, Eds. Sanford Levinson and Steven Mailloux (1988); *Literary Criticisms of Law*, Eds. Guyora Binder and Robert Weisberg (2000); James Boyd White (1985), *Heracles' Bow: Essays on the Rhetoric and Poetics of the Law*.

2. See not only the basically canonical Gates et al. (2004), *Norton Anthology of African American Literature*, but Jon-Christian Suggs (2000), *Whispered Consolations: Law and Narrative in African American Life*; Eric Sundquist (1993), *To Wake the Nations*; Gregg D. Crane (2002), *Race, Citizenship, and Law in American Literature*; William E. Moddelmog (2000), *Reconstituting Authority: American Fiction in the Province of the Law*.

3. "The Nomotop: On the Emergence of Law in the Island of Humanity." *Law and Literature*. 18, 1(Spring 2006): 1–14.

4. *The Signifying Monkey: A Theory of Afro-American Literary Criticism.*

5. See Stephen M. Feldman (2000), *American Legal Thought from Premodernism to Postmodernism: An Intellectual Voyage* throughout.

6. Ellison was anticipated by twenty years when George Schuyler (1931/1989) published his hilarious satire on passing, *Black No More*. But Schuyler was an outrider in black literature, a contrarian and a real wit. The passing novel as a sub-generic response to American laws of race is increasingly the object of scholarly attention. The best known of these is Nella Larsen's *Passing*, a novel of Harlem society. It is generally taught and discussed in college classes. Two that are not so well known are noted here.

Walter White's (1926) novel, *Flight*, tells the story of a young woman who flees Atlanta for New York, has her fatherless baby, becomes successful, marries a wealthy white man while still hiding her child from the world, and decides to give it all up and go to Harlem to live not because she feels guilty about abandoning her race or because she has abandoned her child but because she goes to a Carnegie Hall concert of Negro spirituals and the nostalgia becomes too much for her.

In summary the story seems insipid but it is only the obverse of another story. Wallace Thurman's (1929) novel, *The Blacker the Berry*, is about the indelibility of the indices of inferiority and how they are internalized not only by individuals who might accept a story of their own fate but by the race itself. Thurman tells the story of a dark-skinned young woman from Utah who, rejected by her fellow Negro students when she goes to college because she is dark, goes to New York where in Harlem she expects to find acceptance. In Harlem she finds that light complexions are all the rage. Over the course of the novel she encounters consistent intra-racial color prejudice; She takes every available patent medicine to brighten her skin. She poisons herself with arsenic wafers to grow at least pallid. She is tyrannized by lighter women and victimized by every man, light or dark. Finally she can take no more and manages to leave her brutal lover, leaving behind a disabled child. She determines to find a way to accept her color and make a valid life for herself on the basis of that self-acceptance.

7. Kennedy (1997), *Race, Crime, and the Law*.
8. Franklin (1982), *Prison Literature in America: The Prisoner as Victim and Artist*.

# REFERENCES

Attaway, W. (1941). *Blood on the forge*. New York: Macmillan.

Balkin, J. M., & Levinson, S. (1998). The canons of constitutional law. *Harvard Law Review, 111*(4), 963–1024.

Binder, G., & Weisberg, R. (2000). *Literary criticisms of law*. Princeton: Princeton.

Brown, W. W. (1853/1969). *Clotel, or the president's daughter*. New York: Arno and the New York Times.

Chesnutt, C. W. (1900). *The house behind the Cedars*. New York: Collier-Macmillan.

Chesnutt, C. W. (1901/1969). *The marrow of tradition*. Ann Arbor: Michigan.

Chesnutt, C. W. (1905/1968). *The Colonel's Dream*. Boston: Gregg.

Crane, G. D. (2002). *Race, citizenship, and law in American literature*. Cambridge: Cambridge.

Dunbar, P. L. (1902/1969). *The sport of the gods*. New York: Arno and The New York Times.

Ellison, R. (1952/1995). *Invisible man*. New York: Random/Vintage.

Feldman, S. M. (2000). *American legal thought from premodernism to postmodernism: An intellectual voyage*. New York: Oxford.

Fish, S. (1989). *Doing what comes naturally: Change, rhetoric, and the practice of theory in literary and legal studies*. Durham: Duke.

Franklin, B. J. (1982). *Prison literature in America: The prisoner as victim and artist*. Westport: Lawrence Hill.

Gates, H. L., Jr. (1988). *The signifying monkey: A theory of Afro-American literary criticism*. New York: Oxford.

Gates, H. L., Jr., McKay, N. Y., et al. (Eds). (2004). *Norton anthology of African American literature*. New York: Norton.

Griggs, S. E. (1899/1992). *Imperium in imperio: A study of the Negro race problem a novel*. Salem: Ayer.

Griggs, S. E. (1905/1969). *The hindered hand*. Miami: Mnemosyne.

Harper, F. E. W. (1892/1988). *Iola leroy*. New York: Oxford.

Himes, C. (1945/1933). *If he hollers let him go*. New York: Thunder's Mouth.

Himes, C. (1947/1986). *The lonely crusade*. New York: Thunder's Mouth.

Hopkins, P. (1900/1988). *Contending forces: A romance illustrative of Negro life north and south*. New York: Oxford.

Hopkins, P. (1901–1902, 2004). *Of one blood*. New York: Washington Square.

Kennedy, R. (1997). *Race, crime, and the law*. New York: Pantheon.

Levinson, S., & Mailloux, S. (Eds). (1988). *Interpreting law and literature, a hermeneutic reader*. Evanston: Northwestern.

Moddelmog, W. E. (2000). *Reconstituting authority: American fiction in the province of the law*. Iowa City: Iowa.

Morrison, T. (1987). *Beloved*. New York: Knopf.

Posner, R. A. (1998). *Law and literature: A misunderstood relation*. Cambridge: Harvard.

Schuyler, G. W. (1931/1989). *Black no more: Being an account of the strange and wonderful workings of science in the land of the free, A.D. 1933–1940*. Boston: Northeastern.

Sloterdijk, P. (2006). The nomotop: On the emergence of law in the Island of humanity. *Law and Literature, 18*(1), 1–14.

Suggs, J.-C. (2000). *Whispered consolations: Law and narrative in African American life.* Ann Arbor: Michigan.

Sundquist, E. (1993). *To wake the nations: Race in the making of American literature.* Cambridge: Harvard.

Thurman, W. (1929). *The blacker the berry.* New York: Collier.

Van Evrie, J. H. (1861). *Negroes and Negro "Slavery": The first an inferior race, the latter its normal condition.* Np: Np.

Van Evrie, J. H. (1868). *White supremacy and Negro subordination; or, Negroes a subordinate race.* New York: Van Evrie, Horton.

Webb, F. J. (1857/1969). *The garies and their friends.* New York: Arno and The New York Times.

White, J. B. (1985). *Heracles' bow: Essays on the rhetoric and poetics of the law.* Madison: Wisconsin.

White, W. (1926). *Flight.* New York: Knopf.

Wilson, H. (1859/2004). *Our nig.* New York: Penguin.